Elizabeth T.

Vancouver, B.C.

Portrait of Beecham on his 70th birthday by Douglas Glass

Beecham Remembered

Humphrey Procter-Gregg

Duckworth

First Published in 1976 by
Gerald Duckworth & Company Limited
The Old Piano Factory, 43 Gloucester Crescent, London N.W.1.

Preliminary edition issued privately in 1973 as *Sir Thomas
Beecham, Conductor and Impresario, As Remembered by His
Friends and Colleagues*

ISBN 0 7156 1117 8

Made and printed in Great Britain by
The Garden City Press Limited
Letchworth, Hertfordshire SG6 1JS

Preface

To those who only knew the name, Thomas Beecham seems just a legend in a halo of delightful (or outrageous) anecdotes. To those who knew and those who also worked with him, he was a great deal more than that, probably the greatest conductor in the world and the most vivid musical experience in their lives. To the historian, Handel and Beecham must appear the most potent individual forces in the history of music in England: both operated on a lavish scale and both lost a lot of money. The enormous power of broadcasting in our day is no relevant comparison—it is not an individual impresario, but a vast machine for the dissemination of every conceivable grade and quality of 'music'—Beecham and Handel were autocrats of an aristocratic turn of mind.

I have long wondered how the influence of Beecham could best be preserved. For reasons mostly covered by the first paragraph of Charles Reid's *Independent Biography*, a full-scale biography may never come to be written, and biographical details do not in any case convey the musical impressions so prized and laid to ear by the perceptive among Beecham's colleagues and audiences. I have at last, I think, been led to the most effective way of doing this: to collect the impressions of skilled musicians, friends and critics who remember and still survive his epoch. Among them, I think the contributions from orchestral players have a special interest and near-unanimity. Few of us who appear here are writers, but we are all, in one way or another, professionals who know what we are talking about in professional music: we bear very willing witness to the unique gifts of a genius who for the best part of fifty years was dedicated to the enjoyment and perfecting of musical performance.

A preliminary edition of this book was issued privately in 1973. A new edition has called for some enlargement and re-arrangement. This justifies a new title, one which still retains the book's composite character. It is really a survey of the enormous range of artistic activities and contacts in Beecham's career which, through his recordings and the memories of those who worked with him, can still influence new generations of musicians and music-lovers. Perhaps, too, it may remind them of some of those things which make music sound like music, in days when it so often sounds like some strange addiction to mechanised noise.

Since the first edition, greater detail has come to hand of the extent of Beecham's achievements, and thereby the legendary Beecham comes still more clearly into the light of history.

Hence the present re-arrangement of material. Personal remembrances, of which my own are in a way a summing-up, follow the sketch of his life and work, and they are followed in turn by all that has been selected from his own voice and pen; plus two obituary notices; and the facts listed in the Appendices give an immediate impression of the great span of his work.

As in the first edition, I am grateful for permissions to reprint the quotations acknowledged in the text, to all those who so kindly and willingly made contributions to 'A Cloud of Witnesses', to Denham Ford and Alan Denson of the Sir Thomas Beecham Society for much factual material in Appendices and footnotes; to Maurice Johnstone and Maurice Aitchison for their assistance and to Miss Marion Smith for typing; and last to Walter Harmsworth, John Kennedy Scott, and the Dean of Music at Illinois University for making available further matter by Sir Thomas himself.

And, as in the first edition, royalties will be devoted to the perpetuation of the Beecham name and tradition.

February 1976   H.P-G.

Contents

APPENDICES

List of Illustrations

List of Illustrations

Part One

BEECHAM'S LIFE AND WORK

A CLOUD OF WITNESSES

MAN AND ARTIST

Beecham's Life and Work

Biography is not the principal purpose of this book, but an outline of Thomas Beecham's career is essential for the full appreciation of the two sides of his many-sided personality which are presented herein—the recklessly splendid impresario and the quite magical interpreter of music. The former can only be got into any clear focus after glancing over the whole of Beecham's career. What follows is a summary of his extraordinary life and achievements, with such factual data as I have been able to assemble as evidence of his monumental industry, and with, I think, some gleams of light which my own experiences have been able to shed on a figure for many years familiar throughout the world and still very much alive to musicians and to friends who still survive.

1879–1909

Thomas Beecham was born in St Helens, Lancashire on 29 April, 1879. His grandfather had started what was to become a very big business by personally selling digestive pills which he had invented and later patented. Originally pursued in the back yard, the pill business developed into a concern with a six-figure annual bill for advertising. The grandfather is affectionately portrayed by his grandson in his autobiography, *A Mingled Chime*. Sir Joseph Beecham, Thomas's father, comes into the son's story a good deal, but as a background figure.

As a child, Thomas evinced both a passion for music and a marvellous memory; at the age of nine he could repeat anything he wanted from his reading, including, we are told, the whole of *Macbeth*. His apparently encyclopaedic memory was to surprise acquaintances at all stages of his life; it covered not only a vast repertoire of music but innumerable recollections of literature, pictures, places, means of transport, and comic contingencies from the drawing-room to the bar-parlour.

On reaching his teens this son of Lancashire went to a famous Lancashire School, Rossall. He became captain of his house, and the only boy to be allowed a piano in his study: he acquired a wide knowledge of opera, both in holidays and personal study, and at cricket he eventually bowed to expectations and got into the School Eleven. In after years, when his fame was established, he would take concerts to the School, or drop in to visit his old haunts. In the 1950s I was told by relatives of two schoolboys how one day they had received in their study a funny little old gentleman who knocked on the door and very politely asked if they would be kind enough to allow him to sit down for a few minutes in what he believed to be his old room, just to see what it felt like after sixty years. They thought it very amusing, and apologised for only having 'pop' to offer him, which he drank with solemnity while he listened respectfully to their views on various topics. They were flabbergasted to learn later from their fellows that they had airily been entertaining the famous Sir Thomas.

In 1897 Thomas Beecham entered Wadham College, Oxford. He read desultorily, apparently remembering it all years afterwards. He played football, and snatched clandestine trips abroad to hear opera at the best continental centres. At home he founded the St Helens Orchestral Society: in later life founding orchestras was to become quite a habit.

When he was just twenty Thomas had his first opportunity to conduct a professional orchestra. The Hallé had been engaged for the Mayor's Concert at St Helens. Their conductor, Hans Richter, fell ill, and father Joseph insisted that his son should deputise. The event is merrily described in *A Mingled Chime*. One of the players who took part told me in his old age that the young conductor made a rather ludicrous appearance, and the orchestra was expecting a ludicrous performance; but in the train on the way back to Manchester it was quietly agreed that the lad knew his music all right, and there was 'something about him, they didn't quite know what.' Over the next sixty years, players and public throughout the world were to recognise in Beecham 'something they didn't quite know what'.

The following year the young man, finding he had had enough of Oxford (he modestly suggested that this saved the authorities the trouble of feeling obliged to dispense with his attendance— or non-attendance) continued the travels on the Continent which had so palliated the monotony of undergraduate life. He had, on an earlier trip with his father, already established an acquaintance with America which he kept up throughout his life; an early passion for American literature was soon out-grown, but another —for seventeenth-century verse and drama—strangely survived, as did yet another for early French opera, which provided one of his many innovations to English programmes. Beecham's extraordinary and irregular scholarship may have included a few lacunae, but it contained many discoveries, and was well served by his phenomenal memory. We soon realise from the pages of *A Mingled Chime*, closely sprinkled with historical asides, allusions and footnotes, how readily he could summon up, as he did in casual conversation, odd but apt quotations illustrative of any topic that came along: it seemed that he had never forgotten any music, or classic book, or experience down the years: provided, of course, that it had interested that lively mind, capable too of obliterating from consciousness anything or anyone boring or unpleasant—and generally getting away with it.

In 1902 Beecham, having thrown up his position in the family pill firm, was based in London, and relates with amusement how he joined a small new opera company run by one Kelson Truman. That gentleman, aghast at the young man's request to consider an opera he had composed, was soon relieved to find that the young man knew most of the company's stock repertoire by heart, and engaged him as second conductor on the spot. The company rehearsed at the Old Vic and went on tour, and this was the solid and practical foundation of Beecham's unique professional technique, a technique which happened to be so unorthodox that in routine professional circles he was sometimes dubbed an 'amateur': a superficial jibe doubtless born of envy. His recording of *La Bohème* alone disproves it, for it is arguably the supreme performance in the whole history of that opera. Habitually one adopts a judicial attitude to this so frequently performed opera, weighing up this or that singer, conductor or orchestra. With Beecham one forgets all that, and finds oneself between smiles and near-tears, thinking: What a lovely opera! What enchanting music!

Beecham's marriage to Utica Welles, an American diplomat's daughter, in 1904, marked a fresh period in his life. A family dispute had estranged him from his father—in this Thomas and one of his sisters were in the right; they rescued their mother from an unhappy situation, but it was years before his father forgave him. He had now settled in London, and collaborated with Charles Kennedy Scott in launching the latter's Oriana Madrigal Choir, which in due course became famous; Beecham, in whose room the informal rehearsals had started, sang bass and wrote the programme-notes (see pp. 159–70). Through another friend, Joseph George Morley, the harp specialist, Beecham got more and more into professional musical circles: he studied with Charles Wood, Moszkowski and Frederic Austin, and played for the singing lessons of the justly celebrated baritone Maurel, whose impeccable dramatic style (he had created the parts of Iago and Falstaff) I have heard Sir Thomas in old age discuss with admiration (as he does in *A Mingled Chime*). All this, and musical travels on the Continent, with numerous visits to opera houses and libraries, contributed to the goal gradually clearing before him. No more pill business, no more playing or composing—he was teaching himself, with the aid of a sort of chess-board he had invented (on which the 'men' were players) and his built-in brain-recorder of all the scores he read, to be a conductor.

In 1905 he collected some Queen's Hall players, and gave his first London concert: a French-Italian programme with the additional novelty of the virtually unknown Cyril Scott's *Helen of Kirkconnel*. It had a *succès d'estime* and a bad notice in *The Times*; Beecham's own account is severely self-critical. He retired for more months of intensive study. Then, with the help of the master clarinettist, Charles Draper, he founded the New Symphony Orchestra for a series of concerts in the Bechstein (now Wigmore) Hall; with sixty-five players, and some very stylish conducting duly recognised by the Press. But for the public at large the programmes were a trifle *too* stylish—recondite and unknown classics 'killed' the box office. The programmes were pronounced 'both catholic and esoteric'. It would be more accurate to say that his early repertoire tended towards the esoteric

but that it became, with one or two exceptions, remarkably
catholic as his long career developed.

In 1907 the New Symphony Orchestra expanded and appeared
in the Queen's Hall. The programmes were still too specialised
for popular success, but the standard of performance was unusually high. After the first concert, 'a stranger of arresting
appearance' came round to compliment the conductor and en-
quire about engaging so excellent an orchestra for a concert
of his own music. His name was Frederick Delius, and his visit
proved a landmark in Beecham's career: one of his missions
in life, no doubt unrevealed at the time, was to save Delius for
the world. The revelation came when he heard *Appalachia* a
few weeks later.

Beecham called the 1908-9 season his 'happy year'. It included his first Manchester concert, with the New Symphony
Orchestra, and in due course he conducted *Brigg Fair*, *Appalachia*,
Sea Drift and the first complete performance of *A Mass of Life*,
and walked with Delius in the mountains of Norway. He made
another life-long friend, Ethel Smyth, who engineered a recon-
ciliation with his father after some years of estrangement; and
he founded the Beecham Symphony Orchestra. This became
known as the 'Fireworks Orchestra' (see page 118); it toured
extensively and lasted five years. Its leader was Albert Sammons
and later W. H. Reed. Tertis led the violas, Charles Draper was
the principal clarinet, and it included the first of the famous
Cruft family (double-bass) and Eric Coates (viola). Its performances became legendary, noted for 'string tone and attack', 'resili-
ence and fire'. Beecham and his young players, who would follow
him whatever happened, had been nearly on the rocks a number of times, and his large repertoire of new English and old
French pieces courted disaster. But with his father's financial
assistance he was able to continue and develop his ideas. His
gifts were already evident and noted: fire, flexibility (a favourite
word of his), delicacy, wit and his incredible memory. Beecham
first met Lady Cunard at this time; she became a great asset
in his life and career. The year also included the English première
(six consecutive performances) of *The Wreckers* of Ethel Smyth:
his first operatic success—and financial loss, but that was borne
by an enthusiastic American millionairess, happily named Miss
Dodge.

One has to remember that when Beecham became a legend in musical circles, though he generally had private means at his back (or round the corner), he had no educational or government grants, no discs, tapes, radio, air transit or television: the motor car, telephone and four-minute gramophone were only on the way in. Today the bright young man is heavily dependent on all these and more advantages of publicity—without them could he became a legend on sheer musical personality?

1910–1919

The first of Beecham's many Covent Garden seasons was in 1910. It was backed by his father, and ran in two parts, with a short season at His Majesty's Theatre in the interval. Other activities included his first Royal Philharmonic Society Concert and various concerts with the London Symphony Orchestra. His opera repertoire for the year consisted of over thirty works: of these he conducted fifteen himself, and his assistant or guest conductors included Richard Strauss and Bruno Walter. With repeats, the performances totalled one hundred and ninety, and the repertoire included *Elektra, Feuersnot, Tristan and Isolde, Tales of Hoffman, Die Fledermaus, Carmen, Hansel and Gretel, Tiefland* (d'Albert), *Werther, L'Enfant Prodigue* (Debussy), *A Village Romeo and Juliet, The Wreckers, Ivanhoe* (Sullivan), *Shamus O'Brien* (Stanford), the sensational production of *Salome*, and four less familiar Mozart operas: a phenomenal season, in fact, which landed him with much unforeseen publicity, but with much frustration and heavy losses, a fate often in store for this extraordinary genius.

The tide of his activities swept on in the following years— Beecham Symphony Orchestra concerts in London, Liverpool, Manchester, Birmingham and elsewhere. Sir Joseph (who was knighted in 1911) and he procured the first visit of Diaghilev's Russian Ballet, an outstanding landmark in stage history. Sometimes Thomas conducted for the Russians, and he took his orchestra to Berlin for them and for concerts which inaugurated his international fame—it was the first British orchestra to play in Berlin. His prospectus for the 1912 opera season was not entirely realised (e.g. 'Signor Toscanini will assist Mr Thomas Beecham'), but the season included a great array of celebrities—

Royal Opera Covent Garden

Lessee and Manager, Mr. FRANK RENDLE
For Autumn and Winter Seasons

THOMAS BEECHAM OPERA SEASON, 1910

THIS EVENING'S PERFORMANCE

Wednesday, October 5th, at 8.30

D'ALBERT'S OPERA

TIEFLAND
(In English)

Sebastiano .	Mr. FREDERIC AUSTIN
Tomasso .	Mr. ROBERT RADFORD
Moruccio .	Mr. LEWYS JAMES
Marta .	Miss MURIEL TERRY
Pepa ..	Miss CARRIE TUBB
Antonia .	Miss LENA MAITLAND
Rosalia .	Miss BLANCHE FOX
Nnri ..	Miss MAGGIE TEYTE
Pedro .	Mr. JOHN COATES
Nando .	Mr. MAURICE D'OISLY
The Priest .	Mr. ARTHUR WYNN

Conductor Mr. THOMAS BEECHAM

Stage Manager M. LOUIS VERANDE

Beecham's first Covent Garden Season; a typical programme.

Tetrazzini (her English début), Destinn, Edvina, Caruso, Chaliapin.

1913 was another memorable year; concerts continued as before in England, and were undertaken in Paris in collaboration with André Messager. At Covent Garden in January he added *Die Meistersinger* to his repertoire and also the first production in England of a brand new masterpiece, *Der Rosenkavalier*. At His Majesty's he collaborated with Sir Herbert Tree in the production of Somerset Maugham's English version of Molière's *Le Bourgeois Gentilhomme* with the opera-inset of Strauss, *Ariadne auf Naxos*. He then resigned from the Covent Garden Board, and opened independently at Drury Lane. Here he gave thirteen operas, three of which were with Russian casts (*Boris Godunov*, *Khovanstchina*, *Ivan the Terrible*, with Chaliapin and the beauteous and be-jewelled Lina Cavalieri among the artists), and fifteen Diaghilev ballets, including *Petrouchka*, *L'Après-midi d'un Faune* and *Le Train Bleu*, and incidentally he lent them the theatre to prepare *Le Sacre du Printemps* for Paris. The dancers in this Beecham season included Karsavina, Nijinsky and Bolm, and among the operas given were *Don Giovanni*, *Pelléas et Mélisande* and *Salome*.

In October Beecham generously rescued the Denhof Opera Company, stranded at the Theatre Royal in Manchester, and took over the employment of the British and foreign artists. From this material he built up his own company, with an existing repertoire that included *The Ring*, *Tristan*, *Die Meistersinger*, *Der Rosenkavalier*, *Pelléas* and *Elektra*. Thus began the great days of 'Beecham Opera', with nine weeks in Manchester and seasons in Birmingham, Leeds, Liverpool, Sheffield and elsewhere. This year must have been one of the heaviest in Beecham's career; in range of accomplishment and historic fame it must have surpassed the achievement of any single musician or impresario in the whole history of theatre and concert hall. The inclusion of both the Russian Ballet and the Russian Opera alone made history, and the formation of the Beecham Opera Company added much-needed brilliance to the English musical scene.

In 1914 the immense possibilities suggested by the previous year looked like fulfilment until cut short by the war, which changed so much in human history besides the currents of art

and music. Up to 25 July, ten days before the unexpected outbreak of war, a great season at Drury Lane had included a number of historic names: during the visit on a larger scale of the
combined Russian Opera and Ballet, among the stars were
Chaliapin, the romantic Marie Kousnietzoff, and Frieda Hempel,
the foremost coloratura soprano of the day. The chorus was
brought from the Imperial Opera of Moscow. The Russian
repertoire included the operas *Boris Godunov*, *Khovanstchina*,
Ivan the Terrible, *Prince Igor*, *A May Night*, *Le Coq d'Or* and
The Song of the Nightingale, and the ballets *Daphnis and Chloe*,
Le Sacre du Printemps and *The Spectre of the Rose*. Of the
other performances, Joseph Holbrooke's *Dylan* and Strauss's
Josefslegende (conducted by the composer) were new. *Die
Zauberflöte* was memorable for the Pamina of Claire Dux, which
drew the stars from Covent Garden to hear it. Beecham conducted the German and English works, and it is said that he conducted, *from memory*, *Thamar*, *Scheherazade*, *Die Zauberflöte*
and *Der Rosenkavalier*; this last he was destined not to conduct
again till 1933.

The most remarkable performance of the season, and one of
the most remarkable of any in operatic history, was the opening
night of the Russian visit—the English première of *Prince Igor*,
with Chaliapin in two rôles, the rascal Prince Galitzy and the
Tartar Khan Kontchak, and with the Diaghilev Ballet in the
now-famous dances in Act III in the Tartar Camp scene designed by Roerich. This occasion has been well described both
by Charles Reid and by Beecham himself.

During the war years Beecham was indefatigable. Obviously
unsuitable for the forces (the official reason seems never to have
been published), he was obviously suitable for keeping music alive
in Britain. With his financial and personal assistance he enabled
the Hallé Society and the London Symphony Orchestra to maintain (and increase) their concerts, and his immediate response to
the war was to persuade Landon Ronald to join him in a Promenade season at the Albert Hall. But his greatest achievement
was the touring of his opera company, which gave the provinces
a wider and more exciting repertoire than they had ever enjoyed
before. With no foundation of national opera to build upon, he
gave the theatres large and small over thirty different operas
between 1916 and 1920. Among them were *Romeo and Juliet*,

*Madam Butterfly, Tales of Hoffman, Faust, Carmen, La Bohème,
Tosca, Il Trovatore, Otello, Lucia di Lammermoor, Everyman*
(Liza Lehmann), *The Boatswain's Mate* (Ethel Smyth), *Tristan,
The Fair Maid of Perth* (Bizet), *Samson and Delilah, Aïda,
Louise, Falstaff, The Golden Cockerel, Naïl* (Isidore de Lara),
*Boris Godunov, Prince Igor, The Valkyrie, Figaro, The Magic
Flute* and *Il Seraglio.* The Playfair-Rumbold production of
Figaro became a legendary landmark in English operatic history,
and the Beecham principals became the leading singers of their
generation. (As typical of the philanthropic admission prices for
these full-scale productions, a seat in the gallery of the Manchester Opera House cost 1s. 10d.)

In 1916 Beecham was sent on a diplomatic mission to Rome,
and characteristically took the opportunity to give some concerts
while he was there. On his return to England he was knighted.
He continued to support both the Hallé and the Royal Philharmonic Societies, conducting without fee and meeting deficits
and the fees of visiting conductors. In this year Sir Thomas
conducted his first *Messiah* and gave an autumn season of opera
at the Aldwych Theatre. It was at that time that Sir Joseph's
sudden death threw Beecham's affairs into temporary confusion,
the two of them being deeply involved in purchasing the Beecham
Covent Garden Estate. Years of legal wrangling were to follow,
but an interim settlement procured by the sale of his father's
fine art collection left Thomas in a position to carry on with
more operatic activity—for a time. (Having recently been knighted in his own right, he now succeeded to the baronetcy.) In this
same year he was at last able to see realised what had been, at
considerable personal expense, his own plan to establish a municipal orchestra in Birmingham.

While the financial complications caused by Sir Joseph's death
were accumulating, Thomas reached what was to be his last
season for many years at Covent Garden. In the 1919 season
he conducted nine operas, which included a new production of
Gluck's *Orfeo*, with Clara Butt and Maggie Teyte as outstanding principals. In the two 'grand' seasons of 1919–20, the Sir
Thomas Beecham Opera Company and the Opera Syndicate
were partners. Notable additions to the repertoire instigated by
him were *L'Heure Espagnole* (Ravel), *Iris* (Mascagni), *Il Segreto
di Susanna* (Wolf-Ferrari), *Thaïs* (Massenet), *Djamileh* (Bizet),

Don Pasquale, Il Trittico (with Puccini's supervision), *The Girl of the Golden West, Lucia* and *Louise*. Beecham conducted *Manon, Le Coq d'Or, The Fair Maid of Perth, Falstaff, Samson and Delilah, Tristan, A Village Romeo and Juliet, Die Meistersinger* and *Die Zauberflöte*—these in addition to the nine others in his own season. A soprano, Graziella Pareto, of whom he wrote and often spoke in after years, sang in *La Traviata, The Pearl Fishers* and *Don Pasquale*. I remember her performances as especially distinguished, as were others by Edvina and Ansseau among the numerous fine artists then to be heard in succession to such famous predecessors as Melba, Destinn, Caruso and Martinelli.

But Beecham's splendid manager, Donald Baylis, died; Beecham at last was broke, and reorganising the Beecham Estate kept him out of music for almost three years (1920–23). His company was taken over as the British National Opera Company, and survived precariously almost entirely on his repertory material for seven years. I joined the Company in 1924; that autumn season we toured some twenty operas, all but one with his scenery and mostly in his casts. I think no opera company has ever toured so large a repertory, and in Britain certainly, so fine a collection of principals. Only once, alas, did Beecham conduct for us while I was in the Company. It was a propaganda performance of '*Cav and Pag*' for the Imperial League of Opera scheme; dashing rather than magical, as I remember it. I was present at another propaganda performance, of *Faust* with the Carl Rosa, which was so electrifying and so moving that we all, including the cast, could hardly believe our ears. Thus could Beecham on the instant revitalise his performers' response to an old warhorse.

1920–1923

At this time Sir Thomas was successfully involved in staving off bankruptcy and paying off almost all the debts he had incurred in the pursuit of music. His formal return to music was signalised by a concert, suitably publicised, at the Royal Albert Hall, in April, 1923. Sir Thomas conducted the combined London Symphony and Albert Hall Orchestra in a typical Beecham programme which naturally included Strauss's *Ein*

Heldenleben (A Hero's Life). He renewed his association, both as conductor and benefactor, with the London Symphony Orchestra, and occasionally conducted for the British National and the Carl Rosa Opera Companies. He made recordings, and revised and revived Handel's *Solomon* for its first performance since the 18th century. This was at a concert of the Royal Philharmonic Society, at which he received the Society's Gold Medal. He also arranged and composed the music for John Fletcher's play, *The Faithful Shepherdess*, for the Phoenix Society. He renewed his association with his old friends at Liverpool and Manchester. In the latter city he conducted the first performance of a piano concerto by Hamilton Harty in March, 1923, with the composer as soloist. (In 1920 Harty had been enthusiastically appointed permanent conductor of the Hallé Orchestra on Beecham's recommendation, a post he held for twelve memorable years.)

Sir Thomas now prepared to launch the Imperial League of Opera; a good deal of money had been contributed, and fine plans were laid, but fresh financial difficulties cropped up, and it ended with the subscriptions going mainly to stop-gap operatic enterprises and to Delius recordings. A number of subscribers claimed their money back. (Beecham's financial vicissitudes and campaigns of litigation would fill a considerable volume of biography.) On the more practical side, Beecham accepted the direction of the Leeds Triennial Festival and (later) the Norwich Festival, and, as he had done more than once before, he came to the rescue of the Royal Philharmonic Society when its survival was in jeopardy.

The year 1929 was memorable for the Delius Festival which Beecham promoted in London: a week of orchestral and chamber concerts devoted to the music of his friend of many years. Delius, now blind and paralysed, was brought over from his home in France, and it proved the joy and consolation of his last tragic years. In this year, too, Beecham revived Handel's *Hercules* and began his inspiring association with the Opera School at the Royal College of Music; the opera was *The Magic Flute*, designed and produced by the present writer, who then began to work for him. In 1930 occurred another of his generous rescue operations. A so-called Festival at the Scala Theatre

(London) got on the rocks. Beecham had agreed to conclude the event with one or two performances of *Der Freischütz* (produced by the present writer). When a fold-up seemed probable, Beecham offered to conduct a second week of performances without fee, to save everybody and because he liked the opera! (The Agathe was Thea Phillips, whose reputation was made from then on; incidentally, she became the protagonist of one of the Beecham *Messiah* legends—see page 157.)

Sir Thomas was at this time negotiating with the BBC and the London Symphony Orchestra for the formation of a full-time, permanent symphony orchestra in London. (Hitherto, the only full-time orchestra in England had been the Bournemouth Municipal Orchestra.) Accounts of these negotiations differ, but one should remember that musical politics can be quite discordant and should never be encored. The philanthropic Courtauld family and Dr Malcolm Sargent, whose name was yet to make, participated in further negotiations, but these again broke down with some bitterness on all sides, never forgotten except by 'Tommy', who generally forgot quarrels as fast as he made them. In 1931, in spite of recurrent ill-health and lameness, he again supervised the Leeds Triennial Festival and promoted a remarkable season of Russian Opera at Sir Henry Irving's old theatre, the Lyceum, thus breaking (temporarily) its long dégringolade as a dance hall. Sir Thomas himself conducted *Prince Igor*, *Sadko*, *Roussalka* (Dargomijsky), *The Tsar's Bride* and *Russlan and Ludmilla*, with his old friend Chaliapin in his famous dual role in *Prince Igor*.

These various occupations somehow ushered in a period of intense, even phenomenal, activity which was to last eight years. Abroad, his American concerts established his enduring fame; elsewhere, it was built up in such centres as Paris, Rome, Prague, Budapest and Munich. It was while he was in Munich that he received a telephone call from Dr Sargent to the effect that the orchestral negotiations had finally broken down; his instantaneous reply was that they should form an orchestra 'of their own'. The Courtaulds, who were prepared to finance a series of concerts conducted by Sargent, and other rich sponsors were persuaded to support what soon became one of the great orchestras of the world, and still exists as the London Philharmonic. After a series of most unconventional sectional rehearsals with players young and old, its first historic concert took place in Queen's Hall on 7 October, 1932 (*Carnaval Romain*, the Prague Symphony, *Brigg Fair* and *Ein Heldenleben*—all memorable performances).

Earlier in the same year, while he was a guest of the New York Philharmonic Orchestra, Sir Thomas was invited by cable to open the Covent Garden season with *Die Meistersinger*. His return to this theatre was triumphant; he also conducted three performances of *Tristan*, two of *Götterdämmerung*, and *Tannhäuser*.

1933–1944

The following year he began as joint manager at Covent Garden with Geoffrey Toye, who had been one of his earliest lieutenants in the Beecham Opera Company. During the next three seasons they introduced *The Damnation of Faust* (Berlioz), *Don Carlos*, *Schwanda the Bagpiper*, *Arabella*, *Lohengrin*, *La Cenerentola* (first revival since 1891), *Turandot*, *Koanga* (Delius), *Alceste* (Gluck), *L'Italiana in Algeri* (with Conchita Supervia and her Pomeranian), *Ariane et Barbe-bleu* (Dukas), *Don Juan de Mañara* (Goossens), *The Serf* (George Lloyd), and *The Bartered Bride*. In 1933 and 1934 he again gave his services to the Royal College of Music, immediately after the rigours of the Covent Garden season, to direct and conduct performances of Vaughan Williams's *Hugh the Drover* and Delius's *A Village Romeo and Juliet*. In both works Beecham turned to memorable musical account the freshness and enthusiasm of his young performers.

In 1934 Delius died; at his funeral at Limpsfield Beecham conducted his music and spoke the oration reproduced on pp. 171–3. He planned the Delius Trust. And at Covent Garden he conducted *Fidelio*, two cycles of *The Ring*, *Die Meistersinger* and *Otello*. The opening performance was *Fidelio*, with Lotte Lehmann singing for the first time in London the part of Leonora, a role in which she was always reckoned to have been supreme. The occasion was somewhat damped by Beecham's cutting rebuke—'Shut up, barbarians!'—to members of the audience who applauded as he began the announced performance of the

Leonora No. 3 overture as a transition from the prison scene to the scene of liberation.[1]

During the next year at Covent Garden Beecham conducted *Carmen* (with Conchita Supervia but without her Pomeranian), two cycles of *The Ring, Lohengrin, Prince Igor*; in the Imperial League of Opera season which followed he conducted *Der Freischütz* (with Eva Turner) and Delius's *Koanga*. In the previous season Wilhelm Furtwängler, later to become a friend and colleague of Beecham, made his first appearance with *Tristan*.

In 1936 owing to the resignation of the managing director, Geoffrey Toye, Beecham was left in sole command. He produced a new and distinguished *Tales of Hoffman*, conducted two cycles of *The Ring*, and introduced Malcolm Sargent to Covent Garden in three performances of *Louise*. The year included the débuts of Kirsten Flagstad, Hilde Konetzni. Kerstin Thorborg, Tiana Lemnitz and Ludwig Weber, all of whom left memorable names at Covent Garden. And in these years Beecham invited, among other conductors, Furtwängler, Fritz Reiner, Erich Kleiber, Felix Weingartner and Hans Knappertsbusch—the last was prevented from coming by the Nazis. But Sir Thomas did manage to secure the Dresden Opera for a fortnight; during their visit he conducted eight concerts in Germany, while at home he organised provincial tours of opera. Ernest Newman wrote this year, 'On a hundred occasions I felt tempted to stand up and thank providence for Beecham, and probably would have done so, could I have been sure I was addressing my thanks for so demoniac a phenomenon to the right quarter!'

Once more the German horizon was beginning to darken. But Beecham kept up his entente with Furtwängler, and engaged his expatriate secretary, Berta Geissmar, who was devoted to them both, and who travelled safely under the aegis of Sir Thomas and under the nose of Hitler, with whom Beecham had an amusing encounter during his German tour with the London Philharmonic Orchestra. This was Coronation year. Beecham, when in Berlin, had planned a large repertory for the Spring season,

---

[1] The incident has become legendary and has been misreported more than once. People who were present, and others closely associated with him, can confirm that neither then nor on any occasion whatsoever did this master of language use the common and coarser word attributed to him.

with Furtwängler's *Ring, Parsifal, Orphée* and *Alceste*, Goossens' new *Don Juan de Mañara* and *Pelléas et Mélisande*. For Covent Garden and performances elsewhere he engaged numerous conductors, young and old, who included John Barbirolli, Eugene Goossens, Robert Ainsworth, Lawrance Collingwood, Stanford Robinson and Albert Wolff. Such a list reminds one that throughout his long career Sir Thomas was always ready to give others a chance, while glad to share a season with the greatest of his fellow-conductors, as noted in the preceding paragraphs.

Notable performances during the 1937 season were *Otello* (with Martinelli and Tibbett) and *Carmen* in Harold André's fine production. Despite good performances in the German and French operas, some of the productions fell short of expectations, and a number of critics were so acid as to annoy Beecham, who withdrew their free tickets. In his curtain speech at the end of the season he remarked characteristically, 'Never before in the history of Covent Garden has the Press attained so high a state of excellence. We on our side have not been able to live up to it. We propose to devote the next six months to the careful reading of every word that has been written in the newspapers. We have become sadder and wiser people, for you know how seriously we take everything that is said about us.' Apart from Covent Garden, he again directed the Leeds Festival, and conducted numerous concerts as a welcome guest in Manchester and Liverpool, and extended his Herculean labours as an impresario by promoting Sunday concerts at Covent Garden and the Cambridge Theatre.

While the clouds were gathering over Europe in 1938 the Covent Garden season saw a more cautious repertoire. It was restricted to Wagner, Strauss, *Fidelio, Rigoletto*, three Puccini and two Mozart operas. The most distinguished performances were Beecham's *Zauberflöte* (with Tauber, Gerhard Hüsch, Tiana Lemnitz and Erna Berger), but Vittorio Gui and Erich Kleiber gave a foretaste of the great British reputation each was to acquire. In *Der Rosenkavalier*, conducted by the latter, occurred the historic breakdown of Lotte Lehmann in the first act and her immediate replacement by Hilde Konetzni, who happened to be in the audience. Beecham conducted *Elektra, Lohengrin* and *Die Meistersinger* (in addition to *Die Zauberflöte*), while Furtwängler conducted the two *Ring* cycles. In the concert field he organised and conducted a Sibelius Festival in London; six concerts, with all seven symphonies, *Tapiola*, the Violin Concerto and other works. He conducted concerts in Brussels and Paris, and France made him a Commander of the Legion of Honour.

It is not surprising that such a life began to tell on Beecham's constitution. He acted as artistic adviser to a short additional season of opera in English, but did not conduct himself. The season suffered heavy losses, whereupon he returned to the fray and collected new forces, vocal and financial, for a season in 1939. He wrote to *The Times*, scouting with trenchant eloquence, 'all the jitters and jumps that would bring discredit upon a community of elderly nuns'. His plan to bring the Dresden Opera and a company from Czechoslovakia to London had to be 'postponed' for political reasons, and Flagstad's reappearance unfortunately fell through. But on 1 May, Queen Mary attended the opening performance of *The Bartered Bride*. In this season Weingartner made his début with a *Parsifal* (he was to have become a colleague of Beecham at the Opera for some time ahead), and Sir Thomas conducted *The Ring*. After the Covent Garden season he was to have rested for a year on medical advice, but on the outbreak of war he was conducting concerts with his London Philharmonic Orchestra as soon as they could be arranged in wartime conditions. Asked why he was not resting, he replied, 'I heard that there was a state of National Emergency, so I emerged . . .'

Throughout its history Covent Garden has been the Mecca of aspiring opera singers, but looking back, its galaxies were never more brilliant than during Beecham's many years of control between 1910 and 1939. He seems always to have attracted the brightest stars, just as it used to be said, 'He always gets the best players.'

There followed nearly five years of constant travel and activity abroad, success and failure alternating in a manner characteristic of the war years. First, he crossed to America, then beyond to fulfil an Australian tour already booked. This was a period of very mixed success and frustration, now part of the Beecham legend. He met with mostly second-rate orchestras and temporarily galvanised them into admired vitality, while his speeches sometimes shocked by their merciless criticism more than they stimulated by their wit. On all sorts of topics he told Australians and Americans perhaps too much of the political and social truth . . . and 'it is only the truth which hurts'. Many acts of kindness to young musicians are recorded, and many snubs to the pretentious. One of his finest achievements was a concert for unemployed musicians which the New York press found 'sensational'.

In the course of some sixty thousand miles of travel over both continents, one particular change of circumstances was effected; after some thirty years of separation from his first wife he secured a divorce, and married a young English pianist, Betty Humby, of considerable personality and repute. She often played some of his favourite concertos with him, but ill-health slowly gained on her, which the strain of professional tours could only exacerbate. His devotion to her and constant care were noticeable, and the posthumous dedication of his Delius biography bears touching witness to his affection.

While in America, with his directorship of the Seattle Orchestra as some sort of base, he made tours of the States, Canada and Mexico. His debut at 'The Met' was in 1942, with Bach's *Phoebus and Pan* and Rimsky-Korsakov's *Le Coq d'Or*. He took part in the special tribute to Marjorie Lawrence, the international soprano who had become paralysed, and during the next two years he conducted *Hoffman, Carmen, Faust, Manon, Louise* (with Grace Moore), *Tristan, Falstaff* and *Mignon* at 'The Met', and concerts with the New York Philharmonic and other American orchestras. Years later he promised to tell me in detail about his hilarious experiences during a short season in Mexico, 'when we can get a day in the country together'. He looked back on it with great delight as a fantastic episode; but we never got that day, so I can but hope that his account is embodied in the yet unpublished addition to his autobiography. [The first volume, *A Mingled Chime*, stops short, alas, at 1924. It is packed with wit and wisdom and will bear much re-reading. It appeared in 1944, soon after his return to England in a cargo boat.]

1945–1949

Beecham was now sixty-five; the grey had turned to white, and the face, never florid, was a pleasant pink. But the whole impression was one of sprightliness and benignity curiously mixed. He was known by now round the world (except in the Orient) as much as a personality as a musician; his familiarity as a unique interpreter was to deepen in the last phases of his crowded life. After so many vicissitudes, so many battles on the operatic and concert fields, not forgetting those in financial and legal territory, one might have expected a dignified decline into a quiet retirement. But there were to be two more periods, one of unsettled, almost feverish activities—concerts, broadcasts, authorship, collecting pictures and house-moving, and a final slow sunset of concerts and recordings, in the glow of the last splendid orchestra he was to form. The difficult years were roughly from 1944 to 1950; henceforward the storm-clouds so often hanging around his path were softened and tipped, if not with gold, certainly with glory. There had been crises on the way, two of which, bearing upon his career as an impresario, call for a few words.

In pursuance of a one-sided grievance by John Barbirolli, Sir Thomas was never again invited to conduct the Hallé Orchestra, which he had twice saved from dissolution and with which he had had a continuing association since 1912. Moreover, his presidency of the Hallé Concerts Society, an honorary post which he had held since 1934, was terminated behind his back by a Committee which again disloyally surrendered to pressure. Beecham's jocular letter to the *Manchester Guardian*[2] made those responsible look ridiculous, but the wound was deep, and the

----

[2] 'I desire to affirm, and with all the emphasis in my power, that not only am I still the president of the Hallé Society but that I have not the smallest intention of resigning or permitting myself to be removed from that position. The committee... may succeed even in getting a new president appointed, but that will not budge me from my stand. It will only mean that the society will enjoy the uncommon advantage of two presidents instead of one. Although this duality of appointment is rare in the annals of public institutions, it is not wholly without precedent. For one hundred years during the Middle Ages Christendom beheld the edifying spectacle of rival Popes, one in Rome and the other in Avignon, each periodically addressing the whole body of the faithful as if he alone were the true vice-regent of heaven upon earth. Yet so far as I can read, the cause of religion does not appear to have suffered from this division of authority, which assuredly added considerably to the stock of gaiety among the contemporary communities of unbelievers outside.'

resentment of his many Manchester adherents very genuine; not until 1955 was he asked to conduct a Hallé concert, and then it was with his own orchestra.

Meanwhile Beecham conducted frequently for the BBC in London, and in his native North he conducted the BBC Northern Orchestra in Manchester and elsewhere and renewed his association with the Liverpool Philharmonic Society. Among his studio performances for the BBC were *Tristan*, *Prince Igor*, *A Village Romeo and Juliet*, and a memorable performance of *A Mass of Life*, and later, *Irmelin* (also by Delius), Cherubini's *The Water Carrier*, and his old favourite, Bizet's *The Fair Maid of Perth*.

The other cloud on his horizon in that often tempestuous period gathered over the London Philharmonic Orchestra, which had fought hard to survive without him. Their first happy reunion slid somehow into friction and finally into separation. Beecham was neither blameless nor wholly to blame; fate, as so often in his incredible career, seemed bent on throwing everything into dissolution only to furnish him with the conditions for some new achievement. This time it was the fifth and last orchestra which he collected, rehearsed and launched in 1946, the Royal Philharmonic. Happily both the LPO and the RPO survive, and long may they do so! These splendid instruments each sustained for many years much of the Beecham style. The first concert of the Royal Philharmonic Orchestra was in Croydon, at the Fairfield Hall. By 1950 it had established itself, to quote Charles Reid, 'as one of the key orchestras of the world ... At the beginning of his eighth decade Beecham was the unapproached and unquestioned king of the English musical scene as well as one of the nation's chief symbols in foreign eyes.' Precisely.

In 1946 Sir Thomas gave his second Delius Festival; this time there were seven concerts, split between the Royal Albert and Central Westminster Halls. And at last he appeared at Glyndebourne, where his Orchestra was subsequently employed for a number of years. His great series of late recordings was begun, with the Delius sequence among the first (see page 196). The following year he organised a festival of music by another old friend, Richard Strauss, who, then eighty-three, was received with acclaim at the concerts. And for Beecham the year saw him

. .

embark on more world tours, in the course of which he visited Italy, Spain, Portugal, Vienna, Paris, Switzerland, Canada and the Americas. In 1949 his seventieth birthday was celebrated with wide recognition, a concert at the Albert Hall, and many tributes, of which Richard Capell's in *Time and Tide* and the *Daily Telegraph* are perhaps the best (see Bibliography).

1950–1962

After a lapse of four years, Beecham was summoned again to conduct extensively in North America in 1950–1, and he took part in the Glyndebourne Mozart Festival. He spent most of 1952 in his own country, where, in addition to his London concerts he conducted fifty-two concerts in forty-three towns, and returned to Covent Garden as a guest conductor for six performances of *Die Meistersinger* (see page 86). A small side-line in these years was the holding of auditions, averaging fifty sessions a year. In spare time, when any occurred, he worked at his biography of Delius.

The vitality required for such a life, when summed-up even superficially, amounts to an incredible intensity. One is familiar certainly with touring virtuosi and conductors with engagement lists looking almost as heavy; but they do not have to audition, engage and rehearse opera casts, direct festivals and promote concerts at the same time. Beecham was Hercules and his task-master Admetus rolled into one. Handel, as I have suggested elsewhere, was his only parallel in British musical history, not, of course, as a creative artist, but as a National Institution.

In all this enterprise there were a few—surprisingly few—operatic ventures which misfired. In early life Massenet's *Werther*, as he has told us, was one; it was both before and after its time: in our own day it is now appreciated as a period piece. His championship of de Lara's *Nail* and Joseph Holbrooke's *Dylan* was presumably based on personal regard for the individuals who wrote them, and an attempt to find a viable opera by a contemporary native. And then, in his old age, after the many successes of a lifetime, he proposed to revive, as the most suitable operatic contribution to the Festival of Britain, *The Bohemian Girl*, a favourite of his boyhood (as, up to a point, it was of mine). He had long wished to revive it, and the festival gave him his opportunity, or excuse. He knew what good young singers the Americans produced for their home-product, rather dubiously called 'musicals'. He engaged some of these and supervised a lavish production of the opera which in our youth we irreverently called 'Bo Girl out of the British Ring'—the remainder of the 'cycle' presumably consisting of *Maritana* and *The Lily of Killarney.* Neither of these is in any danger of revival, and the glamour of his most seductive phrasing which Beecham gave to the splendid tunes in 'Bo Girl' failed to breathe new life into the old opera. It was not for Covent Garden; its over-all *ethos* was beyond the rescue even of the Beecham genius. For all his artistry and all its melodic charm, 'When other lips' is for other days . . .

A more worthwhile and successful venture was the first performance, sixty-three years after its composition, of Delius's early opera *Irmelin*, which Beecham financed (the whole of the material had to be newly copied) and produced at the Oxford Playhouse, in 1953. The BBC recognised the significance of the event and later arranged a studio broadcast, but for all its Delian loveliness the opera as a whole was too frail to survive. In this same year Sir Thomas conducted a concert for the Finnish Sibelius Fund at the Festival Hall, and was presented with the White Rose of Finland in recognition of his championship of their greatest composer.

The concerts, tours and recordings continued—his ninety-odd concerts at the Festival Hall are discussed elsewhere. Among his splendid recordings, perhaps the most remarkable is the *Bohème* which he made in New York in 1956—almost fortuitously, as it appears the whole work was recorded in four days in a warehouse, there being no suitable studio available. Beecham's recording is, by common accord among connoisseurs of the opera, regarded as the best performance it has ever had. Beecham remembered that he had been through 'that piece', as he would call his favourite musical works, with Puccini in his youth, and so he 'knew exactly what the composer wanted'. This was true.

In 1955, as noted earlier, Beecham and his Orchestra were at last received into the Hallé Society's concert scheme, to the gratification of his many Manchester admirers, and among other activities he directed Grétry's *Zémire et Azor* at the Bath

Assembly. Ever since the *Tableau Parlant* of his youth he had often wanted to mount another Grétry opera: rather sadly this turned out to be, despite other plans, his last opera in a British theatre.

In 1956, amid much concertising and broadcasting there were several unique incidents: immediately after the memorable *Bohème* already mentioned, came an interlude of some weeks in the University of Illinois, where he rehearsed and directed a Mozart festival which included the *Requiem, Figaro* (in his original version), and two symphonies, and delivered a lecture: soloists, chorus and orchestra all from the university—surely no such artistic enterprise has ever found its way into an under-graduate course? And in May he recorded in England Mozart's *Seraglio*. In June he gave the Oxford Romanes Lecture on one of his Elizabethan favourites, John Fletcher (see page 54). Then at the Edinburgh Festival, where his performances included the Choral Symphony and the memorable Brahms Second Symphony, he finished up with the Handel *Fireworks Music* with the massed bands filling the huge Castle Esplanade, and a fireworks finale: after startling the City with incidental explosions through-out the afternoon rehearsal, the evening performance was mainly remarkable for its rich and perfectly controlled *pianissimos*, while even the fireworks seemed to adopt quite decorous dynamics! Before the year was out he had added a recording of *The Fair Maid of Perth* (Bizet) (not issued commercially), *Solomon* (Handel) and the Liszt *Faust Symphony*, another rarity.

Sir Thomas was made a Companion of Honour in 1957. The following year a bronze portrait head (by David Wynne) was unveiled after a concert rehearsal at the Festival Hall, where it is on permanent loan from the Royal Philharmonic Society. And there was his mainly triumphant season at the Colon Opera House, Buenos Aires, wherein occurred the much-publicised quarrel with the now-veteran soprano, Zinka Milanov, which was politically patched-up amid tumultuous applause. But the season was for him clouded by the illness, now acute, of his wife, Betty. He lavished every care upon her, and when she died, he cancelled one performance, stoically completed his season and returned to England.

In 1959 Beecham saw his scholarly and graceful biography of Delius through the press, and quixotically engaged his old friend and protégé Sir Eugene Goossens to refurbish the score of

Messiah for him; he produced this mildly updated version in Lucerne. He still struggled to record as much music as possible, sensing that the time was short for the only lasting legacy he could bequeath. In the autumn he married his secretary, Miss Shirley Hudson. Sir Thomas's eightieth birthday had been celebrated by a luncheon given by upwards of three hundred colleagues and friends. Two brilliant speeches were made, one by the general administrator of Covent Garden, Sir David Webster, gracefully burying old hatchets, and the other by Sir Thomas himself, blithely recalling the prowess of his players at all times and the modest contribution made by the conductor, his summary of the relationship boiling down to 'I just get the best players and let them play ... At rehearsal they play the piece through; any mistakes they know about as well as I do, so we play it through again; then they know it. And *I* know what they are going to do ... *They don't know what I am going to do ...* so that at the performance everyone is on his toes, and we get a fine performance ...' An extreme understatement, but those who knew him understood ...

But the sands were now running out; plans were still made ceaselessly, but most had to be abandoned. In 1960 he was taken ill in America, and returned to England. He had planned to conduct two of his favourite operas, ten performances of *Die Zauberflöte* at Glyndebourne and *Les Troyens* at Covent Garden, but they did not materialise. His last Festival Hall concert took place in April, and his final concert, admirably described by Charles Reid, was at Portsmouth. He lunched the Orchestra and devoted most of the rehearsal to watching the Cup Final on a specially imported television set. Later he went to Montreux to rest before the Glyndebourne season, but he died on 8 March, 1961, after a second thrombosis. He was cremated at Brookwood, near Woking. At a memorial service in Westminster Abbey his Royal Philharmonic Orchestra was conducted by Sir Malcolm Sargent in a programme mainly of favourite Beecham pieces; it was probably the most moving and beautiful performance Sargent ever gave.

A Cloud of Witnesses

[Placed in alphabetical order, these contributions make an anthology in a rather special sense—a collection of memories and portraits, all individual, and produced in response to a personal request. Their authors were all independent and ignorant of the contributions of the rest: their reports were readily supplied, with no directive as to content, except to avoid tempting anecdotes in favour of points of musical significance.

In consequence it has come about that the reader had better be warned in advance about one or two 'first impressions'. The extraordinary near-unanimity of feeling and sometimes of expression will not surprise those who knew Sir Thomas, or indeed those who only heard him. But the fact that these are spontaneous views of a number of independent witnesses, all of whom are gifted or distinguished in different ways, must be set against any impression of monotony; and it must not only be admitted, but emphasised, that this collection has been made not to sell the book as a titillating entertainment for the casual reader, but as a piece of historical evidence of musical genius. The English have always been ready to welcome and adulate the foreign musician, and the fascination exercised by this Lancashire-born artist is something unique and perhaps a little uncomfortable to acknowledge.

Furthermore, despite his genius, his charm and his undoubted and frequent kindness, Beecham does not emerge as a saint. The perfectionist and the sensitive artist cannot help—can he be expected to help?—moments of irritation, exasperation and even harsh dismissal of obstacles when thwarted, apparently by hostile circumstances, of the grand effect conceived and fiercely struggled for. But I can think of no leader ever more devotedly followed, no conductor so affectionately revered by his many performers almost to a man, from all of whom he exacted such exhausting service. To me, and I hope to the percipient reader, this chorus of sunny memories is something unheard of in a lifetime spent in the world of professional music; and it must be left to the reader for whom his records are still available, to judge whether the few discordant notes in these extracts which I have come across and retained, bring any serious blemish to a handsome portrait. The varying circumstances and approach of the contributors preclude any symmetrical presentation, but the several situations as between contributor and editor should be sufficiently clear.]

LEOPOLD STOKOWSKI

[This name has been put first and out of order because he is the last survivor* of the eminent conductors invited by Sir Thomas to share a season with him. When I asked for his commentary on Beecham I was given an appointment during a recording session on one of his last London visits (1970). He broke off from vetting and selecting portions from two unique takes of the '1812' (to which he had added voices for the Russian hymn!), to dictate to me, very carefully weighing every word, a single sentence, passing from the current popular conception to the true professional verdict on his former colleague. This so curiously and clearly foreshadows the general drift of the ensuing collection of evidence as to make its appearance suitable at the beginning. The key phrase is 'a keen and penetrating musical sense'.]

Beecham was a magnificent musician and great conductor—one of the greatest in the world. Unfortunately, owing to other gifts —he was a brilliant wit and raconteur—people who did not have a keen and penetrating musical sense have come to regard him principally as a famous humorist rather than conductor, and so his musical achievements often come to be overlooked.

NORMAN ALLIN

[Frank Mullings[1] and Norman Allin were the two giants of the original Beecham Opera Company; and for many years after,

---

* d. 1976.

[1] The Wagnerian tenor familiar to two generations, and so justly portrayed in *A Mingled Chime*, chs. 32 and 33.

Allin was the leading English basso. When the following impressions appeared he was eighty-eight and a professor at the Royal College of Music; able to look back on his long career in something of a golden glow—in that way more fortunate than most of us whose view includes at least a storm-cloud or two; fortunate also that he comes alphabetically first in this series of recollections. He died in 1973.

Allin's rôles included Khan Kontchak in *Prince Igor* (in which I, just left school, first saw him—a tall, commanding figure: the nearest thing to Chaliapin I ever saw and heard), Gurnemanz, Ramfis, Hagen, Osmin, of course Sarastro, and in fact the whole bass repertoire. There was not a harsh note in his tremendous voice or in his temperament as colleague in the theatre. We were together in the British National Opera Company, and I particularly recall his sinister Sparafucile, and the sly comedy of his Simone in *Gianni Schicchi*. For this anthology he asked me to quote from the memorial broadcast on Beecham in which he took part, and from his letters to me. He had nothing but the happiest memories of Sir Thomas, and one was delighted to see him sitting with his old chief at the Beecham eightieth-birthday luncheon. On the air in 1961 he said:]

I well remember my first piano rehearsal with him, in the chorus room, for *Seraglio*. It was grand singing and working with him: everything seemed to be to his liking, and he did nothing but smile: nothing could have been easier or more helpful. In piano rehearsal he always seemed so relaxed and in a jocular frame of mind. When it came to orchestral rehearsal, it was very different —very different indeed: in plain English, he was the boss. But you didn't feel you must be watching his stick all the time; you just carried on and he accompanied. He was absolutely grand to work with in every way. I don't know what there was to be afraid of: he couldn't have been more charming.

[In Norman Allin's letters to me, he mentions his own 270 performances of *Messiah*, many of which must have been with Beecham; of whose first performance of the work he recalls that when 'Rejoice greatly' at rehearsal did not seem to go very well, he turned to the soprano and said, 'Shall we go over this jig once again?'[2]]

[Allin here remembers Beecham's performance of Kontchak:]

This must have been at Covent Garden, as I have such a clear recollection of the enormous stage (Albert Coates conducting). TB had an electric effect on the whole crowd as soon as he was noticed sitting in the stalls. Sometimes he expected quite a lot from his principals. I remember during a performance of *Faust* (I forget the conductor), he came up to me on the stage, and asked if I could sing *Boris Godunov* the following Tuesday. I said I could, but I got the unequalled help of T. E. Fairbairn, a master of stage technique. At the performance, Sir Thomas just smiled when the opera was ended. That is how I always remember working for him.

FELIX APRAHAMIAN
(Music critic, *Sunday Times*)

The phone rang, and I answered it. I was alone in the London Philharmonic Orchestra office. Thomas Russell was away, playing viola with the orchestra. A throat cleared, and a familiar voice, drawling yet articulated, inquired, 'Is there anyone there who can tell me the lowest note a bassoon can play?' 'B flat, Sir Thomas', I replied immediately. That was probably the first time the voice of the orchestra's assistant-secretary registered with its Founding Father, who from that time regarded its owner as a potentially useful person. For my part, I never let on that Hans Gal's little primer on orchestral instruments happened to be on my desk at the time. Nor did I ever tell him our librarian's sardonic comment when he heard of the inquiry: 'That's only Tommy's way of establishing that he's actually scoring one of his arrangements himself!' The score in question was the *Faithful Shepherd* suite adapted from Handel's *Pastor Fido*.

Of course I had been hovering round the Green Room and

---

[2] Of course, Beecham was remembering Handel's original version of this famous aria which was in 6/8 'jig' rhythm, quite hilarious in effect; Handel had either second thoughts or some good advice, and sobered it up somewhat in common time.

Ridinghouse Street entrance of the Queen's Hall at every
Beecham concert since the LPO's début with him on 7 October
1932. But, alas, now that at last I was actually working for the
orchestra, Beecham was about to leave it. On 4 April 1940
Beecham gave his greatest Sibelius performances at a Finland
Fund Concert, and after it, the LPO gave their Master supper
in an upper room at Pagani's. With his departure to Australia
and America imminent, I was aware that we faced not only the
hazards of war but what Ethel Smyth would have called 'a period
of total eclipse'. Yet in the event the LPO not only survived but
triumphed during Beecham's absence. And he returned to it.
The intrigues and misfortunes that divided him from it and led
to his founding of yet another orchestra belong to the musical
history of the time, duly recorded and one day to be revealed.

It was, however, during that brief second honeymoon with
his LPO that I came to know Beecham better. His former
secretary, Berta Geissmar, and I had been sharing an office for
four years, and I had been well briefed about his idiosyncrasies.
Sir Thomas enjoyed respectful attention, but hated sycophants.
Amuse him, divert him, but above all stand up to him. The
opportunity to do this came soon enough. He had decided to
arrange a piano concerto from the works of Handel for Lady
Betty Humby-Beecham, and I was sent to the RAM to copy out
some of Handel's borrowings from Gottlieb Muffat's *Componi-
menti musicali*, published by Chrysander as a supplement to the
collected edition of Handel. Although I regarded the particular
object of this exercise as footling—as the result proved—I held
my tongue and produced the required manuscript. I forget what
it was that Beecham said, but I remember being goaded to
express my preference of Bach to Handel rather trenchantly. And
having started a debate I stuck to my ground. Beecham's black
eyes opened wide. 'My God, what heresy!' he roared. But from
that time he trusted me. In the following years he employed me
on more congenial tasks than copying out Muffat, and I learned
much from him and about him.

Quite early on I realised that although he had a quite staggering
knowledge of history, he lacked any appreciation of history as
applied to his own particular subject—music. Musicology passed
him by. Tony Mayer and I provided him once with a spellbound
audience of two in a Paris hotel room when he addressed us just

as if we were a public meeting on the subject of French eighteenth-century history. And yet the researches of Robbins Landon meant nothing to him: on the morning of his eightieth birthday I found him re-marking corrupt nineteenth-century parts of Haydn's *Miracle* Symphony, not with textual corrections but with bowing marks and expressive 'hairpins'. When, in 1946, he asked me to write programme notes for his second Delius Festival, I had occasion to delve into the archives of the Delius Trust. The composer had kept all the conductor's letters, but the conductor had not kept one of the composer's.[3] I reported that the autograph score of Delius's first opera needed first-aid: the paper was so brittle that 'cello and bass parts broke off between the fingers as pages were turned. But I never obtained authority to spend a pound or two on having it bound and repaired by an expert. Sir Thomas would lose Delius autographs as readily as his own working scores, two of which I once found at Foyles and bought back for him. During the course of his essentially nomadic existence, the hotels of several continents must have been littered with some of his valuable musical leavings. To him, musical scores were only a means to a musical end. He had greater devotion to a few pieces of rather grand and tatty furniture than to his musical library.

Working for Sir Thomas sporadically since 1945, I am able in retrospect to assess some of the attributes which made him unique in his profession. On the one hand there was his ability to delegate; and on the other a shrewd, actuarial mind which calculated years ahead. Above all there was that quality he had of being able to communicate his musical thought. This was something far beyond stick technique. Lesser men would be safe beating a clear four in a bar, and leaving the rest to the orchestra. Beecham, who exuded rhythm from every pore in his body, did not have to beat four in a bar; though in fact he often did, for his conducting sobered in later years.

A few personal reminiscences will, I think, illustrate these facets of his character. Sir Thomas's willingness to delegate was not restricted to an orchestra. In this field it was manifest at every rehearsal. He never presumed to teach Leon Goossens or Paul Beard or Frederick Riddle, Lauri Kennedy or Geoffrey Gilbert,

---

[3] Utica, Lady Beecham, in 1963 still owned one early letter from Delius to Beecham.

or a hundred others, how to play their instruments. That was a mistake for which one of his juniors in the business was never forgiven. Beecham employed the best available instrumental talent, and trusted it. Undoubtedly he moulded it to his way of musical thought, but this he achieved with immense subtlety, half persuasive, half hypnotic; so that he was never served grudgingly. His rehearsals rarely ran the full allotted time, and his players invariably looked forward to the evening concert in pleasurable anticipation rather than boredom or dread, as with many others.

In the field of administration, Sir Thomas's delegation was often bound up with his propensity for procrastination. In the autumn of 1947 he was planning his complete recording of Gounod's *Faust*. Everything had been laid on, except the soloists. Studio, orchestra, chorus and technical staff were at the ready, but the conductor would not agree to the singers proposed by the record company. I was sent for—by Sir Thomas, not the record company—and told to go to Paris, find a French cast for *Faust*, and book them. My protestations were of no avail: they were swept aside by a three-figure fee and the prospects of a diverting week in Paris—in exchange for half-a-dozen names on a piece of paper. Since I have never worked in opera, I should perhaps explain that Sir Thomas's confidence in his protesting delegate was based solely on two facts: first, as partly responsible for the series of *Concerts de musique française* at the Wigmore Hall, I was in very close touch with the Paris musical scene; secondly, I had previously brought to his notice that highly musical coloratura soprano, Dorothy Bond, whom he had been pleased to engage on several occasions. (When I phoned him to remind him that I had proposed her specifically for the *Et incarnatus est* and high Mozart concert arias, and not as Debussy's *Demoiselle élue*, my caution was overruled: 'No! no! Miss Bond has just the timbre of voice needed—that of the illegitimate daughter of the village idiot!')

Whichever Sir Thomas believed in most—my ear, or my useful list of Paris phone numbers—this was a typical example of the way in which, having decided on someone's ability to do a particular thing, he would then happily delegate responsibility. It was during this episode that I also gained a little insight into the workings of what I have called his actuarial mind. In Paris, it was not long before, thanks to Roger Désormière and others, I had the ideal cast assembled: I even had time to investigate the musical text, and thanks to Irène Joachim, spent an hour with a surviving Gounod pupil, Henri Büsser, from whom I gathered valuable information to pass on to Sir Thomas. My briefing from the Gramophone Company regarding the fees for the soloists was that the three principals should each be offered a certain outright payment, without royalties. The singers met and decided to ask for exactly *four* times the figure proposed. I phoned Sir Thomas from Paris to tell him this. Quite unruffled, he answered, 'That's perfectly all right. They shall have what they ask for.' Back in London at the weekend, I asked my Gramophone Company contact, Victor Carne, for an explanation of this. 'You said that two hundred was all that could be afforded: now Sir Thomas authorises eight hundred. What is all this about?' 'Well, you see,' replied Victor, 'two hundred each is all *we* can allocate. But Sir Thomas has already calculated that in the first eighteen months of sales, his royalties on the set will come to about fifteen thousand pounds. He is perfectly prepared to spend two thousand of this now if it ensures an unrivalled cast and recording.' I began to get some inkling of the way Beecham's mind worked in these matters. To complete the tale I should add that just when everything was ready, the Director of the Paris Opéra put his spoke in: if Gounod's *Faust* was to be recorded with French singers, it should be recorded here in Paris with our orchestra and a French conductor, was the gist of his objection. Monsieur Hirsch completely overlooked the fact that the instigator of the recording was Sir Thomas Beecham. It was he who had decided to record *Faust,* not a commercial company who might be deflected from London to Paris. When Beecham learned that the singers of my choice might be prevented from participating, he phoned me and asked whether I could arrange for him to see the French Ambassador. Time was short. I pointed out that it would probably save a few days and be no less effective if he were to see the Cultural Counsellor of the Embassy instead. The appointment was made. On the dot, *mirabile dictu*, Sir Thomas stepped from the ancient Rolls as from a band-box, in formally elegant attire. Monsieur Varin and I were awaiting him on the doorstep of 58 Knightsbridge. The builders were in occupation: the library was shrouded in dust sheets, but a little oasis had been created for the interview. This began as a skilfully propelled monologue in which

Sir Thomas gave a trenchant, factual account of his connections
with French music.

'Now, Monsieur Varin, if I had asked my old friend, Monsieur
Rouché, for these artists, he would have sent them by the next
plane if necessary. But Monsieur Hirsch will not let me have
them. Who *is* this Monsieur Hirsch? No one seems ever to have
heard of him.' Monsieur Varin took the point. Then Sir Thomas
went off at a tangent, or so it seemed. 'Monsieur Varin, I believe
I hold some distinction in the *Légion d'Honneur*?' The *Conseiller
Culturel*, nothing if not thorough, had done his homework. 'Yes,
Sir Thomas, you are a *Commandeur* of the *Légion d'Honneur*.'
'Very well, Monsieur Varin, I understand that this entitles me to
twelve rifle shots at my funeral?' The very solid and habitually
imperturbable Monsieur Varin was mildly shaken by the course
of the conversation; but he knew his stuff and was quick off the
mark with: 'That is so, Sir Thomas,' adding something about
'douze coups de fusil à ses obsèques.' Sir Thomas paused a
moment. Then out it came. 'Monsieur Varin, I should be glad
if they could be discharged forthwith in the direction of Monsieur
Hirsch.' To this, of course, there was no reply except the happiest
beam across Monsieur Varin's face. The interview was at an end.
I like to think that the French Embassy did all they could for
their rather unusual *Commandeur,* but the Monsieur Hirsch 'no
one had ever heard of' held the trump card of contractual
obligations, so a compromise was reached in which Sir Thomas
got my Mephistopheles and Valentin, and a Faust and Marguerite
of Monsieur Hirsch's choice.[4]

On another occasion I personally experienced Sir Thomas's
ability to convey his feelings as to how the music should go,
although I was not facing him as an orchestral musician. I had
been summoned to Hallam Street, where the stormy petrel was
nesting for a time. There I found a raging Beecham tearing strips
off everyone. Ian Hunter, the Director of the Bath Assembly, was
there, looking crestfallen rather than perky. No soprano acceptable
to the conductor had yet been booked for the role of Zémire in
Grétry's *Zémire et Azor,* to be given there in 1955, and Sir
Thomas was announcing in no uncertain manner that he would
now see to this himself. 'Mr Aprahamian will proceed to Paris

---

[4] See also David Bicknell's account of the recording arrangements,
Hi-Fi/Stereo Review (N.Y.), Vol. 6, No. 6 (June 1961).

and there he will stay until he finds the singer I want.' I had no
option in the matter, but when the others present had been
dismissed (and, for once, this included Lady Betty Humby-
Beecham) I pointed out to Sir Thomas that he did me a disservice,
for my knowledge of Grétry in general and of *Zémire et Azor* in
particular, let alone the kind of voice he wanted, would go on
the back of a postage stamp. 'Quite simple, quite simple!' was
his encouraging remark as I was led to the piano. Sir Thomas
sat down at the keyboard and turned to the air for Zémire, *'Rose
chérie, aimable fleur'*. 'Now, this is how this goes.' The vocal
sounds he emitted were indescribable, hovering between two
adjacent semitones, swelling and fading into a husky *mezzo voce*,
and supported by a piano accompaniment in which every chord
was spread and no two notes in right and left hand parts were
ever sounded together. 'A charming little ditty,' he confided, and
my briefing was over. A few days later, seated in the empty Salle
Gaveau, I heard an interminable succession of Lakmés and
Zerbinettas, to whom I proposed *Rose chérie* as a sight-reading
test-piece. No sooner had the *ritornello* been played, and the first
phrase sung, than I realised that my briefing had, in a magical
way that I am at a loss to explain, been explicit and complete.
Sir Thomas had imparted to me *exactly* how the 'charming little
ditty' should go, *and* the quality of voice he required to sing it.
And what is even more remarkable, the briefing had given me
confidence enough to leap on to the platform and demonstrate
myself its tempo and the ingenuous manner in which it should
be sung, and to choose a gentle, flute-like voice rather than a
high-powered violin-like coloratura. Since all this was quite
different from the actual vocal and instrumental sounds and
nuances—if they can be called that—produced by Sir Thomas
himself, I realised something of what happened when he
conducted an orchestra, and how, behind exaggerated gestures,
roars and hissings, he succeeded—telepathically, perhaps—in
communicating an essentially precise musical message.

Zémire et Azor, so elegantly designed by Oliver Messel, and so
delightfully produced by Anthony Besch, reached the stage of
the lovely little Theatre Royal in Bath on Wednesday 11 May,
1955. The orchestra was the Bournemouth Symphony, then led
by Hugh Maguire, and Sir Thomas was in stunning form. It was
an entrancing operatic experience, but the tiny house was far

from full for the first night of the last opera England's greatest conductor conducted in his native land.

In 1959 I was privileged to be present at the last recording session he conducted. His eightieth birthday was already behind him, but he was still full of plans for the future. Beecham's post-war activity as a conductor was geared primarily to the making of gramophone records, and that actuarial as well as musical mind never allowed him to envisage a time when he would not be making them. In those last years, his French domicile had led to a recording *entente* with the Paris Orchestra National, and playing over to me the test records of the *Carmen* he had recently made with them, he could not conceal his delight at the result. Now, what other French music could he record with them? On 30 November, Sir Thomas phoned me from Paris:

'Now listen, I have five sessions here this week with the *National* to tidy up a few pieces. I only need three. What would you like me to record in the time that's left?'

'What about a Fauré record with the *Dolly* and *Pelléas* suites, with the *Pavane* and *Pénélope* Prelude as fill-ups?'

'Can we get the parts here?'

'Of course.' But Sir Thomas seemed doubtful.

'I wish I could come over to help.'

'Why don't you?'

'I have to be in town on Saturday morning.'

'Splendid! We can fly back together on Friday night.'

And so it was arranged that I would take the night ferry on the Thursday and go straight to the Salle Wagram for the first of the two Friday sessions, returning to London with Sir Thomas the same evening, after the second session.

I was at the Salle Wagram in good time, and at half-past nine Sir Thomas arrived. Before the players' break, various patches of the Franck and Lalo symphonies had been 'tidied up' in stereo. The play-backs of these Sir Thomas listened to during the interval. After it, he turned to Fauré's *Dolly* Suite, a score evidently more familiar to the orchestra than to him at that moment, although he had known the music in its original four-hand version. 'Pretty piece,' he commented to me after the '*Berceuse*'. 'Played it once as a piano duet with the old man himself.' Cautiously he conducted all six movements, without ever once stopping the orchestra or addressing a word to the players.

At one o'clock he released them, and I followed him into the ramshackle, improvised listening-room in that dilapidated barn of a place with its splendid acoustics. There, as he listened intently to the playback, he made a few pencil marks in the score; here and there a slur, stress, or 'hairpin', and asked for the orchestral parts to be collected. These we took back with us to his hotel.

After lunch Sir Thomas proposed that I should take a rest while he transferred into the separate parts the marks he had made in the score. I persuaded him that I was capable, at least, of copying his 'master' string parts, so that I occupied the luxurious double suite he had booked for me for precisely twenty-five minutes. During that time the industrious octogenarian had been working on the 'master'. Joining him in his suite, I marked the other string parts, while he dealt with the wind parts. We finished at a quarter to five, by which time the car was waiting to take us back to the Salle Wagram.

The evening session began at five. Sitting on the podium at Sir Thomas's feet, I was aware of a change that had taken place since the morning. The music had come into focus, clear and alive. 'How does that sound?' asked Sir Thomas after the '*Berceuse*'. It had sounded lovelier than I had ever heard it before, but, sticking my neck out, I suggested that the first two notes of the canon might be more clearly articulated. 'Very well, bring me the parts.' Two pencilled stresses each for the first bassoon and the first horn, and a look in their direction at the re-play, put the matter right. '*Mi-aou*' followed without a hitch. A small adjustment in dynamics and '*Le jardin de Dolly*' joined it on the tape. The whole Suite was recorded with ten minutes to spare: time to play through Fauré's *Pavane*.

As we walked to the waiting car, my mind was buzzing with questions regarding the interpretative miracle I had witnessed that day. 'What made the difference this evening?' I asked. 'This morning, although the players may have known the music, which you were only reading, they played perfunctorily. And then you marked the parts. This evening both you and the orchestra were giving so much more. But what made the music come to life like that? You? They? The marks?'

Sir Thomas smiled. 'A little of all those things, a little of all those things.' But of course he didn't know. Nor did the happy leader of the orchestra, aware of the quality of the performance they had just given, but unable to explain the magic that had emanated from Sir Thomas. To my questioning glance, all he had been able to utter was: 'C'est un dieu, c'est un dieu.' And so he was, in his life and music, a little of all of them—Wotan, Donner, even Loge. We shall never see his like.

PAUL BEARD

[In the summer of 1932 a violinist on vacation from leading the Birmingham City Orchestra was offered by telegram from Beecham the leadership of the new orchestra he was then founding. Paul Beard's acceptance destined him to become probably the best known English orchestral leader of his day. After some weeks of intensive rehearsal, sectional and complete, the memorable first concert of the London Philharmonic Orchestra took place at the Queen's Hall. Beard well remembers, on going on to play *Heldenleben*, with its particularly taxing first-fiddle solos, Sir Thomas's cheery, 'Come on, Paul, let's show 'em what we can do!'

The following four years were the most gruelling imaginable for any single leader of a large concert-and-opera orchestra (the days of divided leadership for both kinds of work had not then reached England from the Continent), and the strain upon his health (an average of seventy hours' playing per week for months on end) forced him to resign. He then made an even bigger name for himself as leader of the BBC Symphony Orchestra from 1936 to 1962.

In answer to my letter of inquiry, he speaks of how he remembers his first great chief.]

I doubt if I can tell you anything worth while that you don't already know about Beecham, but I must say that, in my forty-odd years of leading, I never knew a conductor who gave me greater pleasure in music. In temperamental make-up and musical feeling we suited each other perfectly, and the absolute freedom I was given to use my own judgment in dealing with technical matters—bowing, fingering, phrasing, and so on—completed a bond of understanding and agreement which always existed between us in music.

The feeling of close partnership and unity with him and the whole orchestra was, I feel, particularly in the early years of the LPO, one good reason for the unique warmth of feeling, musicianship and brilliance he invariably inspired in his players. But above all else was his own great gift of magnetic personality, the essential inborn quality that transports an orchestra to its ultimate peak of artistic achievement.

[Paul Beard has also cheerfully reminded me of one of the true Beecham legends of which he was the amused victim. When Beard went to lead the BBC Symphony Orchestra he soon established a visible discipline and control of the violin section, which was useful particularly in a varied series of unfamiliar and often inexperienced conductors. When Tommy reappeared to do a guest performance, this caught his eye and ear, and before the interval of the first rehearsal, he stroked that immaculately barbered chin, and with a sly glance and smile around the strings, murmured, 'May I suggest to you, gentlemen, that when we reassemble, you pay a little more attention to *this* beard?']

ADOLF BORSDORF

[The Borsdorf family is another well known for the fine instrumentalists it has contributed to English professional music. Adolf Borsdorf, the violist and concert agent, was for some time concert director of the London Philharmonic Orchestra, and his relatives of two generations played for Beecham almost throughout his long career. He has told me with pleasure and amusement of many experiences, both joyous and difficult, of those days more colourful than our own. There were times when Beecham's meteoric orbits threw the whole financial balance of the orchestra sadly awry: it survived in spite of them by its sheer guts; and then Beecham would try to make amends by conducting a number of concerts without fee, and promoting concerts and recordings. Somehow, largely by tact on the part of leading players, and bursts of generosity on Beecham's part, friendly relations were never really terminated, though Beecham pressed on, as by some inevitable destiny, with founding the last of his five orchestras, having left the others to sink or swim as he had also done with a number of the younger colleagues whom he swept along with him—by and large all managing to survive with considerable distinction when the great man swung off on some fresh trajectory. Clever as Tommy was at meeting emergencies and crises, he was sometimes unaccountable over expected appearances and performances when irresistible impulse or his untamable genius rocketed him off on some new path; of such times Borsdorf, like Fenby and others before and after him, had to bear the brunt. On the other hand, he told me how Beecham, definitely stricken with a feverish attack, had forced himself to turn out and conduct a concert by which otherwise the orchestra stood to lose badly, and in the course of performance by some extraordinary process of concentration and perspiring energy, completely ignoring the risk, he threw off the temperature and weakness and effected a cure. A different Beecham came off the platform!

And there were the joyous occasions, apart from the startling performances and away from the concert-room, when Borsdorf would be summoned to attend the maestro on a tour of architectural sight-seeing. Tommy had no love for the ecclesiastical world, but loved cathedrals and knew a great deal about them: in this way they together visited Wells, Bristol, Peterborough and Antwerp, among others, on all of which Beecham had a fund of information. And there was one delightful day when Borsdorf thought he would turn the tables on Tommy by proposing a trip to a place the great man had never heard of—the Wookey Hole Caves. The suggestion was accepted, and the courageous efforts of that normally dignified person to adapt his stocky and substantial anatomy on all fours to the low tunnels bristling with stalactites and stalagmites proved more diverting to Tommy's faithful follower even than the famous witticisms at rehearsal.

And there was one other little story that definitely appertains to these pages. Borsdorf had organised three concerts in Belgium, and a highlight at one of them was a sparkling performance of the Dvořák G major symphony which the Bruxellois had never heard! But at one concert in the Palais des Beaux Arts, the director, Marcel Cuvelier, turned to Borsdorf after the first item, and said, 'This Sir Bichem of yours, he conducts as the bird sings!' Our own best critics could do no better nor briefer than that.]

GWYDION BROOKE

(Son of the composer Josef Holbrooke: Beecham's second bassoon in the LPO and his principal in the RPO; their record of the
Mozart Concerto is well known for its gaiety and brilliance.)

I am pleased I did the Mozart with him. The Beecham label
assured non-stop sales ever since it was made! It was one of his
genial recording sessions: we played it through, and that was *it*.
I remember I thought the orchestra played beautifully. The only
thing he suggested was the little fillip at the end, where I usurp
a few bars of the final tutti. Jolly good idea, too.

In addition to his complete love of music, Tommy undoubtedly had quite an affection for the men who were able to produce these noises. He was full of anecdotes himself about the
players he had known. And at the end of a concert, if he had
diverted the audience with the wise-cracks they hoped to hear,
he would turn round and wink at the woodwind, to see how he
was going down. And at the end of his life, if he had nothing
better to do, he would often be seen sitting in his car as the
orchestra walked out of the rehearsal of some other conductor.
I am sure he had come to see the boys as much as anything else.

Today we have the sterile approach, the heavy teutonic, the
over-emotional, the vulgar, and all the posturing in between,
including the highly polished precision. But Tommy had the
complete gamut of masculinity—allied to *taste*. Who has heard a
Rossini overture like his? And how boring is Delius with anyone
else: he took infinite pains with Delius.

These qualities outweighed the impossible sides of his character. What a Henry VIII he would have made! What a Nero! He
could blow himself up like a bomb about to explode, and the
black eyes would blaze. He had hands and feet like a child, and
a back like a bull. He was amused and amusing: but I never
knew him actually laugh.

The difference? The evidence? Today conductors are making
fortunes. Tommy got through one. Tommy gave the orders.

MURIEL BRUNSKILL

[Near the beginning of a long and distinguished career in the concert hall and opera house, Muriel Brunskill was first summoned to sing *Messiah* with Sir Thomas in 1927. Of that experience, the first of countless happy occasions over the years, she told me:]

I didn't know at all what to expect at the first rehearsal except that it would be different from anything to which I was accustomed. During my first recitative he strode up and down conducting in long, curving gestures which seemed most confusing at first, but soon one began to realise they were the very essence of the fluidity of which he was so great a master. The aria, 'O thou that tellest' was really 'good tidings' when beaten in two instead of the usual stolid traditional six in a bar, and a feeling of real happiness surged into the work.

Of a memorable performance soon after this, a critic's notice said of this aria, and the still more familiar 'He shall feed his flock', 'We were given a pastel picture, full of those lesser lights and nuances that are so acceptable, and yet so rarely to be found.'

For me, Beecham's *Messiah* had a tenderness and joy as well as a deep pathos. I can never forget the effect which at rehearsal he always took great pains to ensure, of the orchestral part of 'He was despised': those falling thirds between the short vocal phrases were like tears wrung from the soul, of quite indescribable sadness, and yet in the performance as a whole there was a life-giving joy. Often after a Beecham *Messiah*, both in rehearsal and performance, despite our fresh enjoyment, we were all utterly exhausted, having given all we'd got. He revolutionised the whole English concept and tradition of *Messiah*: whether historically authentic or not (and who knows?), it had come to need new life breathed into it: Beecham may have shocked some people by doing just that, but he loved the work as much as any of us, perhaps more.

The only other conductor I felt approach him in identifying the singer's thought with his own was Harty, but not quite to the same degree. Other conductors might propel you or follow you: Beecham just drew you with invisible cords into the music and himself: I think he hypnotised people into doing better than they imagined they could.

[Muriel and the writer joined the British National Opera

Company at much the same time, she in 1922 and I in 1924. We saw little of Beecham for some years, but as time went on and as her operatic repertoire grew and made her name, she sang, besides her many *Messiahs* with him, performances of the Delius *Mass of Life*. At their first performance in the Albert Hall she told me that at the rehearsal the orchestral interlude, 'Auf den Bergen' sounded so exquisitely ethereal that the entire orchestra and chorus gasped in astonishment, and it was the talk of the afternoon: in fact the excitement was too great, and the performance, though very good, failed to rise quite to that heart-searching realisation of the Delius vision.]

In performances of *Solomon* and *Hercules* one felt enormous pleasure in the highly telling effects of his new orchestrations, though in the case of the latter there was great last-minute stress to complete in time. Both works he introduced for the first time since Handel's day.

Then there was the one, and to my knowledge, only time he was prevailed upon to conduct Beethoven's Ninth Symphony.[5] Tommy had never liked *this piece* (pronounced heavily, disparagingly), but he took great pains with it, especially over the slow movement.

[Muriel told me of his care in balancing the solo voices, and showed me as an example a passage (Bars 8–11 of 'F' in finale, Peters edition) where an effect once obtained seemed the obvious (though unindicated and probably never before produced) treatment of overlapping phrases in ensemble: he could always make the main tune tell and clarify the best melodic line. She said that of the many 'Ninths', Beecham's gave her most the feeling of being close to Beethoven's mind. But she reminded me too of Tommy's own down-to-earth dictum on all such individual judgments, 'Criticism is only the personal opinion of one fallible mortal.' She spoke also of Beecham's relations with her husband, Robert Ainsworth, the last of the conductors to emerge from the early and middle years of the Beecham constellation, and one of the few who could successfully model some of his readings on

---

[5] He conducted four performances; the first, when he was 67, at the Royal Albert Hall on 21 April 1947. Muriel Brunskill stood in for Marjorie Thomas.

those of the master. Sir Thomas found him a congenial companion on 'free' evenings on tour with the opera, and the two of them spent hours over hobbies of which one would suspect neither of them—the history and workings of ships and trains! But then Beecham had what amounted to a built-in encylopaedia on any aspect of the arts, crafts and history itself which happened to interest him. Finally, Muriel recalled her last meeting with Sir Thomas in his old age, a little incident typical of his attitude to his artists :]

Beecham was the acme of professionalism, always wearing his public mask no matter how he felt. He was frail and far from well at the memorable Sibelius concert at which the Ambassador invested him with the White Rose of Finland. The performance had reached sublime heights and the audience was thrilled and excited—he climbed up and down from the platform many times with all his usual grandeur of manner. I happened to be in the wings and watched him descend for the last time; Lady Betty was waiting for him with two sticks, with the aid of which he literally dragged himself to the artists' room, collapsing into the nearest chair, utterly drained and exhausted. I hung back, but he had caught sight of me and hailed me with the old familiar warmth, 'Ah, Muriel! Forgive my sitting down . . .' That is how I shall always remember him.

JACK BRYMER
(For many years Beecham's principal clarinet)

One of the most fascinating aspects of one's work with Sir Thomas over a long period was the contrast of his approach to a concert performance and a recording. He was no less a perfectionist in either field; but he knew that the supreme moment of revelation in a public performance had to be the one and only culmination of all the preparation and inspiration he could manage or organise; whereas the recording could be, should be, the final resultant of many hours of listening, pondering, altering, re-balancing, and even changing tempo to accommodate that most exacting of media.

I feel sure there can't be many players who fail to regret that some of his white-hot public performances never found their way on to a record. Those would surely have brought a sound to the gramophone, even if the odd cough or rustle would have had to be ignored. In cases where public concerts were recorded, like the BBC Symphony Orchestra's Sibelius's Second Symphony, it is possible to detect a continuity of growth and direction extremely rare in recording. The climaxes are more naturally achieved than in any other performance I know, and there is an immediacy of impact which makes the work sound as if the orchestra were just discovering it for themselves. It seems likely they were, in fact: so often we ended a rehearsal knowing very little of what Beecham intended us to do at the concert; he mostly simply joked his way along, so that there were inevitably great areas of doubt in even well-known works. But between the rehearsal and concert it was his practice personally to re-mark all the orchestral parts in his stubby blue pencil—vital marks which had to be carefully observed, for at the concert he was all eyes, and very much on the *qui vive* for anyone not watching properly. So the concert was in fact creation at work; the symphony came to shape and life before one's very eyes. And I've heard many a hardened 'pro' admit in the bar after one of these occasions, '*That's one I'd have done for nothing!*' A rare admission, to be sure.

But the studio recording was a different thing altogether. To begin with, there was never really any plan. Sir Thomas, at any rate during his last fifteen years or so, had *carte blanche* to record anything he wished at any time. As a result, George Brownfoot, our genial but ever-harassed librarian, used to arrive at Abbey Road, or even Walthamstow, with a huge pile of scores and parts. And there was no saying that the work we set out to record would in fact be the choice of the day. Several cups of coffee and playbacks later, it would be decided that things weren't right today for the *Faust* Ballet, but might well be perfect for that last movement of the Mendelssohn symphony we left undone last month. So Sir Thomas wandered in and out with cigar well alight, issuing instructions to players and recording engineers alike; joking, cajoling, loitering among the stands to discuss details of balance with each of his principals. So the recording gradually took shape; and the miracle was always that tempo and mood were captured and remembered, continuous and perfectly dove-tailed, by that most remarkable little man.

Even so, it didn't always happen quite like that. I myself was

lucky enough to be involved in one of the exceptional sessions
when he did record continuously. We were in Paris, recording in
the wonderful acoustics of the dustiest and ugliest old hall any of
us had ever seen, the Salle Wagram, a place normally used for
'pop' or all-in wrestling, but sorted out by Sir Thomas as the best
Haydn-Mozart hall in the world, and used by us for lots of other
and bigger works with great success and pleasure. Time was
short: we had to leave for London next day, when Sir Thomas
decided to make a recording of Mozart's Clarinet Concerto. He
didn't need to work at it with me, because we had given it together
a couple of weeks previously in London. So we simply played it
straight through, twice, and then adjourned for lunch, after
which we heard it played back. The version which has now been
issued with success for some twelve years consists of Take 2 of
the first movement, Take 1 of the second, and Take 2 of the
third, so far as I can remember. It was, in fact, recording without
tears; but then it always was, whether done in short or long
stretches. I personally wish there could have been more of these
continuous takes, and more of those public-performance
recordings.

Of all the solo performances I have ever given, I should be
willing to forfeit all for the sake of preserving one; a Mozart I
gave with Beecham and the RPO at London's Royal Festival
Hall. To walk on among friends, simply shut one's eyes, and
emerge thirty minutes later with the feeling that it had all
happened as well as one could hope, and that one's inner feelings
had been communicated by a great conductor and orchestra to a
sympathetic audience—this was an experience to be treasured,
and one probably never to be repeated in quite this intensity. It
was mine, and I hope may have been that of many others:
something only the musician and the man that was Beecham
could inspire.

EDMUND CHESTERMAN

(For many years Beecham's principal double-bass, later Professor
at the Royal College of Music)

Few may remember that Diaghilev and Beecham jointly arranged
(and financed) the only tour of the provinces by the Russian
Ballet. This, in the autumn of 1928, gave many people in these

areas their only chance of seeing this astonishing company. As a very young man I played for this tour; we visited Manchester, Birmingham, Glasgow, Edinburgh and Liverpool. I have a recollection that he addressed the audiences during this tour, appealing for his Imperial League of Opera.

A year later I joined the new symphony orchestra formed by the BBC in collaboration with Beecham. After the first season of concerts the individual (characteristically) parted from the organisation, and in 1932 he formed his own London Philharmonic Orchestra. After his long war-time absence in America and Australia he re-joined them, but they soon parted company, he to dally with the Philharmonia for a while and finally to form the Royal Philharmonic Orchestra. Some departments of this were not all they might have been, but his magic soon made itself felt. Audiences clamoured, and many noted players were attracted and joined the orchestra.

Every concert and recording of Beecham's was a distinct creation, even distinct in some cases from the final rehearsal. Often, on arrival at the hall before a concert, principal players would be summoned to his room and informed of an alteration or addition to a phrase or dynamic, and ' kindly inform your henchmen of this'.

His production of *Irmelin* at the New Theatre, Oxford, in May, 1953 was a memorable event. This work, full of glorious tunes (and some pretty banal lines) I regard as unique among productions of an English opera since before the war, Beecham gathered a splendid cast of young singers, and the staging and costumes were first-class. The RPO played, and Beecham conducted all performances but one. It should have been a great success, but this centre of culture and learning where it was produced ignored it. There were often fewer customers than players in the orchestra. A lot of money must have been lost, and in a speech on the last night, Beecham said so, but 'it had been worth it', and 'Lady Beecham had willingly gone without a promised fur coat to help'. A pity Oxford was given this honour: doubtless Poplar or Chorlton-cum-Hardy would have shown more interest.

His last concert, at Portsmouth Guildhall with the RPO, was on 7 May, 1960. He seemed conscious that this was an occasion. He stood us all lunch at the Queen's Hotel, and afterwards at rehearsal said it would not be a long one: 'We must ensure that we start and stop together—what happens in between is of no great consequence!' After about half-an-hour an enormous TV set was brought in; he stopped rehearsal and invited us to watch the Cup Final with him.

This short rehearsal was most unusual: he generally made use of all his rehearsal time; not fussing over details (except possibly for Delius and Mozart), but moulding and creating, and making sure that solo players were heard and allowed to play as they felt they should. This may have been one of his secrets—he always 'let us play', as we say: not shackled and bound with countless facts, figures, intricate details of the length of certain semi-quavers, and so on, that certain gentry love to impose on us. These people usually get an accurate performance like a military tattoo, and with as much soul.

We orchestral players of mature years still miss him. I remember every morning travelling to a rehearsal or recording, and wondering, always with zest, or apprehension, what would happen that day. Something always did! Maybe to laugh at, wish the floor would swallow us, or marvel at. Anyway, we 'lived' and enjoyed it, and were comparatively well paid. How he did it all is beyond my knowledge or powers of description.

EUGENE CRUFT
(Double-bass: father of the famous orchestral family)

[Cruft had been in the 'Fireworks Orchestra', and went to Berlin in 1912 when they were sent by Beecham to play for Diaghilev for his season there. Cruft remembers the bad times with the good, and Beecham's early discouragements when he got no support for English music, and the one or two financial crises. He died on 4 June 1976, aged 88. In his own words to me:]

He was always a cruel perfectionist, and demanded everything from his players, and got it, and gave as much himself. I remember his producing *Rosenkavalier* for the first time in England: he'd been to Germany to hear it, and conducted rehearsals from memory!

Come to think of it, there can't be any of the best players in

London who at one time or another weren't owed money by Tommy. He always had the best; and they'd every one of them go back to him if they could get the chance!'

CLIFFORD CURZON

[Clifford Curzon has spoken and written to me at some length about his work with Sir Thomas, but under the present pressures of a concert pianist's life, he would prefer me to write about it, with liberty to quote from his own words.

Sir Thomas was not always at his happiest with soloists. There was the lamentable lapse, with Cortot, of both their memories; the irresistibly comic but reprehensible bitemporal Brahms No. 2 with Schnabel; the fabulous success in America with Rubinstein, with which neither participant was at all satisfied; but then again, there were the splendid Mozart performances with Clifford Curzon, Heifetz and Szigeti.

About the first of these there is a curious story. Taken and introduced to Sir Thomas at Lady Cunard's house by a distinguished and beautiful London hostess, the young Curzon played some Schubert and Beethoven, and some other composers (no Mozart), what time Sir Thomas, it seemed, appeared more interested in the lady than the music. However, young Mr Curzon was duly commissioned to play a Mozart concerto with the maestro, who would notify him which one. Time elapsed: a date was specified, but no concerto. With only three weeks to run, the only reply to repeated inquiries was an oracular message, 'the B flat'. The young pianist knew there were three, and did not happen to know any of them. Further inquiries eliciting no response, he took desperate measures, hired a room and piano near Landowska who had once coached him, and proceeded to learn all three. In the middle of this gruelling process another message arrived: 'the Coronation concerto' (which is in D!). Somehow this was mastered in time, and played from memory with the success which has now become associated with Curzon's Mozart. But at the time, it was hardly the treatment to endear pianist to conductor, however young and unknown the former and celebrated the latter ... But about the same time, Sir Thomas remarked to a young friend of mine that this same young man 'was the only player he could think of whom he could bear to sit down and listen to playing Mozart for a whole evening'. Subsequently he said much the same to me ... but not to the young pianist himself.

However, Mr Curzon has written to me about the episode:]

It never occurred to my head to feel anger at Sir Thomas Beecham's cavalier treatment over the three 'B flats'—I was far too conscious of my luck in being in touch with him at all musically. No, I felt only a great fear of not being able to justify the faith he had shown in me after only a single private hearing at Lady Cunard's. In his lapse over the choice of concerto, he may, in view of what you tell me of his speed of memorising, have been paying me the compliment of thinking I was as phenomenally quick in learning scores as he was—a very definite miscalculation on his part!

He was always very polite to me in rather a formal way otherwise; and I never felt nervous when actually playing with him—tensed to a high pitch of excitement and anticipation, certainly, but never nervous—because he had the most unusual gift of destroying all self-consciousness in the musicians around him at a performance. Of course, like all artists, he *had* to make himself periodically *incommunicado* if he was to get any concentrated work done; and certainly my letters imploring him for information about the concerto never appeared to impinge on his retirement! Only later did someone tell me that he often put his mail straight into the wastepaper basket unopened—a bold gesture I've often felt, in later years in my humble way, like emulating.

[I ought to add myself at this point that the unpredictable Sir Thomas did make some amends for this behaviour subsequently. Curzon was to play the popular (and perfect) A major concerto of Mozart with him, and at the first rehearsal he said to the orchestra before beginning. 'Gentlemen, Mr Curzon plays *most* music better than *most* pianists; and *some* music better than *any* other pianist.' One must admit the accolade to have been a handsome one.

In subsequent performances with Sir Thomas, Curzon, as I have often heard, always scored a success; but he has told me nothing of that: only of his regret that he was later invited to play the heavier works, such as the Brahms, rather than more Mozart or the Delius concerto in which he had specialised. But it is pleasant to speculate that his reputation as a Mozart player may have originally owed something to Sir Thomas's encouragement and approval, the Beecham-Mozart reputation which I discuss elsewhere being probably the most acclaimed (and disputed) in the world.]

VICTORIA DE LOS ANGELES
(Soprano)

[A message about him reached me the other day through a friend from Victoria de los Angeles, who told of both her intense pleasure in singing for him (her touching Mimi is on the classic recording he made of *Bohème*) and of her experience in recording *Carmen*. She had felt obliged to break off in the middle of making this, for reasons which were really neither her fault nor his: but as more than a year went by before she heard more of it, she decided he must have been offended by her sudden disappearance. But they met again and she was received with open arms and 'Here comes my Carmen!' and the opera was completed to the satisfaction of both of them, and in the friendliest manner. Listeners are quite unaware that the sprightly performance covered two years.]

JOHN DENISON
(Manager, London South Bank Concert Halls, 1965–75)

[Beecham frequently took a mischievous delight in setting his subalterns stiff and unfamiliar duties. I was told of one of these recently, concerning John Denison, who played the horn in the splendid London Philharmonic Orchestra, was later for some years Director of Music to the Arts Council, and has recently retired from the post of Manager of three South Bank London concert halls. In his student days, his RCM tutor recommended him to Sir Thomas, who must have spotted a certain diplomatic flair in the young man, whom he sent for some special study to an expert in Germany. On his return he was summoned formally into the

Presence, complimented in grandiloquent terms (to his own and no doubt Tommy's amusement) on his scholarship and know-ledge of his instrument, and again despatched to Germany to procure an authentic set of the fabled 'Wagner Tubas', over which (and their use in the *Ring* and in the work of Wagner's most devout apostle, Bruckner) much musicological necromancy has always been practised, and many claims of orthodoxy advanced and disputed. Young John Denison succeeded in obtaining a quartet of these trophies, and also the full legend of their almost mystical origin in the Nibelung-craft of Strauss *père*, who in addition to being first horn also appeared to have played a sort of Alberich to Wotan-Wagner. Covent Garden had never possessed these tubas, and while John and his three young colleagues practised-up their precious and rather intractable curiosities, a flood of controversy was loosened among musical scribes and pharisees as to whether indeed there was any *mystique* about them, whether they had been cooked-up by Strauss *père* or a quite uncelebrated horn-manufacturer to whom Wagner had given a sketchy brief of his requirements. At any rate Beecham bequeathed them to Covent Garden, and John Denison pasted all the Press, in which Newman had one of his characteristic wrangles, into a neat little book with nice pictures of the four young tubists, which he kindly lent me: in effect, this purchase of the real instruments was one of Beecham's many conscientious and interesting innovations. (Nowadays, these tubas appear as a matter of course whenever the score requires them.)

Denison said Beecham was always kind to him, and he himself certainly appreciated the genius and the wit; he has the best and most authentic version I have heard of Beecham's unabashed encounter with Hitler, as he played for him in that historic concert in Berlin. The work in those remarkable inter-war seasons was gruelling in the extreme: on the whole he preferred Furtwängler's *Ring* and *Tristan* to Tommy's; but then Furtwängler, of whom Beecham was really fond (though he cooled off when the Austrian truckled to the Nazis) was Wagner-bred, and his most world-famous exponent; and Beecham, as he grew old, came to find Wagner too long and teutonic, saving only in *Die Meistersinger*, in which Tommy found the sweetest and most continuous melody of any conductor ever (I am not sure if John endorses this last point?). He could not write for me at this time, but he gave me a more precious Beecham relic than the Wagner Tubas—a very rare copy of the Romanes Lecture which Sir Thomas was invited to give in the Sheldonian Theatre at Oxford on 7 June 1956. The subject was John Fletcher, a favourite author of Beecham's favourite period of English dramatic poetry. The lecture has, beside its easy scholarship and choice quotations, the real Beecham mellifluous flow: his prose is phrased like his moulding of the dignified melodies of Handel and Haydn, and a pleasant seriousness persists throughout until the final little paragraph, in which, with his ineffable sense of the ridiculous, he bows himself out.]

ASTRA DESMOND

[Astra Desmond's singing career dates from the early 1920s as one of the leading British contraltos, first in the opera house and later in oratorio and as recitalist. She specialised in Scandinavian songs, was an authority on Grieg, Dvořák and Sibelius, and in foreign tours used to sing the composers of twelve nationalities in the original languages. From 1947 she was a Professor of Singing at the Royal Academy of Music. She died in 1974.]

There are many who can testify much better than I to Beecham's musical gifts, but I have one little episode which highlights another side to his character.

Two qualities stand out in my memory of Thomas Beecham: his great loyalty to and affection for the artists who had worked for him; and his understanding kindness of which I have good cause for remembering him with gratitude.

At an early stage in my career I was engaged to sing in a performance at Queen's Hall of Delius's *Mass of Life* under a foreign conductor. The man was of a sadistic type, and for some reason took a delight in reducing me to a highly nervous condition. When, for the performance, we came on to the platform, there in the front row sat Beecham and all the Delius experts and friends. My discomfort was complete, and I gave a bad performance.

Some time after this I happened to meet Beecham in the railway train, and we had lunch together. I told him I had always

Cartoon by Spy

At the railway station – about 1914

felt a desire to apologise for that performance. He expressed surprise, and asked me what had happened, so I told him the story. He just said, 'I wondered why you sang so badly,' and we went to talk of other things.

When the Delius Festival was arranged, to my amazement Beecham asked for me to sing in the *Mass of Life* in Queen's Hall in the presence of Delius himself. This time, with him to conduct, all went well, and my morale, which had suffered a severe blow, was completely restored. Could understanding kindness be more clearly shown than by such an act of faith on his part? Of his great powers in drawing the best out of an artist who gives him trust, many others can testify. He could be merciless to the conceited and cocksure artist!

<h2 style="text-align:center">KEITH FALKNER</h2>
(Director of the Royal College of Music, 1960–74)

[Sir Keith Falkner, lately Director of the Royal College of Music where we were once fellow-students, has both written and talked to me about his recollections of Beecham with whom he often sang in concert and oratorio. Tommy would, as time went on, chaff him: 'I suppose you're earning too much money now to come and sing Hans Sachs for me?' but he seems to have only the happiest memories of their encounters, from his first audition as a young man for *Messiah*. Tommy waved 'Why do the nations' aside, and only asked for 'The people that walked in darkness': when he heard the long phrases sung on one breath, he waved the whole audition to an end, mentioned the time and date of rehearsal, and departed. When the day came, he politely asked before 'Why do the nations', 'How fast do you like to take this?' Keith told me he was green enough to reply, 'As fast as you like, sir', whereupon Tommy belted it along at breakneck speed, Keith somehow staying in the saddle at the hurdles, Tommy interjecting in mischievous aside, 'That fast enough for you, Mr Falkner?' This must, I hope and think, have been only at the rehearsal, as I was told by Keith, as by so many I have consulted, that he always experienced a wonderful confidence in performance; and he used a phrase that has come to more than one of the musicians who have appeared with Beecham: 'Once we got under way, the

3—BR * *

music *bloomed* for him.' My own ears have often told me just what those words mean. He also said:

'When you were singing with Beecham, you were on an altogether different channel from any other musician: wafted, it seemed, on to another element, perhaps half terrified at first, then carried confidently along, yet never hurried: each phrase was polished, and points of daylight were never overlooked.'

While we were talking, he remembered, and got out to show me, a Mozart aria Beecham had found somewhere and scored, called of all improbable titles *Ein Deutsches Kriegslied*. This was always a success, and Keith hoped to revive it at a suitable occasion at the College.

Asked of any particular performance he remembered, he felt they were all enjoyable, but perhaps one he recalled with amusement as well as pleasure was the grand *Messiah* performance at the Crystal Palace, strangely devised by the International Poultry-keepers' Association to celebrate, with due solemnity, their World Congress and Exhibition. It was an unusual audience, and Sir Thomas walked deliberately all through it to the rostrum, surveying the agricultural élite to right and left with respectful attention. Between the oratorio numbers, if not during the music, could be heard from the crowded adjoining aisles the far-off crows of innumerable cocks, and ululations of expectant hens. After the overture, Beecham espied some of the brass slipping quietly from their dais. 'Where are those fellows off to?' he asked the leader at his side. 'I don't know,' came the reply, 'but they've nothing to play for a long time.' 'Perhaps,' said Sir Thomas, 'they've gone to join the exhibits?']

ERIC FENBY

[Eric Fenby, now a Professor at the Royal Academy of Music, is familiar in the last forty years of musical history for his 'realisation' of the music of Delius when the composer was blind and paralysed, for one book on the subject, and another on the composer's music as a whole. He was for a time secretary-assistant to Beecham, and a close witness of his musical activities.]

Beecham is generally regarded as excelling all others in the music of Delius: not that his alone is the one way of playing it: Kempe proved that convincingly at the Bradford Centenary Festival. What can clearly be claimed for Beecham is that no one has projected its poetry more musically. Groves and Sargent may have equalled him in the great choruses of *A Mass of Life*, but in all else Beecham was matchless, especially with the orchestra. Passages such as the marvellous, evocative evening music in the third and fourth movements of the Mass, have never been given with such artistry since. Beecham always insisted on the finest instrumentalists capable of the utmost beauty of tone colouring the threads of Delius's textures. He would lean forward on the rostrum, shaping his phrases in exquisite flow, allowing the music to breathe and speak as Delius intended with pen and paper, but was unable precisely to convey: the stick often seemingly aimless, but poised to point some pivot chord on which the emotional tension hinged in his control of the melodic line. It was direction as if by mesmerism, his eyes anticipating every inflection.

I remember Oda Slobodskaya, after rehearsing Palmyra with John Brownlee in the title-role of Delius's *Koanga* at Covent Garden in 1935, complaining that she could not follow Beecham because he rarely gave a downbeat.

'But you don't need downbeats from Beecham,' cut in John, 'you can *feel* where he is!'

Beecham's fifty years advocacy of Delius in the concert-room, opera house and recording-studio, was the sort of support of which every composer must dream. I ventured to ask him on one occasion what it was in the music that had first attracted him. His reply was hardly what I had expected:

'Here was a composer, Frederick Delius, whom I had never seen or heard of before; whose music was unlike any other, or anything that was being written at the time: that was about 1907. Nobody seemed to know what the devil to make of it! I found it as assuring as a wayward woman, and determined to tame it!' He paused to light a cigar, and added with that characteristic roll of his eyes, 'And it wasn't done in a day!'

He would play through some favourite Delius in rehearsal, the hall empty save for cleaners, and coax the most ravishing sounds from the orchestra as if it were the last time he was ever to conduct it. He often sent for me at these sessions, particularly in his prime in the 'thirties, merely to share his boyish delight in exercising his artistry. There was something endearing about him in such moods, and this is how I usually recall him.

The basic details had been pondered beforehand. He would mark every bar of the score in blue pencil, exaggerating Delius's own nuances of expression, to make the fullest impact in performance. Copyists would then transfer these markings to each of the orchestral parts of the work. The rehearsal existed in the main to familiarise the players, all of them experts, with the way he wanted the design to sound in balance and attack. His verbal comments, often witty, reinforced the scrupulous observance of these editings, or exploded in humorous reprimand or mild rebuke of a player who had somehow missed his entry, 'Cor Anglais! Kindly give me some indication of your presence at four bars after Letter G!'

He would indicate the operative note in a phrase, the pointing of which would make all the difference between telling at once or not at all. 'Clarinet!' he would say, 'A little more time before you get to the C!' Or he would exasperate the first violins by making them repeat a long-drawn melody until he had flighted it to perfection.

His chief concern with Delius was in tending the melodic strands that pass from voice to voice and give the piece its form, and, only less important, the balancing of timbres carrying the supporting harmonies. In the more technical matters arising from errors, he sometimes astonished me. I suspect from his correcting misprints in Delius, that his studies in harmony and counterpoint would appear to have been somewhat perfunctory. I have no recollection of his rehearsing Delius in the highly professional manner of Kempe. I was particularly struck by this at Bradford. Kempe dissects offending passages, and having achieved his purpose, individually reassembles them rhythmically in instrumental counterpoint.

Why was Beecham uniquely successful as an interpreter of Delius? The two men, superficially, had much in common, despite the seventeen years between them. There were certain similarities in their upbringing. Both had come from well-to-do homes in the industrial north of England, and both had fathers who were patrons of music. There was refinement and acute sensitivity in each, though Beecham could be incredibly Rabelaisian in speech, whereas Delius loathed the slightest crudity. Both had been exposed to European culture at first-hand in their teens.

The clue, to my mind, lies in Beecham's temperament, and the kind of music he pursued when left entirely to his own inclinations. Even his superb artistry was but the servant of this obsession, and *that* was the poetry of musical magic.

Some composers have a richer vein of musical poetry than others in their invention; it springs from the quality of their thought. These, it seemed, kindled invariably an instant response in Beecham. There is a musical magic in Schubert wholly lacking in Beethoven. This was the quality Beecham adored. He had found it in his incomparable Mozart, though rarified and impalpable, but nowhere to such excess as in Delius.

Paradoxically, Beecham the city-dweller, like Oscar Wilde, was 'uncomfortable' with Nature, yet was inimitable in his conceptions of Delius's nature music. The Delius Festival in 1929 set the seal on his powers as a peerless exponent of the art of Delius. The entire programmes were conducted from memory, and he barely glanced at his scores in rehearsals. His best recordings date from this time. I doubt if he ever surpassed his performance of *In a Summer Garden* on the old 78s, or of *On Hearing the First Cuckoo in Spring* in the same series. Beecham's recording might well have been labelled 'On Hearing the Last Cuckoo in the Last Spring', so ineffably lovely are the sounds he imparts to it, yet so piercingly poignant is his visionary reading of this little gem among miniatures. In later years his presentations were apt to be marred unaccountably by sudden erratic fluctuations of tempi. His *Walk to the Paradise Garden*—his final version on LP records—is markedly inferior in this respect to his earliest 78. For those who remember his golden years, when each time he faced an orchestra, men knew they awaited an event they were unlikely ever to forget, his passing ended an era. Lancastrian and Yorkist rivalries, though rampant still in cricket, unite in the complementary artistries of Beecham and Delius.

DENHAM FORD

(Secretary to Beecham, 1949–52, and now Chairman of the Sir Thomas Beecham Society (see p. 205), which has been in existence since 1964 and has an active branch in America.)

Although not required to accompany Sir Thomas on his visits to other countries, I invariably travelled with him on concert and other engagements in the British Isles during the period when I was his orchestral manager and secretary.

Most of the journeys were for one or two concerts outside London, but, in 1948, Sir Thomas and the Royal Philharmonic Orchestra undertook an extensive tour of Britain and Ireland during which they gave eighteen concerts in twenty-one days. Beginning in Birmingham, the itinerary then covered Blackpool, Blackburn, Dundee, Glasgow, Edinburgh, Newcastle upon Tyne, Nottingham, Leicester, Belfast, Dublin and Liverpool. In Glasgow, Edinburgh, Belfast and Dublin two concerts were given and it was in Belfast that an incident occurred which aroused echoes of the Irish 'troubles'. Both concerts in the city were sold out and the promoter asked Sir Thomas if disappointed patrons could be allowed to attend the rehearsal for a nominal fee, to which Beecham agreed. At the end of the rehearsal, Sir Thomas was reminded that the orchestra had never played the National Anthem of Eire due in Dublin, to which he replied that he would rehearse it there and then! To anyone unfamiliar with Irish history, this was tantamount to singing the 'Internationale' in the White House and, almost before the rehearsal was over, reporters were demanding to know the reason for what, to Ulster ears, was very near treason! Sir Thomas, as ever, remained aloof and dismissed the whole affair as a huge joke.

Another interesting aspect of travelling with Sir Thomas was that, being a gourmet, he insisted always on having the local delicacy. Thus, in Blackpool, potted shrimps were ordered; in Edinburgh, Edinburgh Rock had to be brought while, on each visit to Leicester a home-made Melton Mowbray pie was left at the artists' room by a lady admirer.[6]

---

[6] With mock horror he once told H. P.-G. that a Manchester devotesse had brought him a 'Toad-in-the-Hole'.

Sir Thomas did not in later years often conduct other English orchestras, but an interesting example took place in 1948 when he planned a concert of English music to be given in the Royal Albert Hall with his own orchestra, the Royal Philharmonic. The programme consisted of:

Falstaff	...	...	...	Elgar
The Garden of Fand	...	...	...	Bax
Paris	...	...	...	Delius
Fifine at the Fair	...	...	...	Bantock

When, a few days before the concert, Sir Thomas learned that advance booking was negligible, he announced, amid considerable press publicity, that he would cancel the whole affair. Immediately, Bournemouth Corporation sent him a telegram stating that, if he would agree to conduct the same programme with their own orchestra in Bournemouth, they would guarantee a full house. Sir Thomas agreed and, within a few hours the box office was sold out and many patrons turned away. In addition to his fee for the concert, Sir Thomas was allowed three rehearsals and made a guest of the town for the week-end and I was fortunately able to share this civic honour. At the first rehearsal, Sir Thomas, after his customary greeting to the orchestra, announced: 'We will begin with the easiest piece, *Falstaff* . . .' and plunged head-long into this great work. An interesting sidelight was that Rudolph Schwarz, then conductor of the Bournemouth Orchestra, asked to be allowed to play the celesta part in the Bax work so as to have an opportunity of playing under Sir Thomas—surely an unusual, if not unique, tribute from one conductor to another!

On another, shorter, tour of Scotland, Sir Thomas was suffering acutely from gout and an invalid chair was provided, in which I propelled him to and from trains, cars, concert halls and hotels. The fact became known to the press and, at Dundee, a photographer was waiting to snap the scene, only to be threatened by an irate Sir Thomas that, if he dared come near, his camera would be smashed beyond repair.

As I have already mentioned, last minute arrangements were the order of the day in the Beecham diary, and I was often called on at very short notice to leave for some provincial town or spot to meet Sir Thomas. One such incident stands out when he and

Lady Betty Beecham had left London for a holiday. Officially no one knew where they had gone, but it was generally believed they were 'somewhere in Cornwall'. After a few days of comparative silence, I received a telephone call one morning asking me to hire a Rolls-Royce in London and drive to Exeter and meet them. No explanation was given, nor any idea of how long I might be away. Arriving in Exeter late that evening, I made my presence known and was told to stand by for further orders in the morning. Next day, an informal conference was held over lunch to decide where was to be the next stop. No decision being arrived at, we left in the car to explore the by-ways of Devon and seek out a suitable spot. This turned out to be Exmouth, where we spent some days until Sir Thomas had occasion to write one of his tirades to the press, and I was dispatched, as peremptorily as I had been summoned, back to London with the letter to meet the press deadline.

In 1952, in order—it was said—to concentrate on finishing the book on Frederick Delius, Sir Thomas rented an island in Poole Harbour. This was reached by a boat from Poole which took some forty minutes, and the only other contact, apart from the telephone with the mainland was the postman who arrived each morning by boat carrying provisions and milk as well as mail. Thus seclusion was guaranteed, theoretically anyway. In practice, it meant once again that I frequently received urgent summonses to catch a train from London, and take a boat to the island. However the tides did not always allow the orthodox mode of travel, and on these occasions, I would be taken by car to a remote spot on another beach, rowed out to sea and transferred to the launch for the rest of the journey to the island.

Such then were some of the incidents which made touring with Tommy sometimes exasperating, frequently hectic but never less than interesting.

Geoffrey Gilbert

[As a youth, Gilbert was picked out by Beecham (who was a great talent-spotter) from one of the English musical colleges he would amuse himself by deriding, and the young flautist soon became one of the leading players always associated with Tommy.

During Gilbert's service in the Forces, he would when on leave be invited to tea with Sir Thomas, who wanted to exchange news of all his players so engaged, and their concerns. Gilbert has spoken to me of Beecham's extraordinary gentleness with young players.]

... Their faults of style he gradually eliminated by suggestion, while seeming to approve of their efforts, never fussing at rehearsal, however seriously he was after fine detail.

He had a curious habit of disparaging composers he really made the most of and enjoyed: this was to avoid discouraging the players over some ineffective phrasing in rehearsal, or just to 'unwind' in chatting with any of them after a particularly concentrated performance. In his later years Beecham managed to obtain an ever-greater technical accuracy in detail while seeming to disregard it, appearing only intent on the interpretation of music as a whole.

[Some time after this conversation, Gilbert, who is now a Professor in an American university (where they have the sense to appoint professors of practical as well as theoretical music) sent me the following commentary.]

His relationship with his players was simple and with a common aim, and it is thus that I think of him as I write. The effect of his genius on those musicians who worked for him and with him cannot be over-stressed. I am sometimes surprised by the fact that his work has apparently left so little influence on the young conductors of our age. There may be some who will admit to the effect of his performances on the development of their own particular talents, but indeed in my opinion they are regrettably few and far between. Be this as it may, for me my connection with him over a period of so many years was the most momentous, and I am glad to say, prolonged, event of my life.

What was it about him that distinguished him from all the others in an age so rich in talent? There were many great conductors, and I think my generation was fortunate in that we met and worked with all of them—Toscanini, Walter, Mengelberg, and so on. But always there was Beecham: developing an affinity with the performers which transcended all other emotions, sometimes even more personal ones. Although it was never so in my own case, there were players who were deeply critical of many aspects of his relations with them, especially in financial matters; but even those strong feelings were never strong enough to diminish their response to his genius during the actual time occupied by a performance.

I believe I said before that upon reflection some of us young players at the outset of our careers must quite often have performed certain passages in a way that may have seemed to him quite outrageously exaggerated; yet I can never remember any hint from his direction that he thought so—not a single hurtful or wounding criticism. He made me feel myself to be a better player than I could possibly have been at that age, and created the impression at all times that what I was doing was exactly how and what he wanted.

I remember one physical characteristic in his conducting which seems to have largely disappeared in the conductors of our present day: this was that he always looked directly at the performers during any vital solo. This established a bond—almost a protective umbrella—over one; the changing expression of his face and eyes is still unforgettable, and always indicated his desires and intentions beyond anything attainable by words at a rehearsal, or stick technique alone at a concert. It is fashionable to describe the eccentricities of his beat, and I have heard it said that he did not have a good technique; this I believe to be false: he had the best technique of all, in that he knew positively what he wanted and could communicate his needs to the players in simple and unequivocal terms. What better can one have?

For nearly all my flute-playing life I was under his influence. Now that my career has changed direction, and I am employed in inculcating into young students and professionals some of those inestimable qualities that I like to think I have acquired from my association with Beecham, I would like to say that I am proud of these effects. Orchestral musicians have lost a friend of rare stature.

LEON GOOSSENS
(Oboist)

I first played for Beecham at the age of thirteen, drafted by my teacher as third oboe for a Liverpool concert, quite undreaming of any such future association as was actually in store: I found it a very exciting experience, and sensed something of his uncanny power of bringing out the best in any player who had anything to give.

Later, when I was more solidly in the profession, and had the good fortune to play for him again, I realised more and more his fantastic and often formidable characteristics. However stimulating to those who could respond to his suggestion, he could never suffer fools gladly: either you rose to the occasion or you were *out*. Once you had gained his confidence (and your own), he made you feel you were doing the whole thing yourself, playing as you always had wanted to play. And in performance something always came out that had not shown itself in rehearsal: he always had some trump card up his sleeve—that extra build-up to a climax, or some caress of a cadence: one could tell from his beat beforehand that something was coming up that he had in reserve.

He seemed often to me to choose his effects like a painter choosing his colours, subtly infusing them with the most telling, seemingly casual strokes. I've known Bruno Walter work in a somewhat similar way, but no one else, as far as I can remember.

Beecham trusted everybody in his orchestra to do his best, and ninety-nine times out of a hundred (leaving some allowance for human frailty) we did our damnedest, and knew it, experiencing a sense of security as surprising as it was exciting.

He was fastidiously considerate with concerto soloists, and understood completely any moments of nervousness or fatigue at rehearsals: he made you feel the whole morning was for you, and you could have a rest while he rehearsed the ensemble, making sure of bowings, details of nuance, etc. He would let you play an awkward passage again until each note was comfortable and secure for all concerned, whether in a concerto or orchestral solo. With singers he was perhaps less indulgent, but they were supposed to have had more previous rehearsal with him and, considering how many British singers made their name in performances under him, he must have inspired them too. Helpful as he was with the young and inexperienced, he could be 'froward with the mighty'.

I am not asked here for reminiscences of his famous gaiety, wit and caprice, which enlivened the days and nights of all who worked and travelled with him: they are related and repeated elsewhere; but do you know the one about getting through the Irish Customs in the days of The Troubles?

We had to cross the border and catch a train for the next concert, but were held up as the orchestra's baggage was suspected of smuggling arms. As endless instrument-cases were unpacked, I think it was myself who suggested to Gwydion Brooke, the bassoonist, that we should establish our *bona fides*; so we struck up *The Keel Row*, others soon joined us, and the conductor's personal version of an Irish Jig proved a conclusive argument of our harmless insanity, and we were rushed through.

But apart from such diversions, my debt to Beecham was not entirely a musical one. His remarkable scholarship, frequent impulsive kindness, and perennial charm, added unforgettable experiences to my own career, of which I would like to include one or two instances. There was an occasion when I had an invitation to break a journey and visit him at Lord Dudley's country house for some music. While there, I discovered that to be taken round the famous library by Sir Thomas, who could quote and turn up many antique references of absorbing human interest, was as much an extension of one's own background as it was to be taken by him round the picture galleries at The Hague and Amsterdam, of which he proved an illuminating connoisseur: as indeed he was of such subjects as the post-Elizabethan poets and dramatists, and it seemed, of any curious literary figure whose name happened to crop up in casual conversation. Amsterdam brings up a unique memory of his unpredictable reaction to life. It must have been in 1932 that a Dutch agent offered me my brother's concerto there. At the same time he asked about a possible British conductor who knew the work. They supposed there was no hope of 'Sir Beecham'—as far beyond their range. I was of the same opinion but promised to make inquiries. As it happened, I was lunching with him soon after, and all I could do was to ask his advice on any possible names. He suddenly smiled whimsically and asked, 'I suppose *I* wouldn't do?' I took it as one of his disconcerting jokes, and protested that he was not serious. 'Well,' he said, 'I *could* be . . . I don't think I've conducted in Holland, and it would rather amuse me: when are you going?' I gave him the date, and he said, 'All right. Leave all the arrangements to me.' I didn't know what to think, but he was expert at all problems of travel, and he sent me full directions next day: my sleeper and hotel had been engaged for me as his guest, and we were to meet at the station. (I had done the concerto with him before.) He looked over all my accommodation himself before getting into his own, and made the hotel change my room to one with a private bath, among other details—I might have been royalty and he the courier. Everything went perfectly, including the visits to the picture galleries . . . and, of course, the concerto.

There are many tales not only of his charm but of spontaneous kindness to his fellow-artists, often in emergency, often saving unpleasant situations. But of course he had his failings—who hasn't?—and there were times when he had to suffer for them. And, of course, having periodically lost fortunes spent on music, he was not always in funds himself, and we sometimes had to wait—to put it mildly.

But it was a great privilege to play with him, and with Beecham every rehearsal, performance or social encounter was an occasion, magnificent, instructive, or just unpredictable, which, indeed, it always was!

[I asked Leon Goossens about any particularly wonderful performances he remembers, and about any special recordings he had made with Sir Thomas. He thought that perhaps on the Berlin tour of 1937, the concert-playing standards had been at its highest; and of the records, he made with the orchestra, he agreed that in the Sibelius Second, the *La Calinda* and *Queen of Sheba's Entry* ('Lollipops') and *Brigg Fair,* he perhaps felt happiest about his own share. I fancy listeners to these records will agree.]

ERNEST HALL
(*Trumpeter: now a Professor at the Royal College of Music*)

[In a tribute broadcast soon after Beecham's death, Ernest Hall summed up in a final phrase: 'Well, I have in my lifetime seen two really great men: one was Churchill, and the other was Beecham.' When I questioned him about a contribution to this Symposium, he said, 'I joined the Beecham Opera Orchestra on being de-mobbed in 1919, and played with him until I joined the BBC in 1930. He conducted us there on several occasions, as you know.' He added this story in a letter:]

As we all know, he was a great character as well as musician; every encounter was an occasion, and I shall always have happy remembrances of playing under him and listening to his witty remarks, which came so spontaneously. One instance I always remember, was at an afternoon rehearsal, and Tommy came in smoking a big fat cigar. On looking around the orchestra, he said, 'Gentleman, I am going to change the items this afternoon and only do Mozart.' He then pointed to the Bass Clarinet and remarked, 'Mr Lear, I shall not need you . . . which reminds me of an epitaph I once saw to a baby who was born at twelve o'clock and died at two minutes past. It said: "Seeing I was here for such a short time,/It was hardly worth coming at all." Good afternoon, Mr Lear, and thank you very much.'

[Ernest Hall also told me a very characteristic story of Beecham's treatment of the Vaughan Williams *Pastoral Symphony*. This work ends with an unaccompanied soprano solo to sound from a distance, and includes a prolonged trumpet solo intended by the composer to be played in the orchestra. Beecham decided that to give the work a more romantically remote effect, he would have both singer and trumpet player in the top gallery of Leeds Town Hall. He said to Ernest Hall, 'Would you be good enough, Mr Hall, to oblige me by ascending to that arcade at the top of the building, where you will find a charming young lady. Try not to pay too much attention to the young lady, but keep in what touch you can with us, and perform your solo up there before rejoining us.' Hall obliged, and at the end of the work

Beecham saw that 'the young lady' and he obtained a particular quota of the applause.

But, though Ernest Hall is as ready as any of us to relish the gay absurdities and witty reactions of Beecham to the routine labours of professional music—and indeed to everyday life—it struck me in talking to him that no one I have come across has a more deep and serious awareness of the purely musical side of Tommy's genius. The personal message of 'the pleasantest of memories and kindest of greetings', written by Sir Thomas on his photograph, clinches the thorough understanding between conductor and player.]

ROY HENDERSON
(Professor of Singing, Royal Academy of Music: long remembered for his Delius performances with Beecham)

Of all twentieth-century composers, Delius wrote the music which fascinated Sir Thomas Beecham the most. The beauty of nature in his orchestral works, and depth of feeling in his choral works, were revealed in a way no other conductor could match. Here was music Beecham loved, which cried out for a flexible beat and subtle *rubato,* for delicacy of phrasing and emotional feeling.

Singing with Fritz Busch at Glyndebourne, I felt rhythm was of paramount importance. With Beecham it was phrasing. Time was elastic, with *rubato* and slight pauses before cadenzas. One felt more like a member of the orchestra than a soloist, ready to follow his slightest whim.

A favourite trick of Beecham's was to whip up excitement by means of a quick down-beat which reached its climax well before its due time, usually accompanied by a loud shout in rehearsal and a grunt in performance. His down-beat was always clear, but he himself told me that I need not expect any direction from any other beats: indeed they were often non-existent.

Beecham conducted all Delius's choral works from memory: a rare feat in the twenties. The effect of his eye, the most expressive human organ, upon choirs and individuals in the orchestra was electric. I remember listening to a rehearsal of Brahms Symphony No. 2 with the Hastings summer season orchestra—a mixed group of players. Beecham conducted each movement without a stop, indicating the phrasing and dynamics with his beat and left hand so clearly that the players responded immediately. At the end of each movement there were perhaps two points he wished to rehearse again.

Beecham's memory was prodigious. Only twice in my experience did it fail him, and in both cases it made no difference to the performance. At the end of one section of the *Mass of Life* he turned to W. H. Reed, the leader of the orchestra, and whispered, 'How many more bars?' At the Leeds Festival he made an unmistakable gesture to bring in the choir *fortissimo* two beats before it was due. Not a single voice responded, and two beats later Beecham had recovered sufficiently to repeat the gesture with both hands: the result was magnificent. Beecham's own jokes during a Delius rehearsal were few and far between. He treated Delius as some people respect a Bible. His magnetism drew the best out of all who followed his beat, and those of us who were privileged to fall under his spell and compelling personality will always be grateful for the experience.

BEN HORSFALL
(For many years a leading violinist in Manchester: now Senior Lecturer in Music, University of Manchester)

In performance Beecham was interested only in the sounds which professional musicians recreated for him. He was the greatest architect of musical phrases, sentences and paragraphs; and had an unerring sense of climax, and ability to restrain the exuberance of orchestral players obviously enjoying themselves. Having from the earliest years, and with complete disregard for expense, surrounded himself with thoroughly professional musicians, he always gave the impression that he was delighted with what they were prepared to give.

Beecham at rehearsal relaxed, and refreshed his memory. He always sat and laboriously turned the pages of his score. His half-spectacles perched on the end of his nose, he appeared to pay little attention to us practising our parts. He never criticised wrong notes, except by a merry quip, e.g. the exposed passage for first violins before Variation 12 in the Dvořák Symphonic Variations: he sniffed and raised his eyebrows, and in a voice without a vestige of reproach said, 'Gentlemen, a *nice discrimina-*

tion between flats and naturals adds greatly to the effect of this passage.' One cold November morning in the old Free Trade Hall, the intonation was appalling; Beecham seemed to bear it for an abnormally long time, and then came the sniff and the inevitable pronouncement, 'Gentlemen, it sounds like an Eisteddfod.'

At performance, Beecham was in complete control. He radiated rhythm and vitality; he firmly believed that music was created for enjoyment, and that vitality in living sounds was unrelated to basic tempi. He stimulated orchestral players to give more than normally could be expected of them in the line of duty. He *inspired* players. There always existed between him and the players the understanding that they were in the same profession. He never 'taught' or gave any indication of how a performance would go. He hadn't any 'technique' in the accepted sense.

His presence was eloquent: he 'conducted' with his knees, restrained us with the palm of his left hand, brought us to order with a clenched fist or an occasional upper-cut or straight-left, and never at any time could I escape his penetrating eyes. The baton was exclusively for audience entertainment: how very often he flicked it like a fan, cracked it like a whip, or slowly dipped it into some imaginary inkwell—all very confusing, for the public. After pre-war Hallé concerts I was often accosted by bewildered members of the audience with the remark, 'I don't know how you follow him!' There was a simply answer—we didn't; we were *with* him, and memorably so.

Beecham's preferences in music are more difficult to define. On his vast experience in opera I am unqualified to comment. In the orchestral repertoire, it was easier to distinguish between the composers with whom he was in tune and those who were thrust upon him in the process of programme building. He was not inscrutable in matters of likes and dislikes. He may not have 'pronounced' against established favourites, though he certainly would if provoked; but he avoided some and shrank from others.

In my experience, every conductor in every concert sets his heart on one piece, at least, being a superlative performance, provided that it is not a concerto: there must be no stealing of limelight or thunder. I took part in more purely orchestral concerts with Beecham than any other conductor, and on the rare occasions when soloists appeared, the performances were least satisfactory, and in some cases almost shabby. Before the war, in the last bar but two of the first movement of the Emperor Concerto, he gave us an enormous straight left, and a grunt which could be heard in Peter Street, on a *silent* beat of the bar. Only a handful of the unwary responded with a squeak. He went on to the slow movement, firmly convinced that the fault was entirely Beethoven's.

The composers most frequently represented, and whose music Beecham obviously relished, were (*a*) Haydn: whether Haydn was an eighteenth-century Beecham, or Beecham a twentieth-century Haydn, I don't know, but they were kindred spirits. A great deal has been written about 'tensions' and 'surprises' in Haydn's music, but the fertility of ideas and inexhaustible invention, particularly in the rondos, seemed to be Beecham's exclusive property; (*b*) Mozart: the immaculate one: Beecham worshipped him; (*c*) Schubert: the Fifth Symphony, in B Flat, was his favourite. Of the Viennese classics, Beethoven was the odd man out. I always felt that Beecham was slightly awed by this giant, who appeared to stand at his elbow reminding him that his music hadn't any tricks, only traps. Beecham sometimes referred to the symphonies as 'grand old pieces', but he rarely performed them more than adequately. He by-passed quite a large number of the heavy breed. Only the second symphony of Brahms, and an isolated performance of the St Anthony Variations (in which he had a lapse of memory), and the Violin Concerto. No Bruckner[7] or Mahler. He appeared to sweep aside great areas of music and act as advocate for some strange bedfellows—Balakirev, Borodin, Mussorgsky and Rimsky-Korsakov. This exotic music was, in Beecham's estimation, surprisingly elegant.

The reputation of Delius is now precarious, and performances of his major works rare; he can so easily be dismissed as 'nebulous', 'spineless', 'shapeless', 'mushy', 'decadently romantic' in a post-war era which worships brutality. Delius had a genius for *divisi* and dispersal of sensuous, indeterminate orchestral sounds.

---

[7] He did, in fact, conduct the Bruckner Seventh Symphony in the Maida Vale Studios for the BBC in 1957 and the Brahms Third Symphony in New York in 1957—an amazing performance which was recorded. In late 1907 he conducted Mahler's Fourth Symphony in London.

His harmony does not resolve; it dissolves imperceptibly into new shapes which in the hands of unenlightened conductors produces a thick yellow London fog. With Beecham I always felt to be on the fringe of a morning mist which was dissipating in sunshine and light breeze. He had an uncanny skill in drawing brief attention to melodic ghosts: there was never 'crisp definition', and the whole impression was one of hazy activity, as if we were involved in a great musical conjuring trick; but it wasn't music, it was magic.

Only once did Beecham entertain us during a rehearsal of Delius. Performances of choral works in the 1930s were like café apple-pie (when fruit and pastry meet for the first time on the plate). Beecham, having rehearsed *Appalachia* with the Hallé Choir on the previous evening, made us aware in the course of the Thursday morning orchestral rehearsal that the work was choral because he sang—incessantly—if 'singing' is the right word (he always groped about in search of the pitch). At one point Tommy became particularly agitated, and sprang to his feet, conducting a mystified, silent assembly. When he eventually composed himself, he sat down and delivered the following address:

'Gentlemen, at letter J the choir will sing a generous portion of this work unaccompanied. At letter K, however, they will have contrived, by some mysterious means, to arrive at a key far removed from that in which they began. I would therefore exhort your collaboration by performing some cues you will observe, if you cast a long and penetrating glance at your music. In this manner we hope to *lure* the choir back, if not to the original key, at least to some nearly related one; and that is all I would like you to remember—beyond the elementary detail of creeping in at the right moment.'

Beecham believed that music was created to enjoy, not edify, and although he never expressed his contempt for Bach and the 'academic' in my presence, I was sometimes embarrassed by his rather naughty public pronouncements against established masterpieces. Occasionally he 'took leave' during performances which were otherwise going well, as was the case once in Beethoven's Seventh Symphony. After the Scherzo he braced himself, and his roguish eyes seemed to say, 'You all believe this to be a great work. I will now demonstrate that the last movement is unutterable rubbish, and belongs to the Old Kent Road.' He then let it rip as if to prove it.

He never rehearsed calculated climaxes: his performances had about them an aura of improvisation. We were on the edge of unnecessary uncertainty at the start of every unpredictable concert, and exhausted at the end of what always proved to be an immensely satisfying musical experience. Music 'bloomed' for Beecham, because he was inimitable in shaping sounds *as they happened*, and although there appeared to be elegant and meticulous attention to detail in the present, he was unique in his conception or comprehension of *whence* music comes and *whither* it goes.

'The evil that men do lives after them: the good is oft interred with their bones' is partially true of this remarkable man. It is some years now since he dominated the musical scene, and it becomes more difficult to denude him of his legendary foibles, whims, caprices, eccentricities, ego, and other manifestations of human frailty. I regard Tommy as the end of an era, and will be grateful to the end of my life to have enshrined in my memory immaculate performances of great works and small ones, which by his genius reached new stature.

FRANK HOWES
(For many years chief music critic of *The Times*, who died in 1975. He wrote the following specially for this book. His obituary leading article in *The Times* is included on pp. 185–6)

In the quotation from *The Times*, of which I was the author, I was speaking anonymously and editorially for the paper. I should like to add to those expressions of opinion some more first-personal recollections of Beecham as an interpreter of music, and by way of supplement, one or two stories of my personal dealings with him.

I mentioned in my leader, written on the morrow of his death, his performance at an Edinburgh Festival of Delius's *In a Summer Garden*, and at a November concert in the Albert Hall of Mendelssohn's *Hebrides* Overture. Both were sun-soaked, but the end of Delius's tone-picture was like the hush of a June night. I have never known a like situation: there we were, listening to an orchestral concert and prepared to behave as audiences normally behave, but as those last strains dwindled and died into silence, no one could move or make a sound; we were in the garden where everything was still, and it took who knows how long to come back to the stolid Usher Hall. At the same festival he gave a performance of Brahms's second symphony, the one of the four nearest to his own warmth of temperament. When it came to an end, the opposite happened: we rose to our feet and roared our instant excitement. How did he do these two things? In Delius it could only have been by phrasing and control of the dynamics of the phrases approaching the final cadence; but in Brahms there was the adventitious aid—so we were told afterwards—of two extra trumpets tucked away among the brass that did not utter till the final coda: dynamics again, of course, but also colours, or tone in the painter's sense of 'tone' for making brighter what was gleaming already.

The removal of Fingal's Cave from Iona to the mouth of the Tagus, the conversion of grey Hebridean water to Atlantic, or even it might be Mediterranean, blue, is not so easily accounted for. Internal balance of the orchestra, extra purity of intonation with a resulting clarity of tone, might have something to do with it; but ultimately it remains one of the inexplicables of personality, the idiosyncrasy of the interpreter, which we recognise even if we can't account for it in the pianist's touch, the violinist's tone, the singer's enunciation. But the odd thing is that Beecham, for all his Mediterranean temperament, could still play Sibelius, whose music comes from the back of the north wind: he was for a long time almost the only conductor to play the sixth symphony; he introduced *The Tempest* incidental music at a Leeds Festival, and in the recordings of the old Sibelius Society (pre-LP) are to be found other incidental music, and among the tone-poems, *En Saga* and *The Return of Lemminkainen.* Finland is further north than Scotland; the conductor shows his ability to play frosty as well as sunny music (such as Chabrier's *España*). It lies, I think, in his power to conjure from his orchestra the most varied tone-colours, at once pure and fully saturated. To make clear what I mean by the corporate colour of an orchestra, I would cite, as contrasts to Beecham's sound, the thick sound evoked by Henry Wood, and the blazing, burnished sound made by Toscanini and Mitropoulos.

The most specific instance I can recall of what he could do by phrasing, is the E minor episode in the development section of the first movement of the Eroica symphony. This, if you remember, sounds rather like a part-song. He made it into a madrigal by the way the lines of flute, oboe and clarinet wove in and out of each other as the bassoon thrust up its line from the bass. This could not have been done by baton, left hand or eye: it was too complex; it could only have been done by the most scrupulous phrase-marking of the individual parts, hairpin dynamics, perhaps by his actual singing of the parts as he marked them.

Here in the context of phrase-marks may be the place to recount a story of gratuitous kindness to me. In 1931 I was providing programme notes for the Leeds Festival of which he was the principal conductor. One evening some months before the Festival, the telephone rang and a voice said, 'Thomas Beecham here. I have just come back from Leeds, and I understand you are writing the programme notes. Is there anything I can do to help you?' To which I replied: 'This is extremely kind of you. As a matter of fact, there is. Could you lend me a full score of the *Mass of Life*?' 'Come round and fetch it from the Dorchester in the morning, will you?' I have called it gratuitous kindness because he took the initiative in helping me instead of merely responding to an appeal, kind as that would have been. The score revealed blue-pencil marks all over pages that Delius had left bare of anything but the notes.

Another of Beecham's achievements was to transform the playing of Mozart in England, as I believe Richard Strauss did in Vienna. Here at the end of the nineteenth century (which means up to 1914) the general approach to Mozart was that he was part of the tradition that ran from C. P. E. Bach through Haydn and Mozart to Beethoven and on from him to Brahms. True enough, he is; but the unexamined axiom behind it was that Mozart was a forerunner of Beethoven, a sort of John the Baptist, but that for a Messiah we must look to Beethoven. The change of style made by Beecham in performing Mozart was part of the process of coming to a new appreciation of Mozart as a composer in his own right apart from his place in a tradition, a change brought about by Edward Dent in scholarship, Gieseking perhaps in piano playing, and Elisabeth Schumann in singing, to mention the first names that come to mind. He wrought a somewhat similar change in the approach to Handel. He was not troubled by the modern insistence on authenticity, and he made attractive, if unscholarly, suites of lesser known pieces from Handel's operas, which he transcribed for symphony orchestra, and which in the event brought out the Italian element that Handel acquired between his leaving Hallé and his arrival in London.

If there is to be one word in which to define the musicality that I have been trying to analyse and illustrate, it would be, I suggest, sensibility. Other words have been used by other contributors with no less authority and containing as much of the truth. That sensibility, I suggest, manifested itself principally in phrasing and tone colour, which is, I confess, to leave out rhythm. This means that his art was primarily lyrical as distinguished from (say) architectural, such as characterised Weingartner's and Sir Adrian Boult's interpretation of symphonies. There is plenty of room in Wagner for long-sustained phrases and the keen sense of orchestral colour. Beecham's *Lohengrin* was almost Italian in its lyricism; his *Ring* was less heroic than Bruno Walter's or Furtwängler's, but it sang from beginning to end.

What about his blind spots? The chief of them was Bach, and it is not difficult to see why. First, texture. Bach's texture is contrapuntal and too thick for Beecham's taste: Bach was too Teutonic, too little Latin. Beecham once, and I suspect only once, conducted the *St Matthew Passion*, at the Leeds Festival of 1937. Yet the one real musical crux, which is the figured chorale at the end of Part I, 'O man, thy heavy sin lament', Beecham negotiated with the ease and inevitability of instinct. The difficulty is to find a tempo at which the perpetual semi-quavers of the orchestra shall neither drag nor hurry. This would not be so difficult if there had not to be accommodated above it in the soprano line the chorale tune in crotchets, which must sound stately because it is delivered one line at a time with gaps between them, and these gaps are filled with the other voices filling in a figuration in quavers. Each element seems to require a slightly different tempo to suit its own motion through a long movement. I doubt if Beecham noticed that there was a problem here. Not all of Vaughan Williams was in his line of country, nor indeed was Elgar, though he helped to give the first symphony its successful start, cutting it about in the process, however. His considered view of Elgar is given in *A Mingled Chime* (pp. 110–11).

On the other hand, he retained an Edwardian taste for Bantock, reviving *The Pierrot of the Minute* and *Fifine at the Fair* for a good while after Bantock's eclecticism had consigned him to subsequent neglect. But this was a product of that strain in T.B.'s psychological-cum-musical make-up which gave us the 'Lollipops'. He took delight in getting hold of some piece of music, preferably of overture rather than symphony scale, that had merit but no pretentions to greatness or immortality, and lavishing on it the whole apparatus of his sensibility so as to make the second-rate appear to be first-rate. One could somehow detect the note of challenge to one's code of values as he played these delicious *trouvailles*. Here was the art of interpretation raised almost to the height of creation, such as in my experience I only once heard excelled when Gioconda de Vito played some footling violin concerto by Viotti, in which one could hear her creating the music as she went along on the skeleton outline provided by the composer.

As a coda to these reminiscences, I should like to add a word about Beecham's feelings for Oxford. In *A Mingled Chime* he describes how he came to go up to the university against his own wish to go abroad, and how he only spent one academic year at Oxford, where, it would appear from a single sentence, he was reading classics. He made the mistake of not living in college but in lodgings where he was freer to make a noise on the piano, and the only collegiate activity he mentions is that he played football for Wadham. His mind was elsewhere, as he fully explains. But something must have stuck, for in later life he enjoyed coming to Oxford. It may be that friendship with Hugh Allen fanned the spark of his affection, for he was most generous to the Oxford Subscription Concerts founded by Allen in 1920, as the following anecdote shows.

These concerts were designed to provide on the thinnest financial foundations a couple of professional orchestral concerts a year in a series of chamber concerts and recitals that were less expensive. They ran for a few years with increasing difficulty, until in 1929 it was thought impossible to call on the guarantors any more. At the committee meeting at which it was sorrowfully

decided to close down the concerts, Sir Hugh Allen asked me if
I would announce their demise in *The Times*. Indeed he pressed
me very hard to turn this non-event into news. So I knocked up
a paragraph and put it in the paper one Monday morning. It
had the instantaneous effect that Allen's uncanny prescience
anticipated, for on his arrival at the Royal College of Music on
that Monday after his weekend in Oxford, the telephone rang,
and there was Beecham on the other end offering help, just as
he offered it to me a couple of years later. He offered an orchestral
concert to Oxford entirely free, a second concert which he would
conduct without fee, and even some financial guarantee which
was not in the event required. For his action saved the concerts,
which have indeed celebrated their jubilee during the 1969–70
season.

In due course Oxford made Beecham an honorary Doctor of
Music, and, an even more striking honour, invited him to deliver
the Romanes Lecture, which he did in 1956 on a non-musical
subject of his own choice [see p. 54].

GERALD JACKSON

[Gerald Jackson's *First Flute* contains one of the best portraits
of Beecham. Jackson first played for him in 1930 at the Scala
Theatre, for those *Freischütz* performances of which I was the
producer, and he soon afterwards became the original first flute
of Beecham's new orchestra, the LPO. He went back to him in
the RPO, and last played for him in 1956. He died in 1974.

What he says here is the more remarkable as, in his official
duties as Chairman of the RPO, so often difficult and far from
agreeable, he had to see the other side of Tommy, harassed by
administrative and financial crises: the other side of that tapestry
which most of us have to hang up before the eyes of the world,
the side so many modern writers love to pull up at the corners,
displaying and describing all the disorderly stitches at the back.
But Gerald Jackson prefers to remember Tommy as we would
all like our friends to remember us, with whatever pattern we
have worked out unblemished by inescapable frailties.]

It is difficult to add to what I have already written about our

beloved Tommy. Perhaps my opinion is best summed up by
saying that to me he represented the fulfilment of an orchestral
player's dreams. Only with him was it possible to give an un-
strained performance. He never dominated to the extent that
the player lost his individuality; always he bolstered one's confidence in one's own ability. When any ex-Beecham player is
asked what was the secret of his truly great music-making, the
reply is always the same, 'He let us play!'

I was very close to him during my years as Chairman of the
Royal Philharmonic Orchestra, and I can vouch for his deep
interest in the personal problems of his musicians. This endeared
him to them and imbued most of them with a sense of loyalty
that none of his famed capriciousness could shake. The feeling
that one was part of a family created a desire to do one's
damnedest for that family. There was no impersonal feeling such
as is engendered by a bureaucracy when it governs an orchestra.
Sir Thomas was so easy to approach, and therefore so very near
to his players when the time came to make music with them.

MAURICE JOHNSTONE
(Secretary-Assistant to Sir Thomas, 1932–35; BBC Head of
Music, North, 1938–1953, and subsequently Head of Music
(Sound), London)

Among the great conductors, only a very few are held in affection
as well as admiration by both performers and audiences. To
them, artistic achievement is the result of a harmonious and
joyful collaboration. In this select company, which in our time
has included Bruno Walter and Pierre Monteux, Sir Thomas
Beecham was unique because he combined inborn musical
authority with irresistible social charm and brilliance. Beecham
the man, was as compelling as Beecham the musician. In both
capacities he captivated his audiences at concerts and his performers at rehearsals.

Sir Thomas, like Walter and Monteux, was, as Sir Charles
Groves has so aptly expressed it, always on the side of the
orchestra. He took their responsiveness and ability for granted,
and assumed that they would resolve technical problems among
themselves. Not for him to explain and enforce his requirements

at rehearsals by tedious instructions and repetitions. Except for witty or poetic illuminations, and an occasional general direction, he spoke very little. His usual method was to play through a movement, or even a whole work, to discover where extra enlightenment or guidance was necessary, and then, after a few observations, play the music again, and perhaps again, until the players were at one with him and he was satisfied with them—and himself.

Orchestras who knew Sir Thomas revelled in and were electrified by his power to express the very spirit of the music without recourse to conventional technique. He could convey style and phrasing and rhythm simply by his unorthodox gesture and demeanour. (Such a routine item as the National Anthem became an unrehearsed act of re-creation under Sir Thomas,[8] and I was not surprised to hear from a friend posted to New York in 1941 that his rendering of *The Star-Spangled Banner* drew delighted crowds to Carnegie Hall.) Inevitably the gramophone record of Beecham at Rehearsal emphasises his inspiring and entertaining eloquence. It cannot convey his concentration of purpose, his wordless expression of interpretation, or the urbane patience with which he obtained the realisation of his concept, without force or frenzy. It took him a full session of three hours to record to his satisfaction the first four minutes of the *William Tell* Overture. The company secretly fumed at such profligacy; Sir Thomas, characteristically, rewarded the individual achievements of the five solo cellists and remedied their nervous exhaustion with champagne.

When Sir Thomas studied and memorised his music remains a mystery even to those who participated in the joyous routine of his daily life. Possibly in the night watches, for the only time when he demanded impregnable privacy was in the afternoon before a concert or opera, for sleep and certainly not for study. His memory for music and literature was as prodigious as Tovey's. His mind contained everything he had ever read or heard. It was not a memory for the minutiae of the printed page, like Toscanini's, but a memory for the contours and total effect of

---

[8] On his welcome reappearance in Manchester in the Hallé season with his own orchestra, the *Manchester Guardian* reported that his rendering of the National Anthem 'would have quelled a revolution'.

work after work, from *Messiah* and *The Magic Flute* to *Rosen-kavalier* and *A Mass of Life*, from Méhul to William Alwyn. He could startle his orchestra into spontaneous applause by giving, from memory, a definitive performance at a first play-through of a work that was new to them as a family. I recall such a stunning occasion in a subterranean rehearsal room in 1932. The work was the first symphony of Sibelius: Sir Thomas saw the score for the first time two weeks earlier.

Elgar marked his scores in even greater detail than Mahler or Puccini. He 'could not bear to see the notes looking naked'. To a very considerable extent, the Beecham sound was due to a similar fastidious marking of nuance, dynamic and emphasis. Especially was this so with his favourite composers. His scores of Handel, Mozart, Schubert, Rossini, Berlioz, Delius (and Beethoven to some extent) looked as if they had had the Elgar treatment. Ironically, Sir Thomas, who was no Elgarian, illumin-ated other composers in the same way that Elgar illuminated his own music. He ensured the vitality and individuality of his performances simply by making explicit what was implicit in the music. For example, he increased the thrill of vigorous music, such as the *William Tell* or *Flying Dutchman* overture, by the simple device of adding one more forte to a fortissimo in the repeat of a fortissimo passage. And conversely, his scaled re-duction of tone in a diminuendo was magical. After a memorable performance of *Hugh the Drover* by students of the Royal College of Music, directed by Sir Thomas, Vaughan Williams said he had no idea his music could sound so beautiful.

The laborious task of transferring these highly significant signs to the orchestral parts was entrusted to his secretary and/ or librarian. Frequently they arose from the inspiration of the moment and the job had to be carried out between the final rehearsal and the performance. Sir Thomas would briefly emerge from his privacy to say, 'Will you be so kind as to put just a few marks in the Schubert symphony, my dear fellow', and leave me or us to thank our stars that the symphony was in the second part of the concert, giving a little more time to insert hundreds ('just a few' indeed!) of marks in the fifty individual parts of a fifty-minute work. During a rehearsal in a provincial city, he had me summoned from London to assist in the immedi-ate transformation of the Jupiter Symphony and the St Anthony

Variations. At all times Sir Thomas alerted his players and his staff by his methods, and his audiences by his results.

The freshness, beauty and ardour of Sir Thomas's interpretations of great and not-so-great music were but one manifestation of an exuberant and original personality. John Osborne's pithy tribute to Noel Coward can aptly be reverted to this prince of musicians: 'He was his own invention and contribution to the century.'

DORA LABBETTE

[One of the most popular of the singers associated with Sir Thomas in concert, oratorio and opera, Dora Labbette may still be heard from time to time in radio repeats of her records of Delius songs with Sir Thomas at the piano. She has written to me of some of those performances which I well remember. I quote from her letters.]

Having been a singer and not a writer, I feel that my words cannot possibly describe the magic with which TB always inspired those who knew and worked with him. You are right: he *was* the greatest of them all, having given his life, soul and fortune (which was considerable) to music; and this makes it all the harder to say anything which would do him justice.

I sang for him over many years, during which time I think he taught me all I know about real music and the art of 'putting it over'. Delius was his dear friend for whose music he had the greatest admiration and understanding. TB took me on several occasions to Delius's home in France, where he lived in retirement, in order that Delius could hear me sing his songs. This was an experience I shall never forget. I sang some of them again for him at the Delius Festival of 1929.

I sang in many concerts and operas under Sir Thomas— *Messiah, Solomon, Acis and Galatea* and other Handel oratorios, songs and arias of Mozart, songs of Schubert, Brahms and Grieg; operas—*Otello, Pelléas, Romeo and Juliet, Faust, Hoffman,* etc.—and *Bohème.* With him at the helm—what extraordinary pleasure! Also in *A Village Romeo and Juliet* (Delius), the only time I think it was broadcast: the cast included Jan van der Gucht, Dennis Noble and Percy Heming.

My last performance with Sir Thomas was in Australia, during his remarkable tour for the ABC, in the Brahms *Requiem*. Of course I had sung it for him before on a number of occasions, but I am bound to remember this performance with great emotion.

NORMAN K. MILLAR
(Administrator of the Royal Philharmonic Orchestra 1948–58)

Out of a multitude of memories of the late Sir Thomas Beecham which derive from my eleven years of association with him, and as the individual responsible for arranging his engagements on this side of the Atlantic (he would never accept that anyone should have the title of his Manager), it is a monumental task to separate one incident or connected series of incidents for the purpose of a short article. The usual story is of his wit or of his caprice, for he was both witty and capricious, or it is apocryphal or quite untrue.

From my earliest days with him it was clear that something which troubled him greatly was the attitude of the authority at Covent Garden towards him. He would tell me how, at a time just before the First World War, not only the Opera House but the market and a considerable block of property in Aldwych, including the Waldorf Hotel, had belonged, if not to him, then principally to his father and one or two others of his business associates, and it had been the scene of some of his greatest, although certainly not least expensive, musical triumphs.

After the end of the Second World War the Opera House was leased to the Arts Council who appointed a Board of Management, which appeared, at least to Sir Thomas, to have as their main object a steadfast resolution to keep him out of the place. This infuriated him. Some time in 1949 he was asked by the Incorporated Society of Musicians to address the Society's Annual Dinner which was to be given in Brighton, taking as the theme of his address 'The Future of Opera in Great Britain'. His only request to me on this matter was that I should find means of furnishing him forthwith of a list of names of the Board of Management and Administration of the Opera House. It was not as easy a task as it sounds. I found many who either did not know or were unwilling to tell me, numbered among whom was the only

representative of the Arts Council I knew and who should have
been able to furnish the information. So I went to the fountain-
head and asked if I might see Sir David Webster, then plain
Mister, and was received with the greatest kindness and courtesy.
I was given all the information for which Sir Thomas had asked.
To this day I am not sure whether the accidental disclosure of
the fact that Sir David and myself happened to be born within
about 16 miles of each other had anything to do with my reception
or not, but I believe it was his natural gentility. Judge of my
feelings, then, upon reading the press reports of Sir Thomas's
address, to find that he had individually castigated every member
of the Board, including Sir David. At this time he offended many
people including among them some very notable British singers.

The aftermath of this was, not unnaturally, an increased cool-
ness between Covent Garden, the Arts Council and Sir Thomas,
and it was only after a strenuous public relations exercise and the
passage of about two years that an opportunity arose of healing
the breach. The occasion was the Festival of Britain when Sir
Thomas was invited to conduct an English opera in association
with Covent Garden, and which would first be seen as part of
Liverpool's contribution to the Festival with one or two performances later at the Garden. Sir Thomas was, I believe, a passionate
Englishman, and it was a source of concern to him that the only
opera he could think of and which had any connection with the
time of the 1851 Exhibition, inasmuch as it had been very popular
at that time, was *The Bohemian Girl* by Balfe, an Irishman.

Arising out of these performances and giving an interesting
sidelight on Sir Thomas as a conductor, I had an informal chat
with one of the two tenors who alternated the principal rôle. He
was a good tenor by certain standards not tenable today. He told
me that often, when he looked at a conductor, the expression on
the conductor's face constricted his throat and put his heart in
his boots, but when he looked at Sir Thomas's face he saw an
expression which said to him that this was to one of the loveliest
sounds Sir Thomas had heard and he found himself producing a
voice he scarcely knew he owned.

This taste of Covent Garden was, of course, fuel for the deep-
seated passion Sir Thomas had for the place, and in course of
time it was arranged that he would give *Die Meistersinger*, but
not, to his great disappointment, a new production. By this time

Sir Steuart Wilson, who had been Director of Music at the BBC, had retired from that position, and had gone to a similar post at Covent Garden. Sir Thomas had it in mind that, if he was not to have a new production he was at least going to have a new sound. I was asked to get in touch with the Garden in the person of Sir Steuart to say 'Sir Thomas wished to have a chorus of about 200 in the final scene'. Dutifully I spoke to Sir Steuart who immediately declared it impossible on the grounds that the Garden could not command such vocal resources. Sir Thomas countered that many local societies would be only too willing to help. This Sir Steuart admitted, but he was not able, by any means within his budget, to dress such a number. Back to Sir Steuart again with Sir Thomas's statement that the costumes from several operas which he named and which were in the Garden's wardrobe department could be used. So it was agreed, and so it stood until the first rehearsal, which was mainly orchestral, with the normal Garden chorus. The production was in the hands of Heinz Tietzen, himself a conductor and a very old friend of Sir Thomas. I met him just after the orchestral rehearsal started and he asked if what he had heard about the chorus was the case. It became clear that this was not the way Tietzen envisaged the final scene and I could not but wonder what the final outcome would be. Tietzen was a man of great charm, of medium build and quietly spoken. At the break in the rehearsal Sir Thomas went on stage to meet him and I just saw Tietzen take him by the arm and walk quietly, arms linked, towards the backcloth. The result was that the opera was done with the normal Covent Garden Chorus.

One other event, arising from this performance, should be recounted. During the course of choral passages, Sir Thomas had been impressed with the voice of a particular tenor. He sent for him to come to his dressing room and asked him what the Garden were doing about the training of his voice. When he was told that nothing was being done, Sir Thomas suggested that the young man leave the Garden and have some voice training, but was told that, since he had both a wife and young family to support, he could not afford such a break. Nevertheless, he did leave, went to a teacher specified by Sir Thomas and was paid a living wage by the management of the Royal Philharmonic Orchestra; after a number of vicissitudes, he now stands as probably the foremost English tenor of the day.

Aida, Act II, c. 1925; Beecham's original 1910 production for the B.N.O.C.

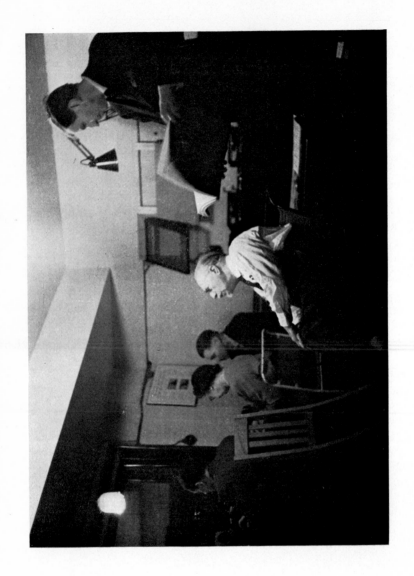

The 'Cave of Harmony', BBC – 1946 (with the author on the right)

IVOR NEWTON

[In a lively book of musical personalities and wide experience, *At the Piano*, the famous accompanist Ivor Newton has drawn a vivid portrait, amusing but admiring, of Beecham in a chapter entiled 'Sir Thomas'. In it he describes how, shortly after Beecham's death, he came across a seat beside the Square Tower at the end of Portsmouth Promenade, inscribed to commemorate Beecham's last concert, which took place in Portsmouth in the spring of 1960. The inscription commemorates the programme, a typical Beechamesque compilation of Mozart, Haydn, Handel, Schubert and Delius. Nearby, plaques commemorate great naval heroes and events in English history. He wrote:]

Somehow it seems fitting that Beecham should be honoured with the fighting men of his country, for his life was a series of battles fought with enormous courage on behalf of his country's music, and enemies included the Press, the Income Tax Commissioners and, at times, the British public itself. When, at the end of his life, it took him to its heart, we knew that he had won his battles . . . While I wonder if this is the only public memorial to one of the greatest Englishmen of our age, I sometimes feel that if Sir Thomas's ghost ever walks the battlements of Old Portsmouth, he will give an approving nod to this simple memorial.

HUMPHREY PROCTER-GREGG

Beecham is so generally set down as this, that or the other, that it is frequently forgotten that he was all of them; in fact much more of a multiple man than any of us who try to describe him. I suppose most of us like to think of ourselves as a whole, single individual, while some of us own up to a certain division, even conflict, of two personalities which we tend to think we harmonise reasonably well, like the clever and engaging old lady I used to know who said, 'I always keep my conscience under very good control.' But Beecham was something rather different: a compendium of several personalities (I think Ethel Smyth's estimate of fifteen[9] was a characteristic exaggeration) each of whom, served by a powerful brain and acute sensibility, could put up a convincing performance as the essential Thomas Beecham, pre-eminent in that particular line of human accomplishment, stimulating and provocative in each field he chose to traverse, and no doubt sometimes destructive as well as creative.

It is no purpose of mine to describe, still less to analyse, the total Thomas, but only to draw attention to certain influences upon the *musical* Beecham of the others; something of them was bound to spill over into his music, mostly as a distinct enrichment: he could make more sorts of music sound splendid than could any other conductor, but it was sometimes, though seldom, a certain disadvantage when the elegant or whimsical Beecham refused to come to terms with a great but serious composer, e.g., Bach, or to try to save a piece he disliked.

And this brings up another matter—the old vexed question of 'versatility, blessing or curse?' Of this problem Beecham was a superlative illustration. So Protean were his transformations that one would be tempted to say he could express and display every human emotion, and that like Terence, the old Roman poet, 'nothing human was alien to him'. But even Beecham had his limitations. A friend who knew him well said to me the other day, 'Beecham could react in every possible way except meanness.' This, as regards meanness, is quite true, as I will show. He was always generous when he had money, and when he had not, with other people's; and always in a fine, or at any rate well-intentioned, cause. But there were other limits: for instance, he could neither be a bore himself nor suffer fools gladly. Generally with a miraculous sense of *tempo*, he could yet, in mundane affairs, show an unreasonable sense of time; and, a past master of sources of human pleasure, giving and taking, he was less good at facing up to unpleasant necessities: if he couldn't walk out on them he would occasionally cut the Gordian knot quite ruthlessly. But is all of this not sometimes characteristic of most great artists?

---

[9] She said of him that at thirty he housed potentially a poet, a savant, a lawyer, a traveller, an actor, a politician, an extension lecturer, an adventurer, a financier, and at least half-a-dozen musicians rolled into one.

Then there were the contradictions in his make-up. He could
infuriate or meltingly acquiesce; exult over or cynically deplore
the same idol of his own or of other people; he could take infinite
pains over a piece, or brush it casually aside as he could any
situation, idea or person when not to his taste. The charming and
impressive 'How do you do?' could be followed after a moment of
suspense by a *coup-de-grâce*, 'Good afternoon.' He could exercise
unshakeable self-control and austerity, or glory in extravagant
indulgence; he could 'whistle a duck off a pond', or consign his
entire environment and predicament to instant oblivion. He could
be passionately patriotic: *vide* his enormous activities in both
wars, and his generosity to English composers and musical societies; and again he could slang every English institution and attitude
for snobbery, ineptitude and a lot of other things. Instances of all
this crop up in the recollections of all of us in this book: I name
them together here to suggest recognisable influences upon his
music. There was very occasionally a careless performance, even
a rather bad one.[10] There was never a boring or a sloppy one: there
was always a rhythmic vitality, something virile and provocative.
And there was that multitude of marvellous performances when
some new musical light and depth appeared in the piece as it
moved along, as though constantly unlocking some new treasure-
house of musical jewels. At other times one forgot to register nice
musical technicalities, and strange suggestions[11] would steal in to
the mind (prompted perhaps by those very technical niceties),
and then the inarticulate longings of the heart at last seemed to
find clear voice and expression. At many of the more exquisite
performances which Beecham coaxed out of his fine players, one

---

[10] Probably of music he did not like: Howes relates his conducting a
pianoforte concerto of Hindemith 'with comic bewilderment'.

[11] In one of his subtle essays Lytton Strachey wrote: 'The purpose of
art is to make suggestions'; a pleasant generalisation, but rather obviously inadequate. Art can have more purposes than one; it may also
involve making a precise, particular statement. Just as an old master
could immortalise a profile by one particular stroke, so Beecham could
get a musical phrase played or sung with such a subtle, particular inflexion that it stamped itself on the hearer's memory ever after—as an
example I would cite the horn solo in the 'Royal Hunt and Storm' of
Berlioz on its reappearance after the storm. (Record ANG S35506)

has experienced what Matthew Arnold says in *The Buried Life* about those moments when

> A bolt is shot back somewhere in the breast.
> And a lost pulse of feeling stirs again, . . .
> A man becomes aware of his life's flow,
> And hears its winding murmur; and he sees
> The meadows where it glides, the sun, the breeze.
>
> And then he thinks he knows
> The hills where his life rose,
> And the sea where it goes.

I have long wanted to put on record something of the impact of Beecham on my own life, in the hope that some faint current may reach others of the powerful stimulus he gave to anyone who had much to do with him. Readers of the foregoing pages will be left in no doubt about this impress on singers and players; in my own case it was both personal and musically technical. The personal side did affect the musical, but it was so extraordinary in itself that I have decided to deal with it first. My contact, after the first year of professional work, resolved itself into a long series of separate occasions, professional, social and simply incidental to his performances, and always in the atmosphere of a long-established friendship, unbroken, and indeed deepening, throughout the years.

But I find it very difficult to write of this, however much I wanted to do so. Of a multitude of congenial friends, I could, if called upon, write cheerfully and with comparative ease. And chance and my professional life have thrown me in the regular way of many musical notabilities[12] both in personal acquaintance and close observation 'in front of' and behind the scenes: of these I think I could also write, though only with one or two of them would the claims of actual friendship arise, nor would I have sought them. Almost invariably one finds real artists interesting, admirable and understandable. But the great artist

---

[12] Should a list be required in justification of this remark, it would have to include Barbirolli, Boult, Delius, Elgar, Harty, Holst, Kleiber, Rachmaninov, Sargent, Ethel Smyth, Sammons, Solomon, Stanford, Stravinsky, Toscanini, Walter, Walton, and innumerable fine singers and players.

is not always congenial: the métier leaves little or no time or room for making friends seriously; the conventional social amenities incidental to business are generally forthcoming, but one meets as fellow-campaigners between battlefields; attractions are momentary and forgotten, or purposefully laid aside. With Beecham everything was different: the attraction was enormous, and the effect unforgettable. Only with four other artists have I experienced so powerful an initial impact—with Rachmaninov at a brief and extraordinary first meeting, and with Kreisler, Eleanora Duse and Calvé: these I only heard and saw several times—Calvé at 63, the greatest singer I have ever heard in range, vocal purity and colour, and dramatic power: she could have carried about Callas and Gracie Fields as accessories in her compact. But with Beecham I felt, as did so many of those who sang and played for him, an extraordinary affinity, in my case even a sort of family relationship which both took for granted. How this came about, and why it persisted when our paths diverged so often, I cannot tell: I was still as surprised as I was touched at one of our last meetings by the warmth of his greeting. I had spotted him sitting in the circle at Covent Garden in the interval of *Alcina*, to which he had gone to hear Joan Sutherland. Sitting beyond him was Miss Shirley Hudson, unknown to me, and soon to become Lady Beecham. After the first handshake and invariably cordial inquiries, he turned to introduce me, saying with gentle deliberation, 'Miss Hudson, this is Humphrey Procter-Gregg, one of my oldest friends.' Well, 'through all the changing scenes of life' that's how it had always been.

I first met Sir Thomas in 1928 at the Royal College of Music, where I had been made Manager of the Opera School, after a good deal of experience as a student in designing, mounting, lighting and producing the operas and repertory performances, and had been sent by the College to study at the Scala, Milan, in Toscanini's last season before his American exile. I had also toured with the British National Opera Company which was, of course, the bold resurgence of the Beecham Opera Company. There I had heard many an adventurous and fantastic item of the Beecham legend: indeed he has been a legend from my school days. Near us in the Isle of Man lived Clare Delius, sister

of the composer: I played his songs for her, which she sang
with complete understanding—I was enslaved by them—and so I
had come to hear of the magic wand waved over his music by
Thomas Beecham. He was Sir Thomas by the time we met, and
round his personality had already gathered an aura of fascination
and considerable awe. This, as far as I was concerned, he was
never to lose: many a time I could imagine, when I saw him in
action, that he might have been just as Coleridge fancied
himself under the spell of music, when

> . . . all should cry, Beware! Beware!
> . . . Weave a circle round him thrice,
> And close your eyes with holy dread,
> For he on honey-dew hath fed,
> And drunk the milk of Paradise.

Only for my part, magician as he remained, he was not either
all that 'dread' or inaccessible, and the honey-dew and the milk
of paradise (to say nothing, on occasions for me, of a marvellous
earthly breakfast, lunch or supper) were often there to be shared
by all who had ears to hear—and still are there, in the records.

In 1929 I was told that Sir Thomas wanted to conduct *The
Magic Flute* at the Royal College, and wished me to design and
produce it for him. I did not know what to expect or how I
should react to this real-life specimen of the Superman. Here,
since I am writing about Sir Thomas and his impact upon my
life, I will refer to his extraordinary effect upon a defect of my
own, an inhibitive stammer—a thing which can poison one's life
in a way no non-sufferer can possibly understand, though its
disablement is obvious enough. From the first encounter Sir
Thomas so charmed and amused me that its hold was released,
and in his company it was at a minimum ever after. It must have
been his innate ability to get the best out of other people.

I wish I could report Beecham at those first rehearsals. I
remember the wit and absurdity that flowed from him perpetually;
consciousness of the hard work put in by everyone vanished; but
the fun of course arose largely out of our various little short-
comings, and was mostly intended for my private ear: in cold
print it might embarrass elderly survivors, so it must go among
the aural anecdotes for select cronies only. But one musical

incidental may be recalled: I can't see any other conductor in the world doing it and getting away with it. When the student orchestra reading *The Magic Flute* through came to the aria for Monostatos in C major with a brilliant accompaniment in presto semiquavers, Sir Thomas casually remarked that he thought the singer would find it easier in C sharp—as all musicians know, a murderous key to play in. The young players gasped, but got it going, and finished it very creditably. Sir Thomas smiled: what might have proved a cruel trick left them with a feeling of professional proficiency which carried them through to the last performance with the panache of a Beecham orchestra.

Sir Thomas enjoyed those performances, as did everybody else. He returned to the College in 1933 and 1934 to conduct *Hugh the Drover* and *A Village Romeo and Juliet*. (Years later, he expressed to me his disappointment that he received no further invitations after the then director, Sir Hugh Allen, retired.) The producer of the Delius opera, John Gordon, has reminded me of another disconcerting trick which Beecham employed: he had several rehearsals of the student orchestra; at the first of the last three he took all the slow passages too fast, and the fast passages too slow; at the next, the procedure was reversed; at the full dress rehearsal everything was at the right speed, and the young players by then could adapt themselves with ease to his most flexible *rubatos*.

When it came to performances of music he was fond of, there was often no question of a fee for the conductor, and he did a number of concerts for charity throughout his career both in England and America. Not long after the *Magic Flute* performances he agreed to do two of *Freischütz* at the end of an opera season at the London Scala organised by an Oxford graduate. The season failed and got badly into debt before his performances came on; whereupon Sir Thomas took on the *Freischütz* there for a week, without a fee. It was the second opera I designed and produced for him, and again a great joy for all concerned. This was before the failure of his ill-starred Imperial League of Opera scheme, in which I was to be in charge of stage and scenic affairs.

From the first encounter over the *Flute* he consulted me, a nervous, not very experienced young man, as a seasoned colleague, often pulling my leg in the most subtle and pleasant way, so that

I was always at my brightest in his company. Early in our acquaintance he told me he wanted someone who, regardless of fear or favour, would go to him about any problem he ought to deal with, whether he was aware of it or not. I did so ever afterwards, and was never abused for my pains, tactless as I now think I may often have been. Indeed, I can only account for his forbearance by assuming his knowledge that I was never afraid of him. I think fear irritated him, as it does so many powerful animals; he was not one of those lesser souls who, in authority, are gratified by the fear evinced by slaves, followers and strangers; he would either take your point or make some crushing rejoinder, and be delighted if you were amused by it, as I was time and again. Once you were on his wavelength you had of course instantly to tune-in to whatever he switched on: with me I think it was often for him some sort of momentary relief, or escape from some intense mental process or problem over music or administration; according to the whim of Prospero, one had to assume instantly the task of either Ariel or Caliban. I had various duties to perform for him over his plans for the Imperial League of Opera. I have just likened him to Prospero: the simile is not inapt. The Duke felt banishment and exile (from Covent Garden) bitterly, and though he could fill his desert isle with 'sounds and sweet airs', the storms of bankruptcy landed him in more than one Tempest! And the Imperial League was not the only one of his magical dreams which never came true; the opera house he offered Manchester, and the orchestra he strove to found in Birmingham were two more, and several cherished productions, for instance, the *Hercules* of Handel upon the stage, referred to later, and his beloved *Trojans* of Berlioz at Covent Garden—his last project of all—were never to be realised. However, Prospero did produce the 'Masque of Hymen'—thrice . . .

Among my duties were the preparation of prompt-scores for a number of operas—the *Village Romeo* to my own designs: these he kept by him to the end of his life, and often spoke of our doing it together eventually. I told him years later I found it, however lovely, almost too harrowing and depressing. He smiled, indulgently, 'Nice nostalgic music . . .' But he was able only to broadcast and record the work, never to stage it again. Among other projects the gifted Russian artist, Polunin, was to design *The Bartered Bride*, and Dulac, *The Snow Maiden*. The former

had done him a splendid *Otello* years before. Harold André was
to do *Carmen* on the lines of his Stockholm production, and
Augustus John the Berlioz *Faust*. André did eventually join him
on his return to Covent Garden. I also had to negotiate with a
young actor who had just made a name for himself at the Old
Vic, one John Gielgud. I asked him to lunch, and did my best to
persuade him to coach the singers in acting, diction, etc. But the
prospect was still nebulous, and he had other fish to fry, as
indeed, when the whole scheme fell through, I had myself. But
years later I recalled the not unusual foresight and intuition of
Sir Thomas, when Sir John in due course produced Tommy's
favourite *Trojans* at Covent Garden: the result would have
delighted Beecham, as it did me, far more than a later attempt.
Gielgud's 'Royal Hunt', a romantic picture in the Poussin style,
and the even more romantic Embarkation scene were outstanding,
and the 'Trojan Horse' perfectly convincing; whereas in the later
'improvement', two pairs of detached legs were apt to be deployed
in dichotomy and unintentional syncopation.

To return to the ill-fated League and its preparations, in which
I was involved. With Sir Thomas I toured North-west London
in search of scene-stores. When one was found (in an old warehouse whose Yorkshire proprietor almost justified Sir Thomas's
Lancashire prejudices), I had to provide a staff. This was not
difficult: a splendid old man who was known to me from touring
days and who ran his stage like a silent, spotless showroom, joined
us, and found most of his staff: he had been both Irving's and
Tree's master carpenter, and knew how to hang, fly and roll
creaseless backcloths—and everything else. Darer was a
distinguished man of the theatre, and I learnt much from him.
We took over scenery, costumes and properties salvaged from
the Beecham and BNOC companies, sorted and repaired them,
and I made models for a number of operas; my scheme for the
Tristan ship, I think a complete novelty, was afterwards used at
Covent Garden, I never heard with what success. It viewed the
vessel amidships, the forepart cut off on the left by a huge Viking
sail, and the afterpart tilted and slightly heeled over towards the
audience, but viewed from outside and above the sea, the visual
pattern and the lighting suggesting both wind and motion. We
came across the magnificent costumes of Roerich for *Prince Igor*,
in the old Diaghilev days, which Sir Thomas lent me later for

an immense production I did in Leicester with concealed
orchestra, chorus of 230, army of 90 and ballet of 50, in stage
conventions and scale of personnel comparable to Fairbairn's
Hiawatha at the Albert Hall. For the preparation of prompt-
scores, Sir Thomas cut some of the operas himself, and left the
others to me: for this and the office work he said I must have 'a
familiar', as he called it, and I found a promising student from
the Academy. There was nothing very Mephistophelian about
either of us: we worked hard till it all folded up when finance
supplied by Sir Thomas ran out, but Maurice Miles went on to
make a conductor's career, I am glad to say.

Once more Sir Thomas's fortune melted away in musical
enterprise. Eventually we got paid an agreed moiety, and all
had a chance to find other work meantime. This was the only
period in our acquaintance so far as I was concerned when he
took his famous evasive action: the stores-staff were paid till
we closed; I had gone a month or two without salary. One day
when in Manchester, about some opera production at the Royal
College of Music there (an annual engagement for me for some
five or six years), I ran Sir Thomas to earth after a Brand Lane
Messiah. Received as delightfully as ever, I hinted at my plight.
'Oh, *of course*, my dear fellow, and why not come to breakfast
tomorrow morning?' I turned up at the Midland Hotel, where
in due course he issued in the familiar dressing-gown, and we
sat down to breakfast. The superlative host, a rôle in which Sir
Thomas excelled, was in full play, and he suddenly said, 'Now,
you're wanting some money—of course you are—can you do with
a cheque?' I of course said, 'Oh yes, thank you', and he returned
to the bedroom, seemed to fumble in his dress-waistcoat pocket,
returned with a folded cheque, and said with a casual smile,
'There, that should help you along for a bit, anyhow, my dear
fellow.' I took it, thanking him, and took my leave without un-
folding it, having no idea what it was—that seemed more tactful
than an immediate investigation. Outside, I looked at it—made
out to *him*, signed 'Brand Lane'—his fee and his fare for his
Messiah the night before: how he paid his hotel bill I had no
idea.

About the same time he promoted the remarkable first Delius
Festival (unaccountably omitted from the Reid biography, as was
the second also)—six concerts representing the large and varied

output of a composer English born and bred, if international in outlook, who will always find a devoted following as long, at any rate, as the Beecham records are available. My guess, like that of Sir Thomas, is that his vogue will mount steadily, if and as sensitive interpreters preserve a love of beauty—the world is without it, by and large, at present, but surely that will pass.

At the first of those Festival concerts, Beecham sent for me beforehand: contrary to his invariable rule of invisibility before a concert, he personally supervised the arrival of the paralysed composer as he was carried early in his chair to the circle of the old Queen's Hall. Sir Thomas wanted me to sit by Delius while the audience gathered, trusting me to talk or be a sympathetic companion in silence, as the invalid might hint. As it turned out, the pianist friend of Delius, Evelyn Howard Jones, arrived and took possession: I sensed that Delius wished just then to make no effort with anyone, and I slipped away to my own seat. Throughout the festival, Beecham was tireless not only in attention to every detail of the performances, but to every possible convenience for his guest. (The inimitable host, always one of Beecham's best 'parts', was admirably described many years later by Sir David Webster, at the eightieth-birthday lunch. His speech and Tommy's I have made many efforts to unearth but without success: some day perhaps someone may be more fortunate.)

Looking back on the Festival as a whole, one impression remained of that singular series of concerts. Loving Delius's music as I did, I still retained my critical faculties, and expected to find its rather restricted emotional range to cloy in a probable overdose. To my surprise, in the orchestral concerts, at any rate, it did not do so. I put this down to the rhythm congenial to Beecham, some melodic line, virile, buoyant and flexible as always. There were one or two out of his huge repertory of composers with whom he could not always find it; in Delius he always could, and often where no other conductors since have done so: why cannot some of them learn the secret? Beecham is quoted more than once as saying, 'The grand tune is the only thing in music that the great public really understands, and flexibility is what makes it live.' But to judge from results, this only defines without explaining the thing: only two conductors I have heard, out of many others with a fine strong rhythm and immense accomplishment, seemed to me to have caught some of the knack of this precise double-trick of Beecham (to which I will return later)—Konwitschny and Matačic.

Except for some broadcasts of opera, I never worked officially with Beecham after the fold-up of the Imperial League, having taken up my post at Manchester University, from which I retired nearly thirty years later: there was then no chair of music, a point upon which Sir Thomas, when he came up for his doctorate, gently upbraided the authorities, '. . . since,' he said, 'you already have the—er—obvious Chairman.' Like so many of his ideas, this only materialised later. We met comparatively often at various times and places, a day in the country, a recording session, rehearsals and concerts in the provinces. His moods varied with the occasion, a serious exploration of some musical or literary problem, a mock-violent harangue, or some fantastic fooling over some recent absurdity in performance the week before. His immediate reaction to any performance was often quite irrational, like a boy let out of school, but hardly ever pleased with his achievement. After a magnificent reading with Feuermann of the Dvořák 'cello concerto (in which the orchestra has an unusually big part to play), and cellist and orchestra had excelled themselves in fire and poetry, and warm, glorious sound, the genial Feuermann, who had smiled contentedly throughout the piece, refused to take any calls till he could drag on the reluctant Beecham every time, and the orchestra were as delighted as the audience. Afterwards I got nothing out of Sir Thomas in his room in response to my enthusiasm but a querulous recital of all the difficulties of balance and phrasing in that particular work, and how insufficient had been its rehearsal. I asked had he ever heard a better performance, and he just changed the subject: he *hadn't*, of course, and knew it.

In relaxed hours his conversation would range unpredictably over almost any topic one could think of, though I never remember him showing any interest in flowers or horticulture: landscape gardening and architecture were a different story; for him, I think, nature required some civilising process to become interesting. But history and all artistic subjects fascinated him. Of food, travel, all social amenities, and literature, he was a connoisseur; he would talk of government rather than politics, and of human idiosyncrasies rather than philosophies. Pleased with all expressions of spontaneous human life, his pet aversion was humbug and cant; he could always enliven or charm the passing moment as he could caress a musical phrase and illuminate a climax. Like Doctor Johnson in perception and authority, he was unlike him in manner and effect. The doctor, we are told, when in splendid conversational form, 'tossed and gored a number of persons present'. Beecham provoked repartee and much laughter, or in serious moments profound reflection and some rethinking. Here are two specimens at random of how he would launch a subject and either leave it in the air or dispose of it in absurdity.

Talking of Russian music, I remember his asking me, 'Can you tell me how it is that so much Russian music—I mean the sort of Russian music that you and I like—is so surprisingly *elegant*? One could have understood it being anything but that —crude, brutal, laboured, sinister, over-loud—but elegant, no!' I offered something about the French style of their nineteenth-century culture, and the influence of Liszt and Chopin; but he could supply strong evidence to the contrary, and reminded me that Balakirev and Rimsky-Korsakov, and in a lesser degree, Tchaikovsky, affected to condemn the French school, were ignorant of Wagner, and looked back as they believed to Glinka, Dargomijsky and their own folk music—'and how much more "elegantly" they treated *that* than we did our own in England!' When one heard Beecham conducting *Thamar* and *Antar* (the latter a portrait of an oriental potentate—and he was almost an oriental potentate himself!), one felt the Russian elegance as he did: his record of the Balakirev C major symphony is another instance. (Some day some choreographer will hear the Beecham recording of it—HMV SXLP 30171—and make of it a splendid ballet.) But as far as I know, this question of his has never been adequately answered.

And another opening comes to mind. One day he remarked dreamily, 'I'm thinking of giving the Delius double concerto— interesting piece, you know—never been given here.' 'But it has been', I said, and gave the place and personnel of the perform- ance. He realised at once he was mistaken, but at any rate I had to be crushed. '*That!*' he cried in mock horror at my ignorance, '*that*, my dear fellow, was not a performance; that was something of an *international scandal*.' One could only laugh and give in.

I recall two occasions in his old age which show two other sides of his musical personality. After one of his later Festival

Hall concerts—a Haydn symphony, *Harold in Italy* (with Frederick Riddle), and the *Tannhäuser* overture and *Venusberg* music, he returned on insistent demand for more, played one of the famous 'Lollipops' and not content with that, gave Delius's most popular miniature, *On Hearing the First Cuckoo in Spring*. From the first bars and throughout, I could see he was taking peculiar pains to communicate something to the orchestra, and the result was different from any performance I had heard before. Strange and exquisite as were the sounds and the phrasing, they spoke not of the magic of the countryside in spring, but of some final irremediable sorrow and loss: so much so that instead of going round to see him as usual, I walked a long way towards my Hampstead home to shake off the depression.

Next morning in the Press appeared an undeserved slanging of Wagner's off-stage voices in the *Venusberg*, and no mention of the encores: the hidden female choir had been as beautiful as usual, if possibly very slightly under-weight. I wrote to tell Sir Thomas this, and asked would he not record that famous old war-horse of his, adding that I had not come round to see him afterwards as I had been so strangely upset by his reading of the familiar *Cuckoo*, not as hearing it for 'the first time in spring', but as though it were the last cuckoo ever to be heard in modern civilisation.[13] He replied in a letter that 'he would think about recording that old piece' (the Wagner) 'if the chance came along', and that, 'for your information, I had twenty-five of our best voices on the Sirens' chorus. But I was particularly interested in your remark about our performance of the *Cuckoo*: such a thought was present with me . . .' The Beecham mesmerism had been at work once more.

The other episode of those last years often comes back into my mind. It was when he had decided to settle in France, since England was 'too expensive to live in and much too expensive to die in'. His last concert in the Festival Hall was to be on Sunday 7 April 1954. I went to the rehearsal in the morning. He led off with the Mozart E flat symphony. I think he intended to make no particular occasion of it: if so, chance upset his plan. The usual equable exploratory run-through reached the first double

---

[13] Since this was written I read with particular interest of Fenby's similar experience many years previously. See page 59.

bar apparently very smoothly and elegantly. Then the successive entries in imitation of the two bassoons petered out, for the simple reason that there was only one bassoon there: he had been covering up previously for his partner, but in this exposed duet that was impossible, and Sir Thomas had failed, as indeed I had, to notice the absentee hitherto. Nettled by his own absence of mind, he called loudly and imperiously for information. An unseen voice from the wings replied, 'We *have* telephoned, Sir Thomas, but they think that he's left home.' Tommy's tone changed instantly to the familiar banter. 'Left home? Very strange —conduct credible enough for young ladies in novels, but highly unlikely for the British wind-player on a Sunday morning . . . go and see if he's around anywhere . . . and make sure he's not still in bed . . . But, gentlemen, what am I to say of your performance this morning of this Symphony? This is a *grand piece*; festive, full of joy, and your treatment of it this morning suggests to my mind nothing so much as the Paris Morgue . . . and several other dismal and unedifying places which I will not name to you . . .' At this point the defaulting bassoonist appeared and rushed nervously to his place to the discreet, ironical desk-taps of applause of his colleagues. Tommy, launched upon his own face-saving harangue, vouchsafed him merely an absolvatory wave of the hand, and continued his castigation of all and sundry. I could not catch the next sentence or two, which were drowned in waves of laughter, but he was evidently inveighing against what would be called in modern slang, mini-Mozart. Then I caught up with 'the notion of little Mozart orchestras and little *pianos* and *fortes* is all pretentious rubbish! Mozart liked the biggest orchestras he could get, and you can read of his delight in finding one day he had forty violins and the rest to match. All this talk of *authentic Mozart* needing miniature orchestras and miniature voices is a lot of musicological nonsense, an *olla podrida* of humbug, heresy, sophistry, pedantry and CANT.' The rehearsal proceeded on these rather preposterous lines: he was not going to let a hint escape him that it might be his last with his last orchestra, as supposedly it was. He sustained the mode of rhodomontade, and when the interval came along he caught sight of and summoned me to attend him, with an imperious gesture. In the conductor's room he became rather more genial, but the façade was still on view, and the moment of truth which was to reveal the modest and deeply sincere musician within was yet some way off. He treated me to a lordly harangue on the impossibility of life in England, the superiority of America in all the amenities of life, transport, roads, medicine, law, business efficiency, and so on, and the superiority of the Riviera to America, all to the detriment of Britain. Hearing the flow of eloquence, one or two amused listeners crept in at the other end of the room behind him. But I had had about enough of anti-British oratory, and when he drew breath I broke in to the effect that no one wanted him to leave us, but we all realised he deserved a real rest and congenial surroundings, and I found spirit enough to add, 'But I think I can tell you one thing!' He sat bolt upright and glared dangerously—who was I to tell him anything? 'And what is that?' he half shouted, still part of the act I was certain he was putting on. I said with what conviction I could muster, 'I think you are going to miss your orchestra.' The shot told: he drew back, and said rather disdainfully after a pause, 'Upon that I will offer you no opinion', and then leaning forward, and in a strange and gentle stage-whisper, added slowly, 'But they *can play* . . .'

Such was his mood on the occasion of what he expected to be his last appearance in England. Happily it was not to be so, and we were to meet again several times at one place or another, when he was in his old familiar vein of pleasant banter.

Examples of his serious style and the cogent expression of considered opinions are given elsewhere, and one can always turn up a page or two of his Delius, and almost any paragraph of *A Mingled Chime* to find him making apparently careless play with a wealth of solid experiences and sharp reflections. My own copy of the latter, inscribed in his beautiful handwriting, 'To my old friend, Humphrey Procter-Gregg, with affectionate regard, Thomas Beecham', is one of my most precious possessions; and when memories of those lost bright hours in his company come back tinged with regret, I take it out and dip into it, and find myself smiling contentedly once more.

FREDERICK RIDDLE
(Professor at the Royal College of Music, and principal violist in
both the London Philharmonic and Royal Philharmonic
Orchestra)

I first played for Sir Thomas when I was a student at the RCM
when he conducted *The Magic Flute* there. The first rehearsal
was electrifying to everybody concerned, and I can still remember
the extraordinary difference in the sound which we produced
when his baton first came down. The rehearsals and the performance were great, and though I don't recall much of the actual
content, I shall never forget the sense of sound and performance
which that man generated from every young musician under his
complete control.

My next experience of him, still as a student, was as a member
of the stage band in *Freischütz* given at the Scala Theatre. The
producer was H. P.-G., and some members of the stage band in
the shooting scene were, like me, students from the RCM. For
our short time on the stage we had the full benefit of the Beecham
temperament, and an introduction to what I think were his
priorities in the world of music-making—rhythm, elegance in
phrasing, sound, and in song the proper respect for our English
language. After our short scene we heard the rest of the opera
imperfectly from our dressing-room situated over one of the large
boxes at the side of the stage. I remember the splendid singing of
Thea Phillips and Tudor Davies, and the terrific drive that
Beecham gave to the Huntsmen's Chorus in the last act where I
was appearing for a small extra fee as a non-singing page-boy.

My orchestral career started with my entry into the LSO and
my chamber-music one as a member of a string quartet with
Harry Blech, David Martin and Willem de Mont, formed by
H. P.-G. and Jack Donaldson, both friends of Sir Thomas. I
imagine they must have told him about us, for eventually Beecham
offered me the position of principal viola in the London Philharmonic Orchestra, in the 1937–38 season. From then, apart
from some unavoidable breaks in my orchestral service with him,
until his death I was privileged and happy to learn and work
with this most lovable man.

During my time in the LPO and RPO he often asked me to

appear as a soloist, in works ranging from the Mozart Sinfonia Concertante to the Rubbra Viola Concerto. He took endless trouble to get as fine a performance as possible, and I have a suspicion that soloists from the orchestra received much better treatment than visiting soloists. I'm sure I never played better than I did for him, but of course it was expected that you played in the orchestra after the interval.

I have often been asked what Tommy was like, and whether I had any new Beecham stories. The stories are legion and by now fully documented elsewhere. To me he was not a funny man, although his sense of humour was at times outrageous; but a most human being, and a musical genius. I sat much too close to him for so long to have what so often appears to me to be the popular misconception of him as a gifted amateur given to showing off in public. I have worked in close proximity to an impressive list of conductors who have played in London since 1932, and the amount of the world's talent which has been directing me and my colleagues is formidable. I would venture the opinion that where most other conductors appeared to have a performance which we all strove to achieve, occasionally successfully, Beecham was always striving to find a better one than the last. He was always listening for the 'tune'. The melody had to be heard, and I think that the hairpins ($<$ $>$) which abound in all Beecham parts are the means of making the players bring out certain notes and phrases, and of getting them out of the way when the tune passed to another part. Nothing was ever permanent: he was always making small adjustments, and always marked the score in his own hand, the librarian transferring them to the parts. Of course this is only one small facet of the way he made music. He expected to have a core of players in the orchestra who he thought played in the right way for him, and in some way these players were responsible for everything else that happened in their sections. There would be some truth in saying that a Beecham orchestra was for him a 'principals' orchestra', but it is not wholly true, as he generally knew everything about everybody who played for him. He loved characters, and I knew several who were employed not for their playing abilities but because he liked them, and they once had been good.

Over the years he became more attached to his friends in his orchestra, and became more like a father with a large family of brilliant, but sometimes impossible, musicians, who could some-times be bullied, but always cajoled, into doing exactly what he wanted from them. Of course he had his naughty moments—who doesn't, especially artists, and during some of the bad patches of health towards the end, he would appear to be failing, and there would be a dull patch; and then he would suddenly come to, the scores would be thrown away, and we'd all give the performance of a lifetime.

I remember Beecham for his unique command of our language; for his never-flagging attention to detail in making music; for his elegance, his temper, his wit, his kindness, his humanity, his generosity, and for his love of music and life.

MALCOLM SARGENT
(Conductor)

[Sir Malcolm, who died in 1967, wrote the following in *The Times* of 10 March 1961 under the heading 'Sir Thomas Beecham, Weaver of Musical Spells'.]

With the death of Sir Thomas Beecham, the world of music has sustained a great loss. For 40 years he has been among the world's greatest conductors—their rival, rather than their col-league, for few people knew him well. He was not a 'clubbable' man, nor did he seek or need the friendship of many. His wit was at times more amusing than kindly, and he had a horror of any expression of sentiment; after a moving performance of great music beloved by him, he would refer to it as a 'nice little piece'. He reserved his affection, and poured out his love on the music itself.

He remained unique in the expression of sheer beauty of phrase. No conductor in my experience has shaped a melody with more tenderness and lustre of tone-quality, and no one has been more diabolically shattering in moments of climax. On the rostrum he wove a hypnotic spell over both orchestra and audience. In his own field he has no equal living today.

I have known him well for more than thirty years, and always loved being in his company. He adored talking music, literature, and politics. His judgments on the first two I felt to be very sound! When dealing with people or circumstances, his wit so easily overcame his true feelings. We were on a Brains Trust together on one occasion, and he made a typically brilliant speech, causing tears of laughter. I replied: 'Sir Thomas has made a most amusing speech—not one word of which was true!' He rose slowly to his feet and with the wicked 'Beecham-twinkle' in his eye said: 'I have not yet decided that it is more interesting to be truthful than amusing.' (A more amusing than truthful remark!)

In his latter days he had become more mellow and more easily lovable with less 'naughtiness' to forgive. I visited him several times during the last few weeks. He was touchingly endearing, frail and obviously physically weakened. But mentally he was alert as ever, planning future recordings and music-makings. We were to have shared his first concerts together, lest a whole evening should be too fatiguing.

His young wife was the greatest comfort to him and the whole atmosphere in his home was peaceful and beautiful. For her I am truly sorry. For him, I am grateful that he did not have to remain too long as an onlooker in this world's music.

'*Gottes Zeit ist die allerbeste Zeit.*'

RICHARD TEMPLE SAVAGE

[Richard Temple Savage has been for many years Librarian to the Royal Opera Covent Garden, as well as bass clarinettist there, previously in the London Philharmonic Orchestra under Beecham. In the former capacity he had to undertake, particularly at times of crisis and inconvenience, frustrating tasks of rush-copying, often with rushed-up assistants. Here his contribution, made as freely as were the others, differs from all the rest.]

I seem unwittingly to have inherited the rôle of Devil's Advocate in the matter of the canonisation of Sir Thomas! I feel rather diffident about giving you my further criticisms as you are self-confessedly 'under his spell'. I have to tell you that except for a few weeks when I first joined as a completely new man in the LPO, I have never been under his spell.

I will try to explain why.

The short spell of my first impression lasted only until I came under such conductors as Busch, Kleiber, Knappertsbusch, Furtwängler, Monteux, and so on. I then felt that so much of TB was superficial and flippant. I think I must be a puritan at heart as regards music, and while I do not for one moment deny TB's inborn musicality, I found his approach grated on me. It seemed to me to lack the humbleness of the very great who are but the servants of the composers, after all. His waywardness seemed to me to be a lack in him of the proper attitude to the works he was conducting, beautiful though many of them were.

TB's much renowned wit was not true wit because it was often based on cruelty and on the using of his power and position to make jokes at the expense of those who were in no position to answer back. I witnessed so many examples of this that his so-called wit turned very sour on me in a very short time. They were cheap.

I by no means equate personal morality with anything to do with the interpreting of music: there are too many examples in history of the morally doubtful being great composers and performers, but I always felt in TB's case that his being rather a spoilt amateur had affected his performances. I know many will not agree with me, of course.

DOUGLAS STEELE

[A change of angle is afforded by the very frank recollections sent me by one of the most brilliant of my past university students. Beecham wanted a music secretary and librarian, and Mr Forbes, the principal of the Royal Manchester College, and I recommended Douglas Steele, who had recently gained a diploma and a degree from our respective institutions. A shy and sensitive young man, he had a remarkable ear and a good all-round technique; the opportunity was not to be missed, however severe the probable strain on mind and body. His account in a letter to me of his experiences then, vividly re-creates that extra-ordinary *milieu*, the 'Garden' under Tommy. Now for many years an established recitalist and teacher, Douglas can gratefully recall the *tempering* process.]

Almost from the very day in 1939 I found him, after tracking
him down to the Scala Theatre, he was demanding. I had arrived
in London, and made a determined series of shots to get an interview with him in his room at Covent Garden. Each shot failed.
He was in conference. After three days I made up my mind to
go and corner him on the stage of the Scala Theatre, where I
was told he was making 'Lollipops' for Radio Luxemburg. The
London Philharmonic Orchestra were playing the Introduction to
Act III of *Lohengrin* when I walked down the aisle and came
near the plank connecting the auditorium with the stage. The
sound was magnificent, the rhythm superb, and it was being
recorded. In the silence when it finished I literally walked the
plank. I stood at his left hand, and said,

'Sir, I have come. If you remember, we arranged this at the
Midland Hotel last month in Manchester.'

He simply said, 'Hullo.'

I thought he very well knew that he had been playing a cat-
and-mouse game with me. Then he said, 'Come to see me on
Sunday, to my flat in Hampstead, and we will talk.'

On Sunday I went, and Smith, his factotum, let me in.

'He's waiting,' he said.

Sir Thomas had red carpet slippers and a flowered silk rose-
coloured dressing-gown. He looked very small, very lonely, and
very old (it was a few days before his sixtieth birthday). Immediately he came towards me, and with great friendliness asked me
to sit down and tell him a little more about myself. He gave me
some sherry.

'Now,' he said, 'you are to come and see how my great machine
works. Come to the Opera House tomorrow morning. I shall
want you to be my odd-job man. You will play any operas, from
score, that Mr Legge and I wish to hear—and I know you can:
Mr Forbes told me so. Next I shall want you to bring my full-
scores from the theatre to me here. You must ask Miss O'Donnell
where my little alpaca jacket is, which you must always lay on
my desk in the mornings—my conducting desk, I mean. When
you have looked after these requirements, I want you to catalogue
all my library—all this library here' (he waved his arms, indicating the shelves of books all round us) 'and let me have many
interesting extracts from them, which I mean to use in a book
I am writing. There is one more thing. You will have to make

journeys to interview people; and I am sending you to Norwich to see a crashing old bore who is the secretary of the Festival. You must stop him from encouraging the chorus-master to perform a wretched old *chant* called—' (he hesitated) '—never mind, it is a dreadful piece. They must not do it.'

I found out that this was Samuel Wesley's Motet for double choir, *In Exitu Israel.*

The next morning, the impression of a little old man vanished as soon as he came across the orchestra bridge to start untangling the confusion caused by Weingartner's being quite out of touch with the *Parsifal* dome choir and, incidentally, with his subconductors. Sir Thomas, looking like a piece of walking electricity, went rapidly here, there and everywhere, all with consummate tact and kindness, and before long, every difficulty was straightened out. This gift of radiating security, charm and kindness was one of the most interesting things in his make-up; in green rooms before a difficult programme the feeling would be that this was going to be a night of nights; he turned on something avuncular, something like a father-figure.

From that morning everything seemed enchanting and wonderful for me, and at the same time Beecham became exacting, formidable and quite ruthless. I was something to shout at and abuse, a kind of whipping boy. He would roar for me, for Lionel Tertis, and for his librarian William Primrose (senior) all over the theatre. Tertis and I would come from wherever we were (generally copying below stage), at the double.

The orchestra disliked the marvellous system of part-marking which Sir Thomas and Tertis had devised. All bowing had to be exact; all had to be exact in accordance with Tertis's system of bowing; and there were hundreds of small details relating to dynamics, phrasing and so on, which went into the parts in different coloured pencils. When I had marked them for a Sunday afternoon performance of Delius's *Paris*, which took place in the Queen's Hall, the rehearsal revealed a series of shadings leading to the wonderful oboe melody, which did not yet absolutely satisfy Sir Thomas. We had spent hours transmitting into the parts, already heavily marked, indications for a slightly different tempo, and a series of complicated and most carefully graded diminuendos. Before the concert, we were summoned to Sir Thomas, and given a mass of entirely new instructions, and there was a roar of abuse when the time factor was mentioned. Whatever happened on these occasions, Tertis would always say, 'No man has done more for British music than Sir Thomas.'

And so we would get our coats off, and start again. The marking of parts was a ritual. Under the ground, within viewing distance of the Ring machinery, we toiled, often all night long. Tertis would come to me, and placing his great Richardson viola under his chin, say, 'Sir Thomas is worried about this little phrase in the slow movement of the *Haffner.*'

He then played the adorable F sharp up to E, down a note to D, and back to F sharp, which I heard Sir Thomas rehearse twelve times that day, and continuing, 'Now, which bowing do you think makes the best sound—this, or this?'

I used to stand transfixed with delight and astonishment, mixed with some fear, because it was a straight question, difficult to answer because of the gorgeous sounds he was making. I think we spent half-an-hour dealing with the various kinds of bowing for those linking notes. At the performance it was the most tender and ravishing sound imaginable; and it was then that all the struggle to serve Sir Thomas seemed utterly worth while, and you became his slave again.

The copies to be marked lay in rows on trestles. Quantities of different-coloured pencils were marshalled alongside the parts—down-bows in red; blue for crescendi; yellow for up-bows, and so on. Sir Thomas invariably worked with a very fat blue pencil, and when he did so he would make a continual rasping sound while he smoked cigar after cigar, and there would be nothing else to listen to but the fierce stubbing out of these, which made a grinding sound in the ash tray. All the time, writing in his curious wavy handwriting, he would turn over each page of the score almost silently. Then call for me; and his eyes flashed, and he would make some frightening forecasts which had nothing to do with the copies I was to take below stage. He would say, 'Now you are to rescore *all* the recitatives in *Don Giovanni.* I do not like the effect of the harpsichord, which does not sustain Mozart's chords. My idea is to score the chord for divided cellos, and they will take over the chord from the harpsichord. So you will ask Mr Primrose to see that this is done immediately.'

On one occasion I was called suddenly into his room, and told, 'You are going to play *Turandot* for Mr Legge and me to listen to.'

When this session started in his room, Walter Legge kept an eye on me, and was out to help.

'Sir Thomas,' he said, 'we have a useful recording of it.'

'No, No!' Beecham roared, 'the boy will do it. Start.'

I did. What followed was indescribable. I did not know the score. What was infinitely surprising to me was that far from sacking me, people began helping. Hands shot to turn the pages over, and I had the sense to realise that they'd probably never heard *Turandot* done this way before. Sir Thomas was coughing and spluttering, and saying, 'Sounds better, what? A good old piece, isn't it? Go on, boy, go on. Good! Now go down to that café in the Strand and get us a carafe of cool orange juice—you understand, a carafe. We are all hot. And it is a hot afternoon.'

What he said to those in the room after I had gone, I shall never know; but I do know that Walter Legge said to me, 'I envy you being so near to him.'

One afternoon, things were reversed. He called me in, and said, 'Have a piece of birthday cake.'

This cake was made every year for him, so he told me, by 'a little old lady in St Helens.' Then he said, 'I want you to turn over for this terrible piece.'

He went to the upright piano and the 'terrible piece' was *Götterdämmerung.* As fast as he roared, coughed, cursed, sang (and what singing!), I turned. When I missed a turn, he cursed, not me but the Ring. 'Damned awful thing, what?—barbarian lot of Nazi thugs, aren't they?'

If complications in turning brought us to a stop, he roared with laughter; stopped, told a marvellous short anecdote about some accident in performance, and the swearing and banging on the piano started all over again, along with the terrible moaning sing-song. The following evening he gave an absolutely majestic performance of the work.

His amazing library of scores was available to me in the small room through which he used to shoot at top speed to evade, among others, two tiresome people who were, I think, his accountants, and he invariably tried to give them the slip by the exit from his music library which led into the opera house circle. He trained me to let them bang and shout at the outer door, 'Open up! Open up!' and when I judged the banging to have gained Sir

Thomas enough time, I would open up. Then they shouted, 'Where is he? Where's the old boy gone?'

And I would say, 'Well, he *was* in here a moment or so ago; but he doesn't seem to be in his room.'

Beecham kept an eye on what he had set me to do, and expected me to work as odd-job boy at Covent Garden in the mornings; do the Hampstead library in the afternoon, and be odd-job boy and copyist at night, and often *through* the night.

He had a fantastic way with books. He knew where things were, and although he said he did not know what he had in his collection, this was hardly true. When the London Festival was on hand, he had to do a BBC broadcast, and he was to describe the events. I was sent up and down to Hampstead to look things up in books. He gave the page and the part of the page. There was a stretch of prose about the coronation of Arthur from Geoffrey of Monmouth's *History*; something from *Henry Esmond* about murders in campaigns being done to military music; something about Cleopatra's 'Water Music'—the sound of hautboys, citherns, viols, played in the barge (taken from *Lives of the Noble Grecians and Romans*, translated by Sir Thomas North); a description of a man with one note in his voice, and a girl without ever a one, from Horace Walpole in a letter to Sir Thomas Mann, 24 February, 1743. The range was very great, as you can see.

Once he said, 'We are doing the Fantasy Overture, *Romeo and Juliet*, of Tchaikovsky at the Queen's Hall on Sunday. I want you to change the markings for the dynamics in the opening wind-chorus. I am revising it now. Look, while I show what I would like you and Mr Primrose to do.'

Knowing the simple-looking chords, I said with temerity, 'Sir Thomas, is that opening very difficult for them?'

He looked up and said very kindly, 'Very, very difficult. It can sound sour unless very carefully balanced. It is a portrait of Friar Laurence, who was a kindly man, not sour at all . . . But this is difficult. Young men like you should learn from Tchaikovsky, and I will show you how great he is.'

He then swivelled round and talked about all the things one would never dare to ask. He also let me ask questions to which he replied in a most practical way. I mentioned a thing which at that time had always interested me so greatly.

'Why did Tchaikovsky, in the last movement of the *Pathétique*

Symphony, at the very opening of it, divide the tune so that first and second violins each take a melodic note in turn?'

He was really pleased at this, and took me into his music library where he turned up very early Delius scores—the composer's name printed as *Fritz* Delius—so that I might see how the young Delius had learned to criss-cross his string writing, in much the same way as Tchaikovsky.

'He wants the maximum *intensity*,' he said, showing me passages from the *Arabesque* and from Strauss's *Elektra*.

The whole of the time I was with him, I observed nothing but a fantastic discipline—while he was working. There was no drinking during the day. The bad times—and there were very many, some of them frightening—are outweighed, now, by the good. All I have to do is to imagine myself handing him the score of *Paris* for a rehearsal (which had been started by a répétiteur pending his arrival), hearing him say as he turned to the orchestra:

'When I came in and you were playing, you have simply *no* idea, gentlemen, how you sound!'—at which his own performance starts in my memory, and the recollected sound of the great oboe tune brings a nostalgia too painful to describe. It does not take me to tell you what kind of a pain this is.

WILFRED STIFF

(General Manager and Secretary of the Royal Liverpool Philharmonic Society, 1946–56)

Beecham's name on the bill guaranteed a sell-out, and people were magnetically attracted to his concerts for a variety of reasons. There was the complete satisfaction derived from his superb musical performances, the joy of hearing him conduct works by their or his favourite composers, and the thrill of hearing an electrifying National Anthem. Some perhaps went simply for curiosity, and others in the hope that he would condescend to address the audience at the end of the concert. In Liverpool there was one over-riding factor—he was adored.

Having spent his early years in that part of the world, he never lost his affection for Liverpool as a city or for its Philharmonic Society, and the reciprocal affection of Liverpool for Tommy only increased as the years went by. He undoubtedly appeared there more regularly throughout his lifetime than anywhere outside London, and a Philharmonic Series which included a Beecham concert sealed its success. If his name was not in the syllabus it mattered little how many other distinguished names there were. It was never the same. The absence of his unique personality created a vacuum nobody else could fill.

It was an unwritten law in Liverpool that first choice of dates offered to guest conductors was given to Beecham, and after numerous telephone calls to his manager one sighed with relief to hear that such-and-such a date or dates looked possible. Fixing a programme was never difficult, and five minutes or so telephone conversation with the great man himself would settle the matter. Invariably one started off by suggesting a work particularly associated with him, in the hope of his ready agreement, and from there the recipe was quickly completed by Tommy with a Haydn or Mozart symphony plus either a Sibelius symphony or a Delius work, with a piece of Chabrier or perhaps a Berlioz overture to end. He was a supreme musical chef and his recipes always worked.

Came the occasion itself, and the anxious search for his small but stately figure in the midst of a milling crowd at Lime Street station. Joining him for the two hundred yards from the station to the Adelphi Hotel in the hired car was like participating in a state drive. And at the Adelphi he was received by a staff whose greeting and reverence could have been no more had he been one of the crowned heads of Europe. Up to the moment of his arrival one always had the fear that he might not turn up, and although he never let Liverpool down, one couldn't relax until he was safely deposited in the hotel.

The noisy tapping of bows which greeted his arrival at the first rehearsal disguised a nervous tension among the players, partly relieved by his obvious pleasure at seeing many familiar faces, and partly by his conjuring up one of those inimitable witticisms which will go on being passed down from one generation of musicians to another. The excellent first percussionist of the orchestra for many years was Harold Ball—and thereby hangs one of the more 'singular' Beecham tales!

Although this symposium is not intended to be a catalogue of his legendary stories, one personal experience is possibly worth recalling because it so aptly reflected his incredible personality.

When acting as host to Beecham for the first time, in my capacity of General Manager of the Liverpool Philharmonic, I invited him to lunch at the Adelphi Hotel. I remember being surprised and rather disappointed that he chose to drink beer, not wine, with his meal, and we had a jug between us. I not being a very enthusiastic beer drinker myself, and TB being thirsty after the rehearsal, he soon accounted for most of it, and we looked around for the wine waiter for replenishment. But wine waiters are never to be found when wanted, and Tommy suggested that perhaps we should begin to make a fuss. This prompted him to tell me how, as a young man, he had first started to use the Savoy Hotel, and he described vividly how he had on one occasion waited for nearly twenty minutes without service and had reached the stage of being able to tolerate it no longer. In his own words, 'I stood on the table and clapped two plates together, and I have had wonderful service there ever since.' At that moment the wine waiter in the Adelphi appeared at my elbow, and I breathed freely once again.

He made his first appearance for the Liverpool Philharmonic in 1911—as plain Mr Thomas Beecham—and from then onwards was a regular contributor to the city's musical life. It was inevitable that he should have the distinction of conducting the opening concert of the Society's fine new Philharmonic Hall on 20 June, 1939, a concert with Florence Austral and G. D. Cunningham as soloists, and no less than ten different items—truly a 'lollipop programme'. However, when he conducted the opening concert of the following season (as he did for many seasons before and after), he confined himself, strangely, to three works of Brahms.

In 1951, the Festival of Britain year, he brought his Royal Philharmonic Orchestra for concerts at the Liverpool Festival and also conducted a special production of *The Bohemian Girl* at the Royal Court Theatre. During his lifetime he did many things with tongue in cheek, of which this was surely one, but one which gave him immense pleasure. With an Arts Council grant at his disposal he must have been at his most impish to choose this particular work, knowing that the production would go on to Covent Garden.

He arrived in Liverpool with much editing of the parts still to be done, and with a copyist who worked the clock round in the Adelphi until the final rehearsal. The first night was memorable for me for some highly amusing but unintentional incidents; however it was all taken very seriously by most of TB's awe-inspired Liverpool audience.

On one occasion we organised for him, after a concert, a private dinner party, bringing together some of his oldest Liverpool friends, and this obviously gave him great pleasure. One of those present was Edith Rose, without mention of whom any reference to Beecham and Liverpool would be incomplete. Here was a remarkable woman, a Liverpool social worker of no personal financial means, awarded the OBE for services to refugees during the First World War, and living in a not very salubrious area of Liverpool but, strange as it may seem, she was the vigorous and successful local representative of TB's Imperial League of Opera. Many years after the League had ceased to function, she discovered funds left in the kitty to the extent, I believe, of about nine hundred pounds, and such was her devotion to Sir Thomas that she persuaded those responsible for its safe keeping to part with it so as to commission a portrait of him from Simon Elwes. This portrait, presented to Sir Thomas in Liverpool, remained in his keeping during his lifetime, on the understanding that it be bequeathed to the nation.

Edith Rose worshipped the ground he trod, and heaven only knows how many complimentary luncheons and dinners she arranged in his honour in their earlier years, and Sir Thomas acknowledged his debt by keeping in regular touch with her up to the time of his death.

But for temporary illness, Miss Rose would have been one of the four special guests of the three hundred and thirty present at Tommy's eightieth-birthday luncheon. As it was, he subsequently arranged for her to come to London for three or four days so that they could quietly celebrate. By then she must have been at least eighty-eight, and the kindness which he then showed to her only served to increase one's personal regard for him. When she died some five years later she was still President of the Liverpool Young People's Opera Circle, founded by her all because of Beecham. I was glad to share with him the close friendship of this extraordinary and fine woman.[14]

---

[14] She died in 1963 aged 92; obituary by Sir David Webster in *The Times*, 9 July 1963.

Thus there was good cause for Beecham's affection for Liverpool to run deeper than was perhaps generally realised, and this he would reflect in the speeches he invariably made at the end of his concerts there. He would positively purr with warmth about the playing of the orchestra, about the qualities of the Hall and the intelligence of the audience, reserving his castigations for Manchester, or other—in his view—heathen cities. He and Liverpool gave much to each other, and both were enriched.

CHARLES TAYLOR

[Now for some twenty-two years the distinguished leader of the Covent Garden Orchestra, Charles Taylor went there first as deputy leader to Thomas Matthews. He had been leading the string quartet I established on taking over the music department at Manchester University, and Matthews wanted to take them all to London. Only Taylor was able to go, and eventually succeeded Matthews as leader. He has led for a number of conductors of note (and a number of *not*), and incidentally for Beecham's last appearance there. He relates how he first played under him.]

As you know, I joined the Hallé from Manchester College when I was seventeen or eighteen, and immediately came under the spell of Harty. I would talk to some of the older players about this admiration, and more than once the answer would come back, 'Ah—but you haven't played for Beecham yet!' It was only late that season, when Beecham came as a guest-conductor, that I realised just what they meant. This completely compelling personality, this wonderful genius for making an orchestral player play his instrument better than he normally could! And the way he would shape, say, a wood-wind phrase during rehearsal, and then give the oboe or clarinet all the freedom in the world to play as if it were his own interpretation . . . His rehearsals to me were always an excitement, and his method of playing all through a movement, while remembering exactly which bars he wanted to go back to for balance or interpretation, stamped his ideas on one's mind without ever a feeling of any time wasted, so that one came to the concert musically fresh and on one's toes.

There may have been conductors with a deeper insight into certain of the ideas of some composers, but none I ever found could approach his vital personality. I shall always remember him in particular for his Mozart, Sibelius and Delius interpretations, and for his last *Meistersinger* series at Covent Gorden.

LIONEL TERTIS

[Lionel Tertis had several claims to the fame he now enjoys. He was for many years the leading virtuoso of the viola, and had been a propagandist for the viola as a solo instrument for seventy-six years, retiring from the public platform at the age of eighty-six. As a result of his efforts there have been a number of viola soloists throughout the world, but his principal successor is William Primrose. Tertis died in 1975 at the age of ninety-nine.

In the early years of Tertis's work, owing to the great scarcity of good violas, he designed in 1937 what is now known as the Tertis Model viola, of which to date (1969) over six hundred have been made in fifteen countries.

His contribution to this symposium has been compiled from two sources: a visit I paid him in 1970 when he talked over many incidents of his long association with Sir Thomas; and his delightful book, *Cinderella No More*, which he lent me with permission to quote: he said he felt it expressed to the best of his ability his recollections of that most remarkable of men.

In reply to my first letter asking for his assistance, he told me that one of the earliest instances to which his memories returned was in 1909 when the then Mr Thomas Beecham, who was attracting considerable attention as a fine conductor, resolved to get a small orchestra of the best players in the country, and make a tour of the provinces in the north, of which the central pivot of travel was Preston Junction. The great English violinist Albert Sammons accepted the position of leader; Warwick Evans, the well-known cellist, led the cellos; and Tertis led the viola section. They were a spirited lot of youngsters, including the conductor, and for some reason, whenever the train halted at Preston Junction, they let off fireworks to the great annoyance of the stationmaster. This episode earned them the name of 'The Fireworks Orchestra of Lancashire'.

When I visited Tertis at his Wimbledon home, he told me many tales of this tour, and of the high spirits of that most un-

Thinking it out

Handing it out

Cartoon by Nerman – 1924 (*Tatler*)

conventional private enterprise which was the foundation of so much musical history made in this country by Beecham. These tales are not for these pages, but I quote Tertis in general conversation in his book.]

I say the 'young' Beecham, but in a sense the word is superfluous: Beecham is a man who has never grown old. What a fountain of musical genius, charm and exuberant spirits he has always been! People will in years to come try their hands at recording his career, but the cleverest pen will never recapture the sparkle of his music-making, or the wit of his speech. From the first, he was a leader of men. Already in those days he possessed a magnetic influence to draw out the best in his players. How much the musical world has owed to his marvellous gifts!

[Tertis emphasised more than once how fine were Beecham's interpretations of Mozart.]

Yes, and Sibelius, and, of course, Delius. No matter what programme Beecham gave, the concert hall was always full, even when on one occasion the programme was entirely made up of weak, sentimental French music. I am sure he had his tongue in his cheek when he gave this concert—to show he could fill the hall whatever the programme; for when I went to see him afterwards in the artists' room, and expostulated with him—*Why* a whole programme of anaemic French music?—he replied, 'Well . . . there is nothing *illegal* about it, is there?' Whatever he did, and whatever you said, with Beecham, you just couldn't win. I once had quite a quarrel with him in one of his seasons of feverish activity, about over-working the orchestra—no amount of work seemed to tire *him*. Our dispute got into the Press, and he became quite caustic about it, and I kept out of his way; but then came a telephone call—'Won't you come to lunch?'—and that was the end of *that*—no word of any sort of rupture or grievance.

He could turn any sort of situation into some delightful nonsense, as for instance when he was rehearsing a new composition in which he showed he had not the slightest interest, for he went on conducting after the orchestra had played the last note. The leader, Albert Sammons, whispered to him, 'Sir Thomas, we have finished the work,' to which Beecham replied, 'Thank God for that!'

I remember on one occasion listening to an orchestral rehearsal of his. I found the viola section rather dull in tone quality. I told him so, and suggested to him that I thought I could improve their tone production if they were willing to take some hints from me. Beecham's astonishing and characteristic reply was, 'My dear fellow, do what you like with them—*boil* them, if you like!'

Beecham had extraordinary attractive power: however much he went for his orchestral players, they never minded it, for they all loved him, and the result was splendid.

PAUL TORTELIER

[The international cellist who has endeared himself to a large public is, among other things, President of Lancaster University Music Society: he has alluded frequently to Sir Thomas in his master-classes. I translate this contribution from the original French.]

The astonishing personality of Sir Thomas Beecham always made an indelible impression on those who came in contact with him, and in my case all the more so in the four concerts at which I played under his direction—they became a decisive milestone in my career, and so left my memories of that unique conductor ineffaceable from my mind.

He had taken a liking for that youthful concerto of Jean Hubeau in which he accompanied me with the Concertgebouw Orchestra,[15] which he frequently conducted: I have always regretted that I could not play that work again under him in England.

Constantly I recall—how could one forget it?—his kind interest in the comparatively inexperienced 'cellist I then was. 'You will succeed in England', he said, 'because you have temperament'. Emboldened by such an opinion from so irrefutable a source, I felt confident that it was my destiny and indeed my plain duty to win, through music, the hearts of the English public.

---

[15] At Amsterdam, on 9 March 1947. Beecham first brought him to England in 1947 to play in Strauss's *Don Quixote*.

EVA TURNER

[It is appropriate, albeit an accident of alphabetical order, that this group of memories from old friends and associates, which began with Norman Allin, ends with Eva Turner, both of them among the very few survivors of Beecham's earlier operatic triumphs in England. Of Dame Eva's enormous repertory (which must rival that of Maria Callas) many of her operatic roles and concert performances were sung with Sir Thomas, of whom she speaks with characteristic vehement enthusiam and affection. What follows I quote, with her permission, from what she told me on the eve of her seventy-eighth birthday.]

I adored singing with Sir Thomas on so very many occasions.[16] He radiated sympathy and warmth—so often that I can't tell you of any one performance I enjoyed more than the rest. Perhaps the many *Aïdas* come back the clearest—such spirit and fire! If I glanced down, specially, for instance, in the duet with Amneris, where she breaks out in a flood of all her repressed feelings, I would see by the smile on his face that he was 'just rarin' to go', and I determined that I too would let him hear every word of it as fast as ever he wanted. You see, we both came from Lancashire, and understood one another—you do too, don't you? Oh, Westmorland? Well, you've just *coom owret dyke*, so you'll do! Well, he was like that: he carried you along on a wave of inspiration. *I* loved singing the grand fugue at the end of *Siegfried* almost more than anything, and *he* 'Elisabeth's Greeting'[17]—he *would* have it on our Celebrity Tour with the new LPO at all the Number One cities of Britain and in the Albert Hall. I said to him at last, 'Oh, not that *again!* They'll think I can't sing anything else.' He simply laughed, and said, 'Never mind, you sing it better than anyone else, so *come on!*'

Many a time after a concert he would want to 'unwind' in company and invite me in his grandest manner to 'a cold collation' at the hotel. At times when we finished late, and had to travel,

---

[16] The first was *Aïda* at Covent Garden, 22 May 1933: the interpretation given by them both was specially noted in the press.

[17] The big festive aria in the Hall of Song, *Tannhäuser*, Act II.

our sleepers being close together, he would stand with me in the corridor talking for half-an-hour about any subject under the sun which he could always make amusing, and he always wanted to hear my experiences and opinion of singers and conductors abroad. What friends we had in the great days!—Flagstad, the most wonderful and simple person—and her Brangäne, Karin Branzell; Claudia Muzio, too, and Stignani, Leider, Olczewska, and of course Martinelli, Gigli and Pinza.

There was one sad and grievous occasion when Sir Thomas was absolutely wonderful and helped me all he could: you may have heard that my father collapsed and died suddenly one night in his stall at Covent Garden at the start of a first performance of the *Freischütz*—my first appearance as Agathe. As there was nothing anyone could do for my father, who had been taken to Charing Cross Hospital, Sir Thomas would not have me told, but sent for my relatives, and at the end of the performance, arranged for them to take me from the theatre by a private door away from the stage-door crowds. The funeral was away in the north, and on the next day I was due to sing Amelia in *The Masked Ball* and could not be replaced, so I had to dash back, and arrived just in time for the performance. His patience and kindness, which I could always depend on, were never more needed or more appreciated.

There was another sad occasion on which they were of no avail, and indeed changed to something else. A tenor from Italy engaged for him by somebody else to sing Radames in *Aïda* was so scared of Sir Thomas and unsure of himself that at the orchestral rehearsal put on for his benefit he sang much of it just under the note. At his own expense, Sir Thomas called an extra rehearsal to help him, and went all through the opera, but it was little better. At the performance I was standing in the wings waiting to go on, and heard 'Celeste Aïda'—we won't say a semitone flat, but anyway well under the note. I turned and whispered to the stage manager, 'The performance is as good as done for, but we must go on and do the best we can.' And it was the opening night of the season, too—quite terrible . . . I tried to give him some confidence by turning my back on the audience and singing that way to help him keep going, but it was no use, and Sir Thomas . . . *was outraged!* That was only one horrible occasion, and there were so many happy ones.

Years later there was a night I remember when I wasn't singing, but teaching for ten years as a professor in the University of Oklahoma. Sir Thomas was touring all over the States. A young harpist on our staff had been to play for him, and he had one more concert in Dallas two hundred and fifty miles or more away. When she told him where I was, he called out, 'Get her over here!'—and that was the message I got on the day of his concert. I'd not seen him for a long time, and wasn't singing then, but it was like a command in the old days, and I wanted to go. A fellow-professor offered to drive me over; we couldn't start till two o'clock, and we drove like the wind and got there soon after the start of the concert. He finished with the Jupiter Symphony, and you know what an exciting field-day he made of that. He was then a very old man, and when I got round afterwards to see him, he was all spread-eagled in his chair and talking to no one, and all the officials and city sponsors of the concert standing round. When he saw me, the old smile broke out and he exclaimed, 'Gentlemen, I would have you know this is Eva Turner, the greatest Aïda and Turandot of her generation,' and he launched into an eloquent oration in his grand style, all about me. He could still come to life all in a moment.

And there was one more occasion when I think of him. I had come back, I think from America, and the BBC had a surprise for me—one of those 'This is your Life' do's, you remember? They had been to friends of mine for information, and asked about any conductor I had specially sung for: they said they couldn't do anything about Beecham who was then living in Nice. My friend said, 'But you could always *ask* him: he could only say No.' So they sent someone over. Sir Thomas had said, 'Certainly of course,' and he recorded a fine piece specially for the occasion: so like him. And there was no one like Sir Thomas . . .'

[While I was with Dame Eva, an advance copy of another 'Golden Voice' record arrived as a birthday present for her from the makers: I noted that most of the pieces had been recorded with Sir Thomas.]

Man and Artist

I. THE CONDUCTOR'S MÉTIER

The late Herbert Withers used to say in the British National Opera Company that the life-blood of every performance has to flow through the conductor's veins. This is very true, and if verification were needed, the history of the conductor-less orchestra in Moscow in early Soviet days would supply it, a tale of endless argumentation at rehearsal, routine performances, and the practical conductorship of the 'leader', or at any rate one leading player: incidentally, soloists would be asked absurd questions in order to adapt their performance to the convenience of the players; and nobody liked it except the dyed-in-the-wool politicians. This does not mean that a really bad conductor is better than none, but that a capable conductor definitely *is*.

Why?

For many reasons, perhaps the first a political one—a strong central government is always better than a disputatious democracy or a party caucus, and all the more so because the purpose of an orchestra is not the welfare and happiness of the inhabitants, but the effectiveness of the music for supposedly cultured listeners who will pay to hear it. Further, there is the sheer convenience of having a beat to follow and a 'reading' to carry out. Then there is the utility of a traffic warden, an engine driver and a guard; also, it is to be hoped, of a diplomat, and an *instant* policeman and first-aid man at any disaster. These are all functions of the conductor, who has also to know the music as a whole, and how to balance the parts. There are also the purely 'showmanship' reasons with the public to consider: the 'personality angle' in our crude modern vernacular, and the convenience—indeed, desirability—of having a recognised spokesman, compère, liaison officer, figure-head; and again the advantage of a possible 'father-figure' who will see to the convenience and contentment of the players under his direction. All these are practical utilities. But then come the artistic reasons: a conductor can be the visionary, the interpreter, and in Beecham's own phrase, the 'searcher after a greater clarity than musical sound, the clarity of musical meaning'—that is where the great conductor has his biggest chance, the highest fulfilment of his métier.

All this sounds a clear and reasonable state of things; but as in so many human affairs, what seems clear and reasonable on paper entails several complications and snags in practice.

It is now a commonplace of musical opinion that the conductor is, by and large, the *prima donna* of our day. And this may be as much his misfortune as his fault; circumstances, including all the above, tend to thrust this form of greatness upon the popular conductor without his necessarily wishing to achieve it. And the term *prima donna* carries with it some unhappy connotations: it implies something of an exhibitionist with such tendencies as the vanity, jealousy, intransigence and spoilt-childishness of the idolised *divas* of the past.

Of most of these traits the great modern soprano can go scot-free. Circling the globe like some satellite, she has no time for tantrums and scene-makings (unless hurriedly manufactured for the press), and all her brains are needed for the continuous rush of work she has to cram in, while her widest channels of communication are the radio and the disc, both requiring cool concentration; and she nowadays has to toe the line for conductors who will only *accompany* her as an act of grace and favour: in short she has to watch her step rather than cultivate her 'image'.

But the conductor is, by the 'whirligig of time' brought into the glare of the hazardous glamour once enjoyed by the *prima donna*. He has become the most vital and sought-after essential of large-scale performances; he is the 'boss' with all the responsibilities thereto appertaining, and he cannot (unless taking over in emergency, which may be his only chance, in Beecham's phrase, 'to emerge')—he cannot just appear, demonstrate, take his calls, and disappear: he has to rehearse and 'carry the can' for the whole performance and for every performer involved; he cannot just flit in and out: his aim is to become 'musical director'. So he becomes incidentally the victim of the highbrow critics and 'fans', much as is the 'pop star' of his lowbrow fans.

With all this on his hands he has to develop a supreme self-confidence, and incidentally to make play willy-nilly with what showmanship he can acquire if he likes it, or stomach if he doesn't. He has to perform with his back to the audience whom he is supposed to be ignoring, while in fact he is for them a considerable part of the show, even in the opera house. Beecham was one of the very few conductors I have known who preferred to be invisible in opera. (He could still on occasion remind the public to be inaudible!) And Beecham was in two most important ways quite different from any other great conductor in history: for much of his career he had not only to call (and shape) the tune, but also to pay the piper—and lose several fortunes in the process. Further, and even more remarkable, he had to acquire his art and fight his way to the top without any of the apparatus available to foreign conductors with opera houses and a national tradition to grow-up in: the only English tradition, of the cathedral and oratorio, was foreign to Beecham's scope[1] and world: as a young man he could only observe, on hurried visits to the continent, the regular life of opera and orchestral music, and use his incredible memory to learn from everything he observed and heard.

If according to the above sketch, one is bound to accept the modern conductor as a sort of *prima donna*, what sort of man must one expect him to be? Brilliant and alert mentally, strong, a born leader of men and women—yes, all that and a little more, and less flattering—ruthless and rather egotistic... It seems inevitable. But on the whole, looking back over fifty years in and out of professional life, I think the conductor who gets all our criticism, expert and amateur, deserves more of our sympathy than he gets: it is a very hard job.

Why does he do it? He is sure to make enemies: I know of no conductor, not one, who has not done so: he has to take hard knocks, and is in general perhaps more sensitive to them than singers who so often, like the splendid cock, crow in their fine plumage with closed eyes (and singers too, for different reasons from the conductor's, deserve our sympathy—perhaps even

---

[1] But after 1944 his London concerts included Fauré's *Requiem*, Schubert's Masses in A flat and E flat, Haydn's *Creation* and liturgical works by Berlioz, Liszt and Beethoven. Before 1940 he conducted Verdi's *Requiem* and Rossini's *Petite Messe Solennelle* in England.

more!). And the conductor is apt to react to the least knock with a harder one in fancied self-defence; the conductor has to take risks, sometimes heavy ones; and if he once falls from grace he has no fine voice to come back with! Given a strong constitution and a good technique he can, once he has gained experience and repute, go on into old age, far more fortunate in that than the singer or dancer. But it is to be feared, or just accepted, that none of these things weigh with the conductor, even with almost all the good ones, so much as one over-riding urge, the longing for power.

Of course they cannot win it without considerable musical ability, but whereas the real singer or player (with the rarest of exceptions—Tauber, for one) prefers singing or playing to conducting; the musician lacking the voice, lips or fingers for performance tends to develop an inordinate ambition to conduct: and it is the besetting sin and saddest vice of the amateur. Most of the best conductors have been, as is well known, rather brilliant orchestral players, maybe just lacking something required for the successful virtuoso, but with acute musical perception and in rare cases, such as Nikisch, Toscanini, Furtwängler, Monteux, and Beecham, endowed with a passion for music itself. Elsewhere I have suggested what turned Beecham into a conductor, a strange amalgam of influences, unique, like most things about him; but when one tries to account for undoubted genius, analysis becomes an interminable failure. One thing is fairly certain: Beecham enjoyed music enormously. This cannot be said of all conductors. They nearly always enjoy conducting, but from my own experence I would say that Beecham did not particularly enjoy it: what he revelled in was the search for and discovery of the exquisite in the music made for him by his singers and players. At the height of his powers, which were maintained into old age, it was not just the perfection of detail that told most with an audience: it was this sense of arriving at a new and unforeseen joy to which he had opened the door.

I was reminded of this one day in a conversation with Geraint Jones, organ recitalist, conductor and impresario who brings first-class music to places where it is anything but indigenous, on this occasion, as often before, to the little towns among the lakes and fells of Westmorland. Telling me how as a youngster he had often heard Beecham and marvelled at the strange beauty of sound that emerged—only Toscanini, he thought, with his terrific intensity of involvement in the music itself, was in any way comparable, however different—he added that later, when he and his wife went to hear Beecham in his old age, the unmistakable sense of enjoyment did not always come at first: a good clean performance might be all that could be said of the first piece, or even more; and then the old magic would break out, to which no one else in the world had the key. And then he wisely added, 'Surely *any* conductor must enjoy the music himself if he wants the audience to enjoy it too.' How many conductors have I heard go through an opera without appearing to enjoy it, often conducting the printed score quite admirably. One exception who shared some of the Beecham flair was Konwitschny, who hated all fuss and all rehearsal, and was delighted when the orchestra and singers performed to his satisfaction: he trusted them to know the music well enough for a hint now and then from himself to be sufficient, which it generally was: he could snap-in in a split second and secure a doubtful ensemble. But when all was going swimmingly, even to a Wagnerian climax, he would beam at the orchestra, stop conducting, check-up with a watchful eye here and there on the massing forces of sound, and very likely blow his nose in apparent unconcern, if need be give a sketchy occasional beat with his handkerchief, and only take over again when he felt it expedient. This was all perhaps a bit casual, but with a British orchestra there is usually no lack of individual enterprise, and the fact that Konwitschny was a bit of a joke somehow produced playing of tremendous gusto, and his performances (when he was on form, which was not quite always) were exciting and enjoyable: this can be heard in his records to this day.

Most great conductors, especially of the Toscanini type, work on different lines: they aim at making a carefully considered and precisely worked-out performance as cast-iron as possible. This is fine. But when I heard all Toscanini's centenary performances of *Fidelio* in 1927 at the Scala, Milan, it was like hearing a gramophone record over and over again: however fine the record, this can bore, a thing of which Beecham was incapable.

The cult of the prima-donna conductor is something he can't be much blamed for. The press are largely responsible, and like to adopt godfather conductors for certain composers—Klemperer's Beethoven, Harty's Berlioz, Furtwängler's *Tristan*, Toscanini's Verdi, and of course Beecham's Mozart and Delius.

In the last example certainly lies the deepest truth. No composer has ever owed so much as Delius to the faithful devotion of one interpreter of genius. But what a pity we cannot all enjoy every composer conducted by every good conductor! Favourites in music are inevitable: it is not a classless society, and what a mercy it isn't! So the feuds and schisms over the great conductors must go on: these men have only one thing in common —the life-blood that Withers diagnosed for every performance. And roughly speaking, there are two blood-groups, one characteristic of the Hebrew Deity, 'the same yesterday, today and for ever'; and the other more typical of Cleopatra whose 'infinite variety' custom could not stale. It is probable that Beecham supporters would opt for the unsaintly 'serpent of old Nile'.

II. IDEAS

I think Beecham's musical activities should be considered from at least two points of view, which one might roughly designate as Strategy and Tactics, in the old military manner. His ideas, if not quite as encyclopaedic as his memory, were prolific and original: no sooner did his rapid brain glance over a set of facts, than it would devise a method of expressing them. Musical facts became a method and then a scheme; for founding orchestras (counting his teenage St Helens venture, he founded five); for building opera seasons, even an opera house; for the artistic presentation of particular operas (casting and designing): for commissioning or suggesting works from composers for particular performers; and for financing all these things. These schemes were not always successful when realised, but enough of them were successful enough to transform the whole musical scene in England. And many of his schemes which were never realised (or sometimes realised later by others) are in hindsight obviously of great artistic merit: in many instances that is an understatement.

His ideas for founding orchestras have been related adequately elsewhere. A glance at the outline of his career will bring evidence of the wide sweep of his strategy in opera repertoire, and in his concert programmes it was the same: only late in his career did the typical Beecham style of programme emerge, and he had already covered a wider range, probably, than any conductor before or since. But in *presentation* I think a number of

his ideas have either been forgotten or never heard of. Here are
a few instances.

There were three small works for the stage which he devised
and produced. The first was *The Faithful Shepherdess* (John
Fletcher) of which he gives a very pleasant description and an
excellent review by Havelock Ellis at the end of *A Mingled
Chime*: it should well repay revival. Then there was his ballet
The Gods Go A-Begging to music of Handel which, when he
conducted it, saved, as Grigorieff relates[2], the last tour of the
Diaghilev Ballet from financial disaster. This still makes
reappearances in the repertoire of professional and amateur companies. And there was the ballet he devised for Bath, *The Great
Elopement* (also to the music of Handel) on the local story of
Elisabeth Linley and Richard Brinsley Sheridan. This seems
never to have 'caught on' until after his death; but revivals seem
to be increasing today, on the continent as well as at home. For
all three of these pieces he delved into the past centuries for
which he had a particular taste—the seventeenth, on whose poets
and dramatists he was an authority, and the eighteenth, from
whose composers he had from his earliest programmes drawn
unknown movements and dances.

Several schemes of a like nature he propounded to me; for
instance, *Le Tableau Parlant* by Grétry, which he had himself
performed privately back in 1908, before he took up professional
opera; *Richard the First*, also by Grétry, with charming music
but mistakenly developed as a farce by Beecham's librettist whom
he sent to consult me: I fear I dissuaded him, for which I feel
no regrets! And there was to have been a stage performance of
Handel's *Hercules* in my little theatre with a fine orchestra pit,
in Manchester. This to our disappointment fell through, as
although Sir Thomas approved the theatre and all arrangements,
he said that no-one short of Callas could sing Dejanira: he asked
me for suggestions, but solemnly assured me in a letter that the
lady I proposed 'could no more sing that rôle than she could
swim the Atlantic'. I was amused to see that he shortly afterwards engaged her with success for an important recording of a
major work! I know of a number of such schemes, all excellent,
but doomed to unfulfilment. But others triumphed.

---

[2] *The Russian Ballet*, p. 253.

Gluck's *Orfeo* has always been a producer's problem: the formality and simultaneous romanticism of the music make the problem of style and period baffling from the outset. Beecham devised an original solution. At the back of his mind was the first *Orfeo* of Peri and Caccini, performed in Florence at the festivities in 1600 at the wedding of Henry IV of France to Maria de Medici. The problem is to fit Gluck's overture, stilted, pompous and festive, and the batch of dances, mostly in similar vein, at the end, as a credible and even artistic frame to the romantic and indeed tragic action and music of the opera proper, despite its rather forced happy ending. Beecham disposed of the incongruity once and for all. He fished out a sumptuous baroque palace-scene left over from the Diaghilev *Josefslegende*, dressed up a royal pair and a courtful of supers, put up the curtain in the overture, and showed the arrival of the opera company graciously received by bride and bridegroom: they passed 'into the theatre' and the court followed them: curtain, and conclusion of the overture. Then the opera in a classico-romantic setting, and a festive epilogue with dances and complimentary leave-taking of the singers in the baroque palace. Orpheus was the statuesque Clara Butt, and Maggie Teyte the slight and graceful Eurydice. The whole effect was excellent.

It was Beecham who introduced the scene of *The Walk to the Paradise Garden* (now famous as an orchestral excerpt, often recorded and broadcast) in *A Village Romeo and Juliet* of Delius. where the lovers, tired and hungry, lose and rediscover their way in the forest; he observed the habit of Delius of often writing his best operatic music when the curtain was down. In this instance he not only saved the embarrassment to an English audience, without opera yet in their blood, of eight minutes in the dark: the twilit picture and his little touches of mise-en-scène added considerably to the poetry and pathos of that lovely last act.

Similarly he introduced into *Hoffmann* a number of amusing pseudo-scientific paraphernalia for Spalanzani, and some weird magical disappearances and effects for Dr Mirakel. Need it be added that he was not responsible for any of the preposterous eccentricities of the film version, which destroyed the whole point and humour of several scenes: but he conducted it *con amore* as one of his favourite operas.

One of his outstanding artistic creations was the *Figaro*

designed by Hugo Rumbold, coached for the stage by Nigel
Playfair, in a new English translation in which he had a considerable hand, and conducted originally by himself: its success
made it a landmark in British operatic history. The whole production was revived years later for the BNOC. I then had to
stage-manage and light it on many occasions: the first act was
eccentric but very pretty and effective, and the rest extremely
stylish and colourful. Some of the wonderful original cast
(Licette, Ellinger, Tyas, Parr, Austin, Ranalow, Radford, Russell)
still survived and it was still beautiful. No *Figaro* since has
equalled it. One scene, as a matter of fact, in recent years deserves
honourable comparison, an Act Three set provided by Sir Barry
Jackson for Sadlers Wells: it was a brilliant essay in eighteenth-
century 'false perspective' and by its apparent vast magnificence
always got a round of applause when the curtain rose upon an
empty stage. Unfortunately, actors had to appear from the back-
centre, and the whole illusion vanished in a moment of comic
incongruity. The famous permanent set in false perspective, a
perfect legacy from Palladio (1580!) in the Teatro Olympico,
Vicenza, is so designed as to frustrate the demand of any
important performer for a grand centre entrance. But that is by
the way. The Rumbold *Figaro* was difficult to set, but worked
perfectly, even to the terrible tangle of garden pavilions in the
last act, which can seldom be made convincing, let alone effective.

Beecham's ideas of *Seraglio*, which he re-introduced to
England, were almost as good. His *Zauberflöte* was mainly
memorable for the exquisite Pamina of Claire Dux; the setting
was conventional, but his Berlin recording shows the superlative
style of his reading of the music.

At this point, some of his proposals for the ideal settings for
the Mozart operas can be recalled. He may have expressed them
elsewhere, but I only know that he put them forward in a dis-
cussion with me. Each work should be set and dressed in the
style of the great painter which seemed to him the most sympathetic both to the story and the music. Thus *Figaro* should be
dressed and set after Goya: *Don Giovanni* after Velasquez;
Idomeneo after Claude or the Claude period of Turner; for *Così
fan Tutte* he appeared rather unsure, but when pressed, said,
'perhaps Longhi'; the *Flute* he considered a pantomime fairyland
requiring ever fresh invention and fantasy. It all sounds so simple

and even obvious when set down like this, but I fancy it took a wealth of experience and taste to think it out in the first place. Apart from Mozart, I am tempted to think that for his beloved *Trojans* (certain musical scenes of which I have heard him describe with an almost schoolboy enthusiasm) he would have chosen David or Delacroix for Troy, and for Carthage gone back to Poussin. I know of no conductor who has ever shown such breadth of vision and imagination in the matter of operatic repertoire: Beecham's taste covered Italian, French, German, Russian, and when he could get it, English, opera; his classical outlook went back to Gluck and Grétry, but hardly further—are not most of us, perhaps, in secret agreement?—with a single universal exception in Monteverdi.

His operatic ideas, summarised in terms of repertoire, changed the whole situation in Britain. When he began, there were in London little more than the annual Covent Garden 'Grand Seasons', with a repertoire at which Bernard Shaw tilted for years, consisting almost entirely of about four Verdi, three Puccini, three French, and one or two earlier eighteenth century operas, with a little Wagner thrown in as a luxury. In the provinces there were the noble but strictly limited Carl Rosa and Moody-Manners companies and an occasional tour by some pitifully small, if vocally robust, company, whose repertoire usually consisted of *Carmen, Faust, 'Cav and Pag', Trovatore, Maritana, The Lily of Killarney* and *The Bohemian Girl*, sometimes, for a treat, a *Tannhäuser* which was anything but that, and occasionally *Mignon* and *Hoffman*. The Beecham repertoire cannot be computed exactly; the records show that he conducted over a hundred. Revivals and different productions would bring that total well on towards two hundred, and Reid says that Beecham's own computation was two hundred and three. The total number of theatre performances he conducted can only be guessed at—he conducted two hundred and fifty at Covent Garden alone. In my first tour with the British National Opera Company (the legatee of the Beecham company), we took out on an autumn tour over twenty operas.

Among Beecham's musical ideas in other spheres were the appointment of Hamilton Harty to the Hallé; that Walton should write a viola concerto for Tertis; his own salvage operations both for the Hallé and the Royal Philharmonic Societies; his two

Delius and Sibelius festivals; his recordings of seven operas; of all the Salomon Symphonies of Haydn; and for his private prescription, the famous 'Lollipops'. Speeches and manifestos flowed from him; there is as much wisdom and musical insight as gaiety and wit packed into *A Mingled Chime*; and there is the sober scholarship and deep sympathy in his masterly Life of Frederick Delius. His mind seemed infinitely inventive.

But why should such a mind have turned from the serious and fluent studies in musical composition which we know he undertook?

Beecham was very strange, and he knew it. He who from his early twenties could and did dominate players, singers and audiences, wherever he went, almost always arousing their keenest and best apprehension of music, was known by many who knew him intimately to be a 'shy', 'modest' and 'lonely' man in many moments throughout his life. Two of his recorded sayings suggest evidence of this. 'I always wear a mask in public', and, jestingly, to a nervous soloist before 'going on' with him, 'Strange that we, who give our lives to this, should often say we would give our life not to have to go on and do it.' I have never known him pleased with, or preen himself over any performance: always the reverse; but always there was the complete conviction with which he tackled everything, successful or sometimes unsuccessful.

I think one might not unreasonably speculate that what turned him from making his own music to evoking music from others, was his particular Lancashire heredity. As he grew up, they wanted him to join, or at any rate supply advertising ideas for, the family business: he joked for the purpose with some none-too-modest doggerel. A true son of Lancashire, with his genial impatience with the inadequate, he found commerce totally intolerable, being fully conscious of a burning musical sense and infallible memory. There came that moment of his father's exhibitionism over the Hallé for the Mayor's celebration: Thomas must then have felt his true *public* as his father and grandfather had done before him: composition would appear too introverted and unprofitable: he would manufacture his own musical commodity to his own prescription, a pill which should *work* with the public, whether it paid or not, and work 'to some tune'. It did.

III. TECHNIQUE

A number of technical devices, and even tricks, contributed to those seemingly spontaneous performances we heard when Beecham was alive, and can still hear almost as magically recorded on the modern machines available in his old age.

Part of the phrase employed above is his own. More than once he has said, when asked how he pulled off those unique performances, distinguishable from those of any other conductor, 'It is quite easy: all you have to do is select the finest players—I mean those who are not merely skilled in every *technical device* of their instruments, but also conversant with every *interpretational resource*. And then—you *let them play* . . .'

So much for initial tactics. But these were supported by an artillery of devices of his own, and a sort of 'air cover' of the most buoyant rhythm. A word or two first on this score. The whole subject deserves analysis, if only for the benefit of young conductors who still think that the conductor's first duty is to 'beat time': and they mercilessly do so all through the movement, which suffers horribly. The first duty, as Beecham fully realised, is the purely technical one of *setting a tempo*, quite another matter. Beecham's ideas of tempo, incidentally, were usually beyond criticism: there were exceptions, but very few: of the too-fasts, several have passed into the legendary; very few too-slows were ever remarked; but his last movement of *Eine kleine Nachtmusik* has often been disputed, though generally highly approved: the opening three quavers melted so daintily into the crotchets, and the whole had such an air of quiet *chic* that most critics even called it 'authentic': in music, who knows the accuracy of that much-traded word?

Well, after having set the tempo (over which he often took quite a few bars of almost bandmasterly orthodox conducting), what happened? Usually a sort of magic in which one's analytic faculties were dulled in the sheer fascination of the musical sounds themselves and the flexibility of the musical stream and its endless, multiple flow. But when a forced critical attention and considerable experience of his ways insisted on analysis of how it was done, a wealth of carefully contrived details came to light.

First in the rhythm itself. Why was it so buoyant? Of course there was a unique rhythmic sense in the man himself, and there was his universally acknowledged 'magnetism' which conveyed it to players and singers alike.[3] But what emerged and caught the ear unawares? Mainly an aristocratic economy of 'privilege' and 'class-distinction' in the matter of *accent.* How few conductors really distinguish and differentiate their accents! With Beecham there was always the main accent in a phrase, the minimum required for purposes of lilt or subordinate accents, and these were graded to a nicety, sometimes by his marking of the parts, sometimes by his guidance of eye or hand in the actual conducting. This was something instinctive, but he used accomplished stratagem to make it explicit: I am told he invariably remembered his marks, and if his mood or the acoustics of the hall suggested a new scale of nuances in some passage, the marks would be adjusted before the concert, or even in the interval: performers would be summoned to his room before going on, to note and memorise some change of detail in subtle effect. No conductor I have come across could give such a sense of 'occasion' to every performance: a case of 'living dangerously' perhaps. But in practice the chances of a particular touch of fantasy always outweighed the risks of disaster, though these were not entirely unknown; and legends have gathered around one or two lapses of memory which Tommy would carry off with unblushing panache.

I will quote two instances to give some idea of his style in the matter of accent: the first I was interested to see quoted by McCallum in the obituary tribute of Beecham players on the radio: it had long been on my mind to quote before I heard this. At the opening of the Schubert Symphony No. 5 in B flat, one usually hears the following obvious accents:

---

[3] The reluctance of one singer to absorb it made one of the legends: Beecham was very patient, and having at last coaxed her into it, he whispered to the leader, 'Sshh! Don't look round—I think we are being followed!'

—a pretty steady *mf*, the internal combustion engine going strong.

But Beechamesque it was somehow thus:

—a gradual lift in each figure to the eighth bar, and slight diminuendo with the change of accents to the second of each two bars, giving an airy lightness and grace.

The second is a similar case, the completely hackneyed bravura tune from the *William Tell* overture.

Overture, *William Tell*, as usually:

or *sometimes* with the alternative accents not quite so loud.

As conducted by Beecham:

... —the third *sf* slightly louder, and perhaps a slight crescendo in the first bar. In performance one would not notice the subtleties, only the *spring* in the rhythm; and in listening to his recordings one is frequently struck by the new charm given to a familiar phrase by a subtle distribution of stresses, relaxations and 'inflections', never exaggerated into mannerism but somehow hallmarking a musical personality.

The aim, had he put it into words, of this vigorous economy of accent was to avoid over-emphasis on the one hand, and flabbiness on the other, and monotony half-way between. Now I am well aware that most conductors maintain a show of vigour by conducting every bar, and putting in lots of accents (often abetted by some of the more popular and cymbal-prone composers); also, that far more money than has been deservedly earned has been made by what is now called 'pop' and 'the Beat', which amounts to a frightfully insistent series of benumbing regular accents—simply and only 'music' for the unmusical. I venture, on this score, to point out that we now have lived more than half a century in the Age of the Common Man, and however much your great man, our Thomas Beecham, is 'of the earth earthy', there was nothing of the Common Man about him, nor about any fine art and craft throughout the civilised centuries. The Common Man is not interested in refined economy of accent, but responds readily to any primitive stimulus to mass-hysteria. I have heard audiences joyfully applauding a Beecham performance, and asking for more, but never hurling themselves into that automatic ululation, that abandonment to the heaving, twitching, grinning, yelling intoxication of the 'pop' *succès fou*. The refinement of Beecham had the effect of refining his audiences, even if it came to shouting at them to 'shut up' on rare but unfortunate occasions at Covent Garden. And we can still savour his neat, virile economy of accent in the records with an appreciative smile: he can still make a listener feel himself something of a connoisseur.

There is much more in fine phrase-moulding than a musical accent. There is what one calls a 'singing quality', and one means by that a beauty of actual sound or voice plus all the nuances of colour and inflexion, or, if you will, 'timbre' and 'dynamics' in more mechanical parlance. Great conductors of course cannot be without this, but Beecham possessed this secret in a unique degree. One has heard of Toscanini's maxim, often shouted to his players, 'Cantare, cantare!'; and when I was working at the Scala, Milan, as a student guest, the splendid result of this was evident in what was of course a magnificent orchestra. I never heard, after he left Italy for America, that rich, warm flood of sound familiar in Milan: there was a military precision and authority, the master-scholar lecturing on musical correctitude, awe-inspiring, impeccable, but no impression of spontaneous joy. With Beecham there was a remarkable difference: he did not shout at his players to sing: he sang himself. The incredible phenomenon of Beecham's singing has been well described elsewhere. Here is his own description as I have heard him deliver it in the familiar drawl

of pained surprise at the incomprehension of mankind in general:
'One thing no one will ever give me the slightest credit for, is
doing any *work* ... But I do: on my own, of course ... I sit
down quietly over my orchestral score, and sing all the parts
through, one after the other ... My powers of 'voice-proe-
duction' (sic) leave something to be desired, but I can make some
sort of onomatopoeic reference to the various instruments ... and
so I sing all through their parts. And if I cannot sing a work, I
cannot conduct it.' This process evidently satisfied his own sound-
stream; it is anything but evident how it managed to convey anything beyond the ludicrous to his players: but it did: they
responded to his own established mental picture and even to an
example of that esoteric burbling, with complete understanding
and a beauty of tone and subtlety of phrasing that I have never
heard equalled.

I think it is worth while to recall, if only for the attention of
critics and young conductors, two other characteristics of
Beecham's technique, practised no doubt by a few other conductors, but perhaps less noticeably and adroitly—his handling
of a climax, and the 'fade out', to borrow radio jargon. The
stunning effect of a typically Beechamesque climax was due to a
combination of preliminary tactics according to its nature, whether
steeply to a peak of highest pressure, or the smooth summit of an
arch. In either case a reserve of power was made and the approach
engineered to appear natural and not pumped up either visually
or aurally. And there was a minute fraction-of-a-second survey
before the climax itself to ensure sufficient breath and bow for the
supreme effort.[4] That however, was graded to the structure and
mood of the piece: his climaxes were never out of proportion,
nor, except perhaps sometimes in a long Wagner act, was one
climax ever allowed to steal the thunder of the most important
one. Again, in passages of prolonged fortissimo, there were subtle
inflections in the shrieking or crashing of the storm, as in his
recording of *Tapiola*. Beecham as a young man, when, for instance,
introducing *Elektra* and *Salome* to England, was often criticised
for over-noise: as he aged, this could hardly have been held

---

[4] Occasionally the process was reversed and the explosion came a hairs-
breadth before expectation when a startling effect was, for him, in the
music.

against him, and he leaned more to the sunny melody of *Meister-singer* than to the many violences of the *Ring*.

Then there was the Beecham *diminuendo*: no conductor I have ever heard could engineer that prolonged retreat of the music into the distance of time and space as could Beecham. Frank Howes described it most eloquently in his obituary (*The Times*, 9 March, 1961) instancing the close of Delius's *In a Summer Garden*. I would like to instance another occasion, a performance of *Appalachia* in the Albert Hall. At the end the withdrawal of sound was so prolonged and mysterious that the mighty Mississippi seemed to flow back into the past of primeval forests, a living silence unbroken by human voice or footstep, a music telling of a world before music was born. Actually this had been stage-managed by a careful grading of previous accents with faint, dying stresses and then the steady slow melting of sound by all the instruments concerned, each of them following that barely quivering stick which was sometimes as eloquent as it often appeared to be! Tommy often scorned his own stick, and players got what they required from something else, some movement of wrist or little finger, but mostly, as he himself said, from the eyes. 'There is, you know, a certain current which passes ... from the eyes.' But those grand diminuendos were organised well in advance: his powerful imagination had pre-conceived the exact reality of sound that was practical, and he kept in the softest as well as in the loudest effects a reserve of cool, calculating appraisal of practical possibilities: his controlled excitement was one of his best assets. In conversation with me, Edmund Chesterman (see page 47) said: 'He had a great trick of holding back a climax, which, when it came, electrified us all as it did the audience, just as did the suspense he could maintain on a diminuendo; and with him every rehearsal was, like every performance, an occasion.'

Reporters would ask him, 'How do you feel, Sir Thomas, when you are carried away by the music?' and he would indignantly retort, 'But I am *never* "carried away!"'—if I were carried away, *what would happen to the orchestra?*'

He relates in *A Mingled Chime* his preoccupation with the matter of 'balance'. It was here that his 'singing' habits proved so useful: there was always some sort of melodic as well as rhythmic line in his performances even when the pattern and lie of the parts would not suggest any sort of tune: with him the music flowed without any suggestion of there being an engine in the background faithfully firing on all cylinders, which is what one so often fancies from so many professional performances. And while the rhythm never flagged, there was always the 'flexibility' which was Beecham's name for his own particular brand of *rubato*.

It has been said fairly often—and contradicted, too, by David McCallum for instance, who long 'led' for him—that Beecham had no formal or proper 'stick technique'; rash critics have even said 'no technique'. But nobody need believe that; nobody, not even Beecham, could conduct over eighty different operas and close on two thousand concerts without very considerable technique. It just happened to be a technique of his own—and why not?

This, I think, brings up a point that, however apparent from the foregoing reports from his players, may well be reiterated in any survey of his musicianship. All Tommy's music was Beecham-*plus*, an act of creation shared by him with the performers; they were not only the instrument upon which his imagination played, they were fellow-artists with imaginations of their own. That they were so and could be heard to be so, and were enjoyed in their own individual right, perhaps constitutes Beecham's greatest technical triumph.

Consider for a moment the position of the good orchestral player—and Beecham always got the best—he (or she) has spent hard years in gaining mastery over a difficult instrument, and has subsequently to spend hard years under the mastery of difficult conductors; following the good ones, adapting to the indifferent, and often saving the bad . . . and the rare great conductor will inevitably strain the concentration and staying-power of the player in a fine performance, which in itself may come sometimes, but not always, as some compensation. It follows that the conductor is the natural enemy, and always the occupational hazard, of the player. Courtesy, and maybe professional necessity, usually preclude overt friction, and orchestral players (save sometimes in Union matters for the Union-minded) are a highly sensitive and courteous crowd. But they feel a lot that they don't say outside the band-room. I have in my time talked to so many players about Beecham, and been so impressed with the certainty and

near-unanimity of their judgment that I feel a particular value
attaches to their contributions to this book; their recollections
come out of years of hard physical and mental work, and where
'Tommy' or 'Sir Thomas', as they may happen to call him, is
concerned, a rare happiness and fascination emerge. Charles Reid
dedicates his biography of Beecham to them, the people 'who
made the world resound with his gifts and their own'.

IV. REPERTOIRE

The Beecham repertoire was enormous. Indeed it is probably the
largest yet amassed by any conductor of international standard
in musical history to date: so large in fact, over his six decades
of performance, as to have become finally immeasurable.

At the same time his musical preferences were so strong as to
earn him, in many a superficial estimate, the reputation of being
limited and biased in outlook. But strictly speaking anyone's
repertoire can only properly be recorded as the number of works
performed to the public, and it cannot be reckoned on the number
most frequently performed: at what number of performances
could the line be drawn? And one must assume that any work
once rehearsed and performed could, if desired, be repeated, and
is therefore in the repertoire. Some patient biographer, piously
stirring the dust of sixty years of this century, may succeed in
unearthing a fairly complete corpus of the work tackled by
Tommy in that epoch: no one has yet managed to produce more
than some local estimates of the music he conducted in separate
seasons and places. Throughout his career very many theatres
and concert-halls, and in his later years, a number of recording
studios, were the scenes, up and down the civilised world, of his
extraordinary activity. This cannot now be of any great interest
to the ordinary reader of today, except as evidence of the amount,
sort and standard of music that one Lancastrian with the help of
a private fortune (or two) could offer to the western world in his
life-time: evidence, too, from the repetitions, of the kind of music
he most passionately believed in and loved so courageously.

Beecham's repertoire grew, rather haphazard and in separate
stages. First the old standard operas known, if only by name,
in the England of his youth; then the early English vocal school
for which, in Kennedy Scott's Oriana choir, he annotated pro-

grammes of music which has, since then, so reblossomed in this country (see pp. 158–70); then his research abroad into old French opera for which he was to retain affection for the rest of his life; then his persistent championship of music by his contemporaries at home—his first financial disaster (of this patriotic enterprise Charles Reid writes with unnecessary disparagement); then Beecham's discovery and revelation of Delius to a largely unreceptive public; then his presentation of the whole field of contemporary European opera, particularly Strauss; then his delighted realisation of the marvels of the still-unknown Russian school of opera, ballet and orchestral music; at the same time unearthing the unknown wonders of Mozart in opera, symphony and concerto ... At this stage several hiatuses appeared in his middle age, between campaigns, over many an operatic battlefield; and last, in his old age, a vast output of recordings largely of unfamiliar music.

A reasonable deduction from the various estimates made after his death, would be that he instigated or shared in his time some two hundred different operatic productions, and himself conducted some eighty different operas, many of them from memory. And his innumerable concerts were, till his last years, much more often than not, conducted from memory and with enormous relish.

Without attempting even an outline of his concert repertory, some idea of its character may be obtained from a brief analysis of one field of his activity, his concerts at the Royal Festival Hall. Neither he, nor many of those brought up in the old Queen's Hall, were enthusiastic about the new building, acoustically or decoratively considered; its auditory physiology was always in need of surgery, undertaken with partial success only after Beecham's day. But with characteristic promptitude in emergency he decided, once the thing had got going, that it was all he had left to get going in himself. (His imprimatur on the Festival Hall, delivered privately in its early days, was, 'It is indeed a curious contraption ... If your performance is *immaculate*, the dry acoustic is not inadequate ... I have myself found it quite acceptable ...'). In the ten years before he died Beecham gave ninety-two concerts there, interspersing them with opera, concerts and recordings round the civilised world.

Here is a glance at the repertoire involved in these ninety-two concerts. The first was on 17 October, 1951, and the last on

6 April, 1960. There were four in 1951, seven in 1952, seventeen in 1953, twenty in 1954, fourteen in 1955, thirteen in 1956, two in 1957, nine in 1958, five in 1959, and one in 1960. The following list of composers represented, with the number of performances of music by each, is arranged in descending numerical order. This plan must be regarded with some caution in forming opinions on his tastes and limitations. He had long learned since his early days of playing what he liked, what he thought others should like and what he thought should be given a chance, that one can't discount the Box Office. Up to a point even a Beecham programme had to 'draw': hence the typical 'Beecham programme'. But hence also the inclusion of a number of safe cards to play which he sometimes had no particular pleasure in putting down. Another point to bear in mind is that beside a number of his own idiosyncracies to be aired, were some personal and political choices. Finally this list includes a number, but not all, of the encores, whether his famous 'lollipops' or not: all that he gave do not appear to have been reported. With these considerations in mind, the list of a septuagenarian's repertoire in one concert hall is both interesting and impressive.

Number of performances for each composer

46 MOZART, including 5 symphonies, 6 concertos, Requiem, extracts. e.g. King Thamos Music.
26 BEETHOVEN, including all symphonies except the Fifth so often done before.
23 HAYDN, twelve symphonies and Flute Concerto.
22 WAGNER, overtures and excerpts.
21 DELIUS, extensive repertoire.
21 SIBELIUS, including four symphonies.
19 SCHUBERT, including eight symphonies.
15 BERLIOZ, including Te Deum, four overtures, *Harold in Italy*, *Grande Messe des Morts*, opera excerpts.
14 BRAHMS, including three symphonies, four concertos.
14 TSCHAIKOWSKY, including four symphonies, concertos, tone poems, etc.
10 SAINT-SAËNS, including one symphony, four concertos, etc.
 9 HANDEL, various, and Beecham arrangements.
 9 MENDELSSOHN, including Italian symphony.

8 BIZET, including Symphony.
8 DVOŘÁK, Fourth Symphony, concertos, etc.
7 DEBUSSY, *Images, Nocturnes, Après-midi d'un Faune, La Demoiselle Elue*, etc.
7 ROSSINI, overtures.
7 STRAUSS, R., *Heldenleben* and tone poems.
6 RIMSKY-KORSAKOV, including *Antar, Schéhérazade*.
5 GREIG, LISZT, WEBER.
4 ARNELL, CHABRIER, ELGAR, LALO, MASSENET.
3 BORODIN, FRANCK, GOLDMARK, GRÉTRY, SUPPÉ.
2 BALAKIREV, BAX, BOCCHERINI, DELIBES, GOUNOD, SALZEDO.
1 ADDISON, ALWYN, AUSTIN, BACH, BARBER, BERKELEY, BERNERS, BRITTEN, BRUCH, CHAUSSON, DALAYRAC, DONIZETTI, GHEDINI, GODARD, D'INDY, MACONCHY, MANFREDINI, MILHAUD, MOUSSORGSKY, OFFENBACH, PUCCINI, RACHMANINOV, RAWSTHORNE, RAVEL, RUBBRA, SCHUMANN, JOHANN STRAUSS, SULLIVAN, VILLA-LOBOS, WALTON.

The one Bach work was the Double Violin Concerto; Balakirev, Symphony in C; Ghedini, Viola Concerto; Ravel, *Daphnis and Chloë*.

V. THE MAXIMUM

Though obviously impossible to reduce so gigantic a personality to any simple-sounding analysis, an attempt can be made to summarise the more important influences left upon successive generations by Thomas Beecham. There is the amazing extent of his public activities, both in themselves and in their effect on music-making in general; there is the aura of a grand legendary figure—almost, if not quite, the last likely to appear in modern democracy (or might one venture to say proletariology?). There is the remarkable fascination he exercised on practically everyone who worked with him (this, and the vast number of his gifted associates, will be surely evident from the foregoing pages), a fascination which clearly made for human happiness and much that is still life-enhancing.

And lastly there is his clarifying influence upon the intellectual and mechanical technique of music-making as an art in practice.

For those who cannot have had the privilege of working with or for him, this is still something all aspiring musicians can lay to heart and emulate. It has been here and elsewhere analysed quite ably several times. In the 1954 edition of Grove's *Dictionary of Music and Musicians* (ed. Eric Blom), the summary by Terence White Gervais covers much of the ground:

'His career is unique for two reasons, his peculiar services to English music, and his interpretive powers as viewed internationally and objectively. The second is to some extent implied in the first. His combination of supreme talent and will-power has improved vastly the standards of British orchestras, impressed on the public mind hitherto little-known music of all periods, above all that of Delius, Strauss, the early Stravinsky and certain Berlioz works. To Beecham is due the initiation and maintenance of the Mozart cult, especially during the first war. In addition, as a brilliantly gifted dialectician, he has constituted himself an outspoken critic and adviser-in-chief on the condition of the musical world, and his good sense is none the less evident for being sometimes uttered with a deliberate disregard of tact.'

Beecham's ultimate greatness, however, lies in his musicality as judged by universal standards. Thanks to his many and faithful recordings, his art will remain for future generations to judge and enjoy. He excelled in music of the eighteenth century; to Haydn and Mozart, as to the Italianate Handel and lesser French and Latin composers he lends a unique perfection and subtlety of phrasing, a blending of grace and vitality that seems to baffle analysis, though all these qualities are immediately recognised by sensitive listeners; and many of the foregoing observations on the man and his style will help to account for them.

But I think the best analysis that can be given is one of Beecham's own, unique, I think, in its brevity and deep implications. He said many things to me over the years about music and its performance and conveyed many telling points by rumbustious treatment of the pianoforte (almost as inaccurate as my own), or by his incredible travesties of vocal illustrations; but there was one occasion when he left me speechless, as by some sudden revelation. I had been putting up some of the problems, as I thought, of securing what could be regarded as a really fine performance, and he said, 'My dear fellow, for a fine performance, only two things are absolutely necessary: *the maximum of* virility *coupled with the maximum of* delicacy.'

I can hear the half-mocking rhetoric of his delivery, and the tone of underlying seriousness, of his piercing thought; and of all the maxims and injunctions and rules and aesthetic principles I have ever come across in print or from conductors or performers or teachers, this goes home as the deepest and clearest utterance of the highest demands of music upon the interpreter. The implications of it cover so much in the way of purpose and detail that is, one way or another, lacking in so many respectable, accurate and even sensitive performances; it supplies such a yard-stick for musical criticism as journalists, performers and audiences would do well to keep by them for constant use; it is simple, easily memorable, and when deeply reflected upon, marvellously complete: it is, I feel, Beecham in a nutshell.

All the same, it is rather unfair to think that Beecham could ever 'be bounded in a nutshell'—he who in music could well be 'counted . . . king of infinite space'. Even so deep and searching an aphorism as the one of his own I have quoted, which strikes at the root of the matter of musical performances, leaves some of his expertise unexplored. No summary of his total value to musicians can be short: one quality, for instance, I think has not been stressed in this consensus of opinions, or indeed elsewhere in the many accounts of him written so far—his *courage*. Sensitive as he was, and easily hurt by any musical or human infelicity, he never showed weakness or slackness: often worn down with weariness after sustained effort at the highest pitch, often denuded of all financial support, often in debt, he always returned to the fray, 'breasted the blows of circumstances and grappled with his evil star'. Gifted with almost the eloquence of Hamlet, he never cried, knowing the British musical world all out of joint, 'O cursed spite, that ever I was was born to set it right!' Instead he cursed British inefficiency and insensibility, and flung himself neck and crop into the fray to set it, as he saw it, musically right.

At his eightieth-birthday lunch he concluded a grand rambling jocular speech about his relations with his players, with a sentence very typical of this intrepidity: 'If there is one word which I would leave with you on this happy and unique occasion, it is this: whatever you, my musical friends, do in life, whether singing, playing, conducting ... or misconducting ... *do it with conviction!*'

In his obituary in *The Times* (see p. 185), Frank Howes has a happy phrase about the extinction of 'the vital spark which had illuminated English public life with its music and flashing wit'. But we still have the records which speak clearer than any words, and we have the legend and the two splendid books, the Gibbonian *A Mingled Chime* and the sensitive, serious *Frederick Delius*. And we still have a rich handful of musicians who made music with him, teaching his secrets to their young successors.

Though there will never be another Beecham, perhaps after all the vital spark will not be extinguished?

Part Two

BEECHAM'S OBITER DICTA

'MR BEECHAM, MUSICOLOGIST' (1906)

'FREDERICK DELIUS, 1862–1934'

'MOZART' (1956)

THE *TIMES* OBITUARY (1961)

'THE MEMORY LINGERS ON' (1971)

Page from Mozart's Flute Concerto in D with Beecham's markings
(*Jackson*)

At the piano – 1948 (*Keystone*)

Beecham's Obiter Dicta

Just as one always remembered particular details of any performance one heard him conduct, so almost everything one heard him say or heard repeated, tended to remain in the memory. The following is a rather arbitrary selection from the large store of Beecham sayings which I recall over the years. By no means an attempt to reflect his whole personality, they do display certain facets of his outlook on life as well as music: they help to explain that sense of spontaneity and surprise in his performances that could startle or even shock, tickle or console, or stir one's deepest and most serious intuitions of the heart. And incidentally some of them reveal his uncanny facility for dressing-up the ridiculous in the grandiose, and wrapping-up a bitter truth in preposterous exaggeration. It was part of his fun that some people should never quite know how to take him: he was a completely sophisticated *enfant terrible*. Of course many of his best quips were private jokes, and never meant to be repeated, nor should they have been, though among his surviving and discreet cronies they can still be exchanged with relish. I have resisted the temptation to include dozens of these, even when I know the authentic version, and an inferior one has been in print. I am not, you see, at any rate in public, a subscriber to the Permissive Society.

But I hope that the following sayings of his which certainly gave me to think myself, will evoke some reflections among readers.

About himself (in the early nineteen-fifties):

'I am thankful to have been born when I was, so that I had my heyday when England was at the top of the world, with an Empire wider and at least better-run than any in human history: now she's a second- or third-rate little country that must just sit back and do as America tells her.'

6—BR * *

(In conversation with H. P-G. he conceded, when pressed, that much of the decline was due to two sacrificial wars to reprieve civilisation, but insisted that 'crazy governments' and 'soft socialism' were largely responsible.)

About America

'I have known America all my adult life, and always rather liked America: but in order to get on in America one has always to "get" a little bit "tough" . . . As for any real *culture*, it will take them fifty years to discover what the word means, and probably another fifty to absorb what Europe has had to bequeath them in that respect . . . But you can say what you like about America: it's getting bigger and richer all the time, and we're getting poorer and smaller . . .'

[About 195(?)]. He deployed much social and economic evidence for American superiority over Britain. I didn't cross swords on that, but tried, 'Well, you've given the Americans in your day a bit of good old Lancashire spirit to get on with'— this quite diverted the onslaught on to Yorkshire, including:

On Lancashire and Yorkshire

'Now I always had difficulty in getting on with Yorkshiremen. In *my* county, where *I* come from, we're all a bit vulgar, you know . . . but there is a certain heartiness, a sort of *bonhomie* about our vulgarity . . . which tides you over a lot of rough spots in the path.'

(So far, in an indulgent adagio drawl—then in sudden asperity)

'—but in *Yorkshire*, in a spot of bother, they're so damn-set-in-their-ways that there's no doing anything with them!'

On France in the late forties
—which was getting a new government every few weeks.

'France is never any good without a figurehead, a father-figure who can conjure up dreams of glory. They'll just have to fish old de Gaulle out of his chateau . . .'

(This was not in the air at that time)

'—disagreeable fellow, but he's the only thing that could pull France together and deal with the Communists.'

(Here I interposed, 'Well, and *how do you* deal with a Communist?' He turned the whole fire of the argument on to me with withering superiority.)

'Well . . . if you're a *man . . . you cut his throat before he cuts yours!*'

(Without stopping to ask myself whether he was serious or not —it might have been either—I instantly recalled all that had happened to my Latvian, Polish and (Singapore) Chinese friends: I had no come-back for Sir Thomas.)

In the 1950s

'When the history of the first half of this century comes to be written—properly written—it will be acknowledged the most stupid and brutal in the history of civilisation.'

On Great Music (as told to me by himself)

'One of those pressing press-gentlemen cornered me the other day on what in my opinion was "Great Music". I thought I knew, but hadn't time to say: so I thought quickly and offered, "that music which penetrates the ear with the greatest facility and quits the memory with the greatest difficulty". He thought that grand, but it wasn't. Of course there's a lot more to it than that, and naturally I wasn't including the catchy tune that haunts the idle mind for a day or two. Great music, as you know, my dear fellow, *does something to you*: I think the least you can say is that it leaves with you, whatever its subject and mood, tragic, comic, loud or languorous, feelings of *wonder and contentment*.'

On Modern Art

'Modern Art is a gigantic racket, run by unscrupulous men for unhealthy women.'

(Passed on to me in Australia, where it was said to have originated.)

On the lack of public response to Delius

'As I have frequently told you, it is the barbarous age we live in.
This is an age in which no new work can possibly appeal if it
reveals evidence of breeding, delicacy, a sense of regret and a
craving for beauty.'

On Stravinsky

'Unfortunately taste and intelligence are not of themselves sufficient for the creation of enduring art, especially if they don't grow
up. I do not find in Stravinsky's newest productions convincing
signs that he has arrived at wisdom even yet. He is still a remarkable innovator, or, rather, a ringer of fresh changes. Naturally he
appeals—he always has appealed—to the young and emotionally
inexperienced . . . (he is) clever as a hundred musical monkeys. I,
once an ardent admirer, find him now sometimes boring: once, as
in Cecil Gray's description, he was Diaghilev's greatest creation.'

On musicology

'A musicologist is a man who can read music but can't hear it.'

At rehearsal

(On the *Venusberg* music:)

'But gentlemen, this is a *Grand Piece*, an *Erotic Piece*—and
you're playing it like a lot of schoolgirls! I want you to play this
piece *like a Welsh Bard in a rage!*'

(On the *Scala di Seta* overture—at the start of the fast tune
for two oboes, who had been revelling the night before—musicians
will imagine those skirling sixths with a hang-over:)

'Oh, my God! Sunday afternoon in the Highlands!'

(On the Sibelius Second Symphony:)

'Gentlemen in the bass department—you will observe in this
movement a prolonged *obbligato* passage for the contra-bass mean-

dering through the lower reaches of the orchestra like an amiable tapeworm—may we try it?'

(On a new piece, produced for one rehearsal, with the concert the next day:)

'Gentlemen, I know very little about this work—I shall follow you.'
(Conducted on the morrow *from memory*.)

To the Control Room before a studio broadcast of *Tristan*. (Some readers may not be conversant with radio procedure: in a sealed-off sacrosanct apartment with glass windows insulated from the performers, sit the technicians, music coach, and prompter, time-keeper, etc. before the complex of instruments of balance and control with which the experts toy from time to time. Enter Sir Thomas, very debonair.)

'And how is the "Cave of Harmony"[1] this evening? . . . I have asked Mr Beard kindly to conduct the orchestra for the moment, what time I propose to turn your inviting knobs and press your buttons to my satisfaction. When I have done so, you will be good enough to leave them as I have done, for I do assure you, without the slightest exaggeration, that this will be the loudest *Tristan* you have ever heard . . .'
(Polite consternation of the engineers accustomed to doctor the 'volume' down in loud passages. But Tommy had his way, smiled his way out, nothing was done, and all was well.)

To an audience in Liverpool between items

'Ladies and Gentlemen, in upwards of fifty years of concert-giving before the public, it has seldom been my good fortune to find the programme correctly printed. Tonight is no exception to the rule, and therefore, Ladies and Gentlemen, with your kind permission, we will now play you the piece which you think you have just heard . . .

---

[1] The title of a well-known contemporary team of night-club minstrelsy.

'This is the so-called "Paris" Symphony of Mozart, composed when as a very young man he was on his first visit to Paris. All I can say about *that* is that the Paris of *his* day must have been very different from the Paris of *mine* when a very young man: or Mozart would certainly never have had the time or the inclination to write a symphony . . .'

To various Pressmen

'I never conduct above an audience's head—it is an impertinence to do so. It has paid to be pleased . . . And great music invites many different treatments.'

'The grand tune is the only thing the public understands, and flexibility is the only thing that makes music appeal.'

On criticism for speeding

'The average ear confuses strong accent with fast tempo, and the frequent use of *rubato* with tempo itself.'

On being praised for a lyrical first act of Walküre

'My concern was for higher clarity than that of sound, to wit, a clarity of musical meaning.'

In defence of opera

'Opera is the most highly-developed and complete form of art in music, and to sing in opera should be the aim of every vocalist. All vocal performance should be dramatised, and opera should be the goal of every composer. And the utility of concerts should be to train audiences and all concerned for opera.'

On contemporary composers

'No composer has written as much as a hundred bars of worthwhile music since 1925. *Wozzeck* is ingenious but uncivilised and uncharming. I am not interested in music—or in any work of art—that fails to stimulate enjoyment of life, and what is more, pride of life.'

On Handel (a tabloid biography he wrote for the postcard repro-
duction of the portrait in the National Portrait Gallery):

'George Frederick Handel (1685–1759). Born in Halle and died
in London, a naturalised Englishman. Greatest of the international
composers, he wrote with equal success in the styles of France,
Germany, Italy and England. His career, like his personality, was
stormy and brilliant. The downfall of Italian opera led him to
English oratorio and his masterpiece, *Messiah*. He loved pictures
and children, endowing liberally the Foundling Hospital. Afflicted
with paralysis and blindness, he died wealthy and the idol of the
nation. Buried in Westminster Abbey.'

On Mozart (from the Glyndebourne lecture, 14 July 1948)

'He emancipated music from the bonds of a formal age, while
remaining the true voice of the eighteenth century. His new sentiment or emotion, as expressed by a matchless technique, was his
supreme gift to the world. That sentiment was an intimacy, a
masculine tenderness, unique—something confiding, affectionate'
(as reported by Richard Capell, *Daily Telegraph*, 17 July
1948).

Capell also wrote[2] of his 'Brighton Oration' on British Opera
to the Incorporated Society of Musicians: 'Beecham spoke for a
solid hour and a half with irony and with passion, with audacious
generalisations and with living instances; he spoke with the
prestige of a glorious veteran's achievements behind him, and
with a young man's fighting spirit . . .'

The (true) Messiah *legend*

After a faultless week of *Freischütz*, Miss Phillips was invited by
Sir Thomas to sing soprano solo in *Messiah* some few weeks
ahead. She nervously confessed to complete ignorance of oratorio,
and was soothingly bidden to learn it. Meantime they met again
by chance, she with the score under her arm. To his smiling,

---

[2] *Daily Telegraph*, 8 January 1949. Address delivered 5 January. See
also TB's article rehearsing some of his Brighton address, *Daily Telegraph*, 17 January 1949; and his biting letter in the issue of 28 January,
replying to the taunts of Lord Esher.

'How goes *Messiah*?" she nervously replied, 'Oh, I *hope* all right!
It goes *everywhere* with me, to work, at meals, up to bed at
night ...'

'Then may we trust you will have an Immaculate Conception
of the part?' ...

Of his famous 'Lollipop' encores

... 'As in the majority of cases the programme ends with a grand
bang or explosion of sound, my practice has been to play an encore
in complete contrast. The piece selected has generally been of an
essentially syrupy, soapy, soothing and even soporific nature, and
the effect upon the audience has been that its emotional temperature, raised to a high point at the conclusion of the actual programme, is gradually reduced to the normal, so that everyone
walks out happy and comfortable.

'The idea is not wholly original, for it is to be found in the old
Athenian Drama, where tragedies were followed by satirical
comedies or other forms of fooling. Of course, when, as in the
case of a symphony such as the sixth of Tschaikovsky, there is a
quiet ending, the character of the "Lollipop" suffers a slight
change, and the former 'tranquilliser' is replaced by something
of a more genial type.

'But in every instance these little epilogues, corollaries or after
thoughts are short, taking and popular in style. In other words, a
musical sweetmeat or, to make use of a Transatlantic idiom—a
"candy".'

'Mr Beecham, Musicologist'

In his twenty-sixth year Beecham wrote Programme Notes for the second and third concerts of the Oriana Madrigal Society which he had helped Charles Kennedy Scott to found, and which subsequently became famous. At their first concert Mr Thomas Beecham led the list of basses, among whom his name does not subsequently appear. (Could it be that even then his vocalism showed signs of the style later to become so familiar to generations of orchestral players?) At any rate he wrote two sets of programme notes, from which I omit one or two details of technical reference to the pieces then heard which are not at hand for readers today. His general introductions evince considerable understanding and powers of judgment, and lucid, concise expression, also a genuine love of that old music which was then quite new, indeed practically unknown in its native country.

His snapshots of Elizabethan genius are apt and attractive—one possible under-valuation is that of Thomas Weelkes, who is now accepted as one of that immortal quintet of madrigalists whose miniatures convey so beautifully the poetry, pathos and often humour of the Elizabethan culture: Byrd, Gibbons, Morley, Weelkes and Wilbye. Incidentally only one Weelkes masterpiece is included in these two programmes.

Mr Beecham appears among the Honorary Members of the Society until its fifth concert on 11 June, 1907. Programme notes were mostly by Charles Kennedy Scott, occasionally by J. A. Fuller-Maitland. These reproductions are by kind permission of Mr John Kennedy Scott and Mr Walter Harmsworth who sent me two bound volumes of the Society's programmes.

THE ORIANA MADRIGAL SOCIETY

From the Second Concert, Thursday 8 February, 1906, in the Bechstein Hall. Analytical Notes by Thomas Beecham. (Some verse texts and all un-annotated items omitted.)

'When shall my wretched life' (6 parts)   *John Wilbye*
(From '*The First Set of Madrigals*', 1598)

There is no more curious fact in musical history than the complete obscurity in which the life of John Wilbye is hopelessly buried. While nearly all his contemporaries found during actual lifetime their chroniclers and eulogists, not only is there no one who has performed a similar office of kindness for him, but there exists a general and inexplicable disregard of both the man and his work. Our loss here is so incalculable that we could not over-express our gratitude for even the smallest scrap of information illuminative of the character or doings of one who, besides being among the few foremost writers of his time, is a unique and fascinating personality. A comprehensive genius in the sense that Byrd and Gibbons were comprehensive he certainly was not. His sole instrumental work is a volume of *Lessons for the Lute*, and he scarcely contributed to the literature of Church music. He did one thing only, but that supremely well. Identifying himself with the Madrigal form (to the exclusion of all possible rivals as far as English music is concerned) he has utilised it for the expression of nearly every shade of emotion communicable through the medium of choral sound.

And this has been successfully accomplished in a spirit of the most complete obedience to the limitations of purely musical effect. Wilbye is essentially the perfect artist; and it would be difficult to point to a single passage in the whole body of his work susceptible of incurring the charge of ugliness or extravagance.

But what so markedly distinguishes him from the entire group of contemporary choral writers is the possession of an inexhaustible flow of the loveliest melody together with a style whose pervading characteristic can only be described by the term poetic. Of this hardly a better example can be mentioned than 'When shall my wretched life', which may be said to stand toward all other Madrigals in the way that Byrd's 'Tristitia et Anxietas' does towards all other Motets. It is a beautiful expression of profound and poignant sorrow, but uttered with such charm of manner as to almost carry with it a degree of consolation.

'Lightly she tripped over the dales' (5 parts)   *John Mundy*
(From '*The Triumphs of Oriana*', 1601)

John Mundy takes a high place among sixteenth-century choral writers of the second rank. He was organist first of Eton College, and afterwards of Windsor Chapel. A celebrated performer both on the organ and the virginal, several of his compositions for the latter instrument are to be found in the collection known as 'Queen Elizabeth's Virginal Book', one of these being a decidedly quaint *Fantasia* intended to convey an idea of 'fair wether, lightning, thunder, calme wether and a faire day'.

His madrigals reveal the hand of an undoubtedly able crafts-man, the present example being a finely-written piece of work, full of power and imagination. It may be that there is some want of variety and contrast between the different sections, but there is such a broad and uninterrupted flow of charming and vivacious melody that one can readily overlook any formal imperfections.

A Carol for Christmas Day   *W. Byrd*
(From '*Songs of Sundrie Natures*', 1589)

Familiar as one may be with the historic development of music in the sixteenth and seventeenth centuries, it is almost in the nature of a lesson to hear in actual performance a work like this carol of Byrd. Its simple division into two admirably contrasting sections—a song for solo voice with accompaniment for stringed instruments and, following each verse, an unaccompanied choral refrain for unbroken voices—shortens the task of analysis.

Glancing at the first section we at once realise how entirely we are dealing with two branches of the art as yet in their infancy. The string writing, thoroughly vocal in style, betrays no sign of a comprehended existence of an independent instrumental tech-nique; the solo part, closely woven in the web of contrapuntal accompaniment, of which it forms merely one thread, is equally devoid of individual significance. But turning over the page and coming to the second section we find in ripest artistic development a beautiful fragment of choral writing, absolutely Byrd, clear cut and vigorous with a sense of exaltation. It begins with twelve bars of an almost rollicking six-four measure which, pausing on a full close, leads into a more dignified but equally joyous section in common time. Observe how the same imitative point—though the device contributes little to the real unity of the work—is used here as in the preceding solo for the setting of the words 'this day'. The music as it continues grows in strength and jubilation, culminating in a delightful passage six bars from the end, where Byrd sends the second alto rolling down to the low F, and then to halt on a pedal C, while the upper parts rush on triumphantly to the final bar.

'See See the Shepherds' Queen' (5 parts)   *Thomas Tomkins*
(From '*Songs of 3, 4, 5 and 6 parts*', 1622)

Thomas Tomkins, a native of Gloucester, was a pupil of Byrd, and during the earlier part of his life was (like his master before him) attached to the Chapel Royal. Subsequently he became organist to the Cathedral of Worcester and it was here about the year 1622 that he wrote the work known as *Songs of three, four, five and six parts*, in which is contained 'See See the Shepherds' Queen'. That Tomkins was esteemed highly by his own generation is evidenced by the presence of one of his Madrigals in the *Triumphs of Oriana* collection; but it is difficult after a fair survey of his best work to assign him a place in the front rank of the great choral writers. His style is inclined to be lacking in individuality, he has no great fund of original emotion and his form has little of the clear outline and perfect balance of such men as Bennet and Morley. It is curious to note that Burney, who ought to have known better, places Tomkins on a higher level than Morley, declaring that 'he seems to have had more force and facility'. 'See See the Shepherds' Queen', however, is a charming piece of work, the themes being all distinctly good, and the feeling fresh and buoyant. It is even more interesting on the formal side. The ordinary structure of the Ballet is

A B

that is, one section followed by a second and different, the whole repeated according to the number of verses. But in this particular composition Tomkins having arrived at the end of his second section B, instead of finishing in the usual manner on a full close, rests on a chord of the dominant and then dashes off again into a third and entirely new section C, which completes and rounds off the whole work. The effect on a first hearing is certainly surprising and has a suggestion of modernity about it: for at the close of the middle section and the return to the original key, it is not at once we realise that we are not listening to a movement in the later form of

A B A

The last conclusion one is tempted to form is that Tomkins has essayed a sort of union between the two forms of the Ballet and the Madrigal, and that the result, from an artistic point of view, has not been altogether successful.

'Mother, I will have a husband' (5 parts)   *Thomas Vautor*
(From '*The First Set*', 1619, republished in Vol. II '*Euterpe*')

If there is a work of the Madrigal species against which it is impossible for any one to direct an accusation of archaism and monotony it is certainly this of Vautor, a writer of whom we know next to nothing. The themes are direct, vivacious and tuneful even to the point of 'popularity'; the construction is as clear cut and roundly balanced as that of any modern composition. There are simply two sections, one in common time, the other in three-four time. After the conclusion of the second, the first is repeated but in a much shortened form.

From the third Concert, Tuesday 12 June, 1906, in the Aeolian Hall.

'In fields abroad' (5 parts)   *William Byrd*
(From '*Psalmes, Sonnets and Songs of Sadness and Pietie*', 1588)

It is hardly necessary to insist on the fact that Byrd's finest work is to be found in other branches of the art than that of Madrigal writing. He does not seem to have comprehended—certainly not in the manner understood of men like Bennet or Wilbye—the inexhaustible possibilities for artistic expression contained within the limits of this most elastic of antique forms. It may be that, taken collectively, his Madrigals do cover a fairly wide range of thought and feeling; but it is equally true that judged as separate compositions they are often inclined to be lacking in variety of mood, colour and pictorial effect, and if it is for the utterance of what is deepest and tenderest within him that we are looking, we must go elsewhere—to the Mass, Motet or Psalm.

These limitations being admitted—and of course such a criticism is based upon the very highest standard of comparison—it becomes the easier to assert confidently that, viewed from the purely artistic and technical standpoint, his achievements in this line are often extremely beautiful, bear the clear impress of their author's high seriousness and sincerity, and as specimens of choral writing are always masterpieces.

'In fields abroad', though of comparatively small dimensions, is a work of considerable interest, and no better example could be cited of Byrd's peculiar and complete mastery of one at least of the most important resources of his art. The whole is founded on and developed out of the little phrase which is given out by the First Bass in the four opening bars. Naturally it endures inversions and other metamorphoses, but there it always is, and there is nothing more heard in the way of new thematic material. It is a striking idea this of a short introduction where two voices only lead off, followed almost at once by the entry, like a thunder-clap, of the whole choir. Observe the splendid climax attained at the words, 'do overspread the ground'! It is interesting and a trifle amusing—and a careful listener may hear without diffi-culty—how into the music, interpretative of a text entirely martial in feeling, has occasionally been intruded a ring curiously ecclesi-astical. The bias of Byrd's mind is unmistakable, even when dealing with subjects essentially secular.

'If my complaints' (4 parts)   *John Dowland*

(From '*The First Booke of Songes and Ayres of foure parts*', 1597, republished by the Society in Vol. III '*Euterpe*')

This is a beautiful and quite unfamiliar example of the lyrical art of the greatest lutenist and most popular composer of his day. Of course any attempt to compare Dowland with such supreme masters of their craft as Byrd and Gibbons is out of the question. He never essayed anything on a large scale, and his work accordingly is slight in dimensions and limited in range of expression. Moreover, he was by no means a prolific writer, and his contribution to contemporary musical literature amounts to little more than a handful of love-songs. But these are of such exquisite beauty and of so decided originality as to secure for their composer an unquestioned immortality. It is a true test of genuine art that, whatever the lapse of time since its creation, it should never appear antiquated, and this is particularly evident in the case of these few lyrics. Nothing more delightful of the kind has ever been written than 'Awake, sweet love', and the music sounds today as fresh and modern as when it was first heard in 1597.

One noticeable feature in the love music of Dowland is an almost ever-present underfeeling of devotion. The homage offered to the one beloved is coloured by a fine flavour of tender respect, and we miss, without much regret, the violent and spasmodic outbursts of overcharged emotion which are the rule in similar compositions of a more recent date.

'The silver swan' (5 parts)   *Orlando Gibbons*
(From '*The First Set of Madrigals and Mottels of 5 parts*', 1612)

'What is our life' (5 parts)   *Orlando Gibbons*
(From '*The First Set of Madrigals and Mottets of 5 parts*', 1612)

That wonderful school which in England began its artistic life about the middle of the sixteenth century reached its zenith of achievement at the close of the same, and which within the space of thirty subsequent years had closed the chapter of its history, finds an altogether fitting climax in Orlando Gibbons, its last great master. For sheer native ability and fertility of production he is inferior to none of his predecessors. It may be that many of the especially attractive qualities which are present in their work are almost entirely absent in his. We find there little of the grace and fresh spring morning atmosphere of Bennet and Morley, as little of the direct simplicity of Weelkes or the sweetness of Dowland, while for actual melodic invention he ranks below Wilbye, nor is his personality so unique and fascinating. But in point of versatility, loftiness of idea, breadth of expression and incomparable musicianship he is superior to all—Byrd alone excepted.

Of choral writing, looked at from the point of view of pure craftsmanship he is possibly the greatest (certainly the most interesting) master this country has yet produced. This is hardly to say that his success in manipulating a large number of parts is more pronounced than that of Byrd, Weelkes or Morley. It probably is not. But the line of Gibbons' melody is infinitely more rounded and flowing, and as he treats every part with the greatest independence imaginable, the results are always of absorbing interest and frequently of commanding and impressive effect. His polyphony, in short, stands in very much the same relation towards that of the earlier men, as the polyphony of Brahms & Wagner does towards that of Mozart and Beethoven.

The prevailing tone of Gibbons' music, like that of Byrd, is one of austerity. But while this characteristic in the case of Byrd generally assumes the shape of exaltation and religious ecstasy, in that of Gibbons it is something more akin to philosophic meditation. In the madrigal his fondness for 'texts' which are moralistic and reflective (and they are nearly all of this kind) amounts almost to a weakness on his part. Even that exquisite lyrical fragment 'The Silver Swan', is made to close with a line presumably of didactic import, but of so quaint a character as to quite upset one's gravity on listening to the work. Though from beginning to end a contrapuntist in style, Gibbons' method of employing simple harmonies for certain effects is all his own, and it is in slow and sustained passages that he has achieved some really remarkable results. For example, in the case of 'What is our life', in spite of the splendid level of writing maintained throughout, the poetic atmosphere is of such an emphasised hue of grey meditation as to bring the work well within the risk of incurring the charge of monotony. But exactly in the middle and on the words 'our graves' occurs a wonderful modulation, and then without in the least disturbing the artistic unity of the composition follow thirty bars of searching beauty and so entirely different in actual sound from what has gone before or comes after that our interest, quite prevented from flagging, is sustained until the final chord. Special attention should be given to the concluding section, 'Thus march we', etc., etc., which is one of the finest bits of choral writing that even Gibbons ever penned and which rounds off in admirable fashion a work which, taken as a whole, is altogether worthy and representative of his genius.

'Ah, dere heart' (5 parts)   *Orlando Gibbons*
(From '*The First Set*', 1612)

Though but thirty odd bars in length, there is a world of concentrated feeling in this little Madrigal. The themes are of great beauty, the sentiment rings true, and the writing is of wonderful mastery and interest—even for Gibbons. Observe, for example, how the bass part on its first entry in the fifth bar marches slowly, step by step, from the lower A to an octave and a half above, while the upper parts swell in correspondingly increased intensity of emotion! Also how at the close of the first section the music glides in the most natural manner and without break into the melancholy but lovely contrasting passage, 'The day breaks not'! There is in the concluding cadence a charming touch of indefiniteness and want of the sense of finality, which makes us regret what we consider to be the premature close of the work and ardently wish to hear more. Perhaps this also should be placed to the credit of Gibbons' insight into the endless subtleties of his art.

'As Vesta was descending' (6 parts)   *Thomas Weelkes*
(From '*The Triumphs of Oriana*', 1601)

In this Madrigal, his contribution to 'The Triumphs of Oriana', we have the essence of all that is best in Weelkes. Deficient as he is in breadth, elegance and emotional depth, if compared with Byrd, Bennet and Wilbye, there is no denying his real genius and extraordinary capacity. In the sheer technique of fine, clear part-writing he has no superior; and his individuality is of a marked and highly interesting order. None of his contemporaries communicate in their work to us in any the like degree such a keen sympathy with the breezy out-of-door existence essentially English. It is true that all the Madrigalists have sung charmingly and lengthily of rural life and customs, of Chloris, Amaryllis and Shepherds Swain. But in Weelkes we really catch a faint breath of the sharp, cutting country air and a flavour of the sense of exhilaration obtained only by early morning walks down lanes and across fields dripping with dew.

Again, the 'Ayres or Phantasticke Sprites' reveal a decided faculty of humour superior to and unlike anything of the sort possessed by any other writer of the same period.

With regard to the present work one may point out how the exquisite feeling of lightness in the opening section is effected by the delay in entrance of the basses until the twenty-eighth bar. Then after a short contrasting passage comes the setting of 'to whom Diana's darlings came running down amain', a delightful piece of word painting. At 'and mingling with the shepherds' the music becomes richer and closer in texture, and presently a series of chords ushering in the refrain, 'then sang the shepherds and nymphs of Diana' lead into the final section. This, which is of some length, is formed entirely out of a short two-bar phrase, and is a capital example of the ingenuity and resource for which Weelkes was in his day so admired. Attention should be paid to the bass part, especially on its repetition towards the end, which is of course a lengthened version of the two-bar theme already alluded to.

'Ah, dere heart' (5 parts)   *Orlando Gibbons*
(From '*The First Set*', 1612)

'Weep, O mine eyes' (4 parts)   *John Bennet*
(From '*Madrigalls to Foure Voyces*', 1599)

There could not possibly be a greater contrast between this work of Bennet and the 'Ah, dere heart' of Gibbons, sung in the first part of this programme. Between the two compositions, judged as things of art and beauty, there is little to choose. Each is in its way a masterpiece, and both are short, but highly successful expressions of a mood of tender and moving sorrow. But just as Gibbons' Madrigal is from every point of view a characteristic production of its author, so, in a like manner, is this completely typical of the genius of Bennet; and in style as well as temperament the two men are at opposite poles of thought and feeling.

The part-writing of Gibbons is in this case, just as it has been described in the note on 'What is our life', curved and irregular in outline. That of Bennett more than any of his contemporaries is elegantly smooth, regular and diatonic. The grief of the former is of a kind that in its direct poignancy (possibly more telling on a first hearing) stretches the limits of its artistic medium of expression to their fullest extent. That of the latter, more restrained and dignified in character, is kept well in hand throughout, but underneath we can always feel the throb of profoundly sincere emotion. It is an interesting instance of a similar result effected by widely differing means.

'Arise, awake!' (5 parts)   *Thomas Morley*
(From *'The Triumphs of Oriana'*, 1601)

'Now is the month of maying' (5 parts)   *Thomas Morley*
(From *'The First Booke of Ballets'*, 1595)

Morley, if not the greatest, was certainly the most versatile and active of the great English musicians of the sixteenth century. In addition to himself producing a large quantity of original work— a good deal of it of the highest merit, he has earned our warmest gratitude for his editing of several important collections of compositions by different composers of the time, including the celebrated series *The Triumphs of Oriana*. He was, moreover, the first Englishman to write and publish a treatise on music which, known as *A Plaine and Easie Introduction to Practicall Musicke*, may still be read with a certain amount of profit and a good deal of interest. He attempted, and successfully, nearly every branch of composition, and, though much underestimated in his own day, his reputation has since steadily grown until now he is perhaps the most popular of the Elizabethan Madrigalists.

The key-note of his style is facility. Everything he wrote moves with a graceful freedom and perfect naturalness of manner. His technical equipment is first-rate, and his ingenuity and resource are adequate for the solution of any difficulty. As an inventor of melodic ideas, he is more prolific than any of his contemporaries, Wilbye alone excepted. On the other hand there is no doubt that the quality of his inspiration is lower than that of several of his other fellow-writers. He has infinite charm, grace, fancy and lightness of touch, but neither his thought nor emotion soar very high or indicate a mind given to inquiring at all into the reason for things. But if this is so, it is only fair to add that he hardly ever falls below a certain level of a kind that is wonderfully consistent and always satisfying.

The two works of his included in this programme are so very familiar as to render comment quite superfluous.

'Frederick Delius, 1862-1934'

[A last tribute spoken by Sir Thomas Beecham at the graveside, Limpsfield parish church, in Surrey, on 24 May, 1935. The ceremony at Limpsfield was recorded and played to his wife a few hours later in the nursing home where she died.]

We are here today to bid farewell for ever to Frederick Delius, a great Englishman and a famous man. You have read that it was his wish to be buried in the soil of his native country.

I think it may be said that nowhere in the breadth of this land could a fairer spot be found than this to satisfy his wish, nor a more auspicious occasion than this beautiful day.

It may have struck some of you as requiring a little explanation as to why Frederick Delius, who left these shores as a very young man, a wanderer and almost an exile, has returned to them finally only yesterday. You may like to know why it was he wished to lie here amid the countryside of the land which gave him birth. I think I am able to give you the explanation.

The England that we live in today is not by any means that in which Delius was born, some seventy-five years ago. He was born in those days which excited and provoked the rage of the sages of the time. Carlyle, Matthew Arnold, Ruskin raged and preached against the brutality, inhumanity, and insensibility of that age.

England at that time seemed to be a country given up to the worship of commercial prosperity and little else besides. It was a country that revolted the finer spirits of that time, and in certain cases drove them out of it elsewhere, where they hoped to find, and they did indeed find, a more sympathetic environment.

Delius was born in a part of the world which was particularly odious to him and to the kind of critical intelligence I have mentioned. It was the arid, hard, business north.

It was into this environment and these conditions that Delius was born, and among which he grew up—and he grew up a rebel and a dissentient. He strove to escape, and he did escape, and when he left this country as a young man he went to other countries and finally settled in the country which, in the opinion of everyone at that time, provided the outlet for his activities and the fitting soil for the reception of his great gifts, as well as circumstances in which he could work in peace and enjoy the sympathy of those about him.

He returned to this country about twenty-five years ago, but for brief visits, and he did not find such a world of difference.

War broke out, and something strange happened, which revealed this country in a different light to the entire world. To the astonishment of the world, this country turned its back on the idols of the market and the counting house, and embarked upon the greatest adventure of idealism the world has, perhaps ever known.

From that moment the eyes of this great musician turned inquiringly and wonderingly towards the shores of his native land. Also, in the meantime, another strange thing happened. His music, which I venture to say is extraordinarily redolent of the soil of this country and characteristic of the finer elements of the national spirit, became known, it became loved, and came to be understood. It had always been respected.

Six years ago, yet another event took place in London. It was without parallel in the musical history of this country. A festival was given of his works at which he was present—blind, paralysed, but none the less present, and able to listen to every note.

That also was a revelation to Frederick Delius, our friend. In his departure from England back to France after this festival, he turned to those in charge of him—for you must remember he could not see anything—and said, 'Place my chair so that my eyes may be directed upon the shores of England, which has given me the recognition that I have not obtained anywhere else.'

I am proud to say that the greatest respect and understanding of his works proceed from the people of this land, that it grows daily, and it shows no sign of diminishing—and so far as it is possible to foresee, if there is any music that will remain honoured and immortal in the memory of the people of any one country, it is the music of this composer.

I said we were here to bid farewell for ever to the mortal remains of Frederick Delius. I do so in no spirit of sorrow or regret. The most precious part of this man is the immortal part—his spirit as revealed in his work; and in whatever sphere that spirit is, I should like our greetings to pass beyond the confines of this earthly sphere, and let him know that we are here not in a spirit of vain regret, but rather one of rejoicing that his music is with us and will remain with us for evermore.

'Mozart'

[On 26 April, 1956 Beecham gave the Introductory Talk at the University of Illinois Mozart Festival 1956. The following is transcribed from the original tape recording.]

Mr Brannigan, Ladies and Gentlemen,
It is quite correct that I told Mr Brannigan I did not know what I was going to talk to you about. He looked a little incredulous a few minutes ago, but I must tell you that I *never* know what I am going to talk about. I always wait till I arrive on the scene. I scan my audience, I gauge to the best of my ability, after a long experience, their joint standard of intelligence and receptivity, and then I go ahead...

Well now, ladies and gentlemen, I have to bear in mind that this is a scholastic institution—at least I am told so. And I have also been asked here to conduct works of Mozart, and therefore I think it better on the whole if I link up what I'm going to say now in the form of a short talk—or whatever you like to call it— I wouldn't dignify it with the term 'lecture': that sounds formidable—with the composer whose works I have been playing and am going to play in the concert hall. I suggest this because for a long time now I have been under the impression that the composer Mozart is insufficiently estimated: that is to say, he is under-estimated in two particular ways: first, as one of the most original geniuses the world has ever seen in the way of spontaneous creation; the other, as *the* composer of all the composers who have ever lived to whom all succeeding composers are most indebted.

In a book written some fifteen years ago, it said that Mozart was born in a very artificial time, the eighteenth century, and that he became the apostle of artificiality in music; and then it went on to say that he was deficient in melodic invention as compared with certain other composers—Bizet and Puccini. I at once sat down and wrote down something like two hundred titles of melodies which in my opinion were exceedingly beautiful. I then did the same with Messrs Bizet and Puccini, and between them I wrote down about fifty. All other composers, any other composers such as Bach—not Handel, who wrote magnificent tunes—Haydn, Beethoven—not Schubert—but Brahms I could hardly get the whole lot up to one hundred. On thinking it over again I increased the number of splendid tunes that Mozart wrote to nearly 250, and I will champion those tunes as tunes of beauty, of grace, splendour, or charm, of humour even, against any other tunes written by any other composer since the world began.

Now if this matter is thought out coolly, without prejudice, and without all the hopeless rubbish, nonsense, baloney and twaddle that's been written about music, the music of the period 1700–1820, let us forget all about it—and I'll tell you the first thing you've got to forget, in considering this rightful position of Mozart in music—what historians, musicologists, and other queer people (*laughter*) used to labour when I was a very young man, was that Mozart was some kind of tenuous link between the giant figures of Bach and Beethoven, and the giant figures of the nineteenth century, Beethoven and Wagner. He was a hangover of the first two; and a kind of small prophetic voice of the latter two. Well, that was what I was taught when I was a child. Accordingly I approached the works of Mozart with a slight contempt, and a feeling that I was wasting my time. Why didn't I hurry on to the greater men, and leave this little fellow behind?

However, I was happy with the operas of Mozart. I did not think much of the sonatas—I haven't thought very much of any sonata anyway—that's mainly for the reason that I don't play well. But the tunes, the operas—*Die Entführung, Seraglio, Figaro, Don Giovanni, Magic Flute, Così fan Tutte*—those I knew all off by heart by the time I was ten or eleven. I have never wavered in my devotion to them as tunes—never. They are to me still the best tunes in the world, and no one has written anything like them, with the possible exception of one or two of Handel, a few Schubert, one or two of Schumann, and that's about the lot. These pieces of Mozart have been *going around* for about 175 years and they're now given to every student in every academy and college of music in the world, and the said students just wrestle with them, endeavour to grasp the meaning, and perpetrate them on the unhappy examiners, just as they do with me in London. In fact the man in some respects has become a damn nuisance, this Mozart.

Well, ladies and gentlemen, what I am expressing is a personal view. You need not swallow it all as gospel. In fact I should be the last person to suggest that anything I said on any subject should be accepted as gospel, but I will maintain simply this: that no one has written such a large number of splendid gracious tunes as this man.

Now what is a tune, anyway? If you want to know what a tune is, set about writing one, and get it played, and see if it would be recognised as a tune. A tune is an idea: it's a musical idea; it occupies the same place in music as an expressive phrase, or even more than a phrase, in literature. It must convey something that has not been heard or said before. It may resemble something—naturally—everything in the world resembles something else that's been done or said before—but it must be heard and couched in a phrase that is novel. Shakespeare had the happy knack of putting thoughts of the Greeks and Romans into new language that has come down to us as the most fitting medium for the thought contained—so fitting that hundreds and hundreds of lines and phrases have passed into our current living consciousness. Now, so far as I am concerned, so far as all the great musicians of the last fifty or sixty years that I have known are concerned, whether Richard Strauss, Sibelius, Saint-Saëns, Massenet, Rimsky-Korsakov—all the rest—Gounod in France, Tchaikovsky in Russia, Grieg in Norway—have all said the same thing—this same kind of musical currency has passed into their consciousness. None the less, professors!—pedants!—pedagogues! have gone on denying it. All right! *Who is more likely to be right?* We will leave it at that—for the moment.

Now then: I have asked you to consider the exact position of this man, the station he occupies in the history of—let us call it—modern music. I date the birth of modern music not from the arrival on the scene of either Mr Gershwin or Mr Cole Porter: those of course are very earth-shaking events, I know. I date it from the arrival on the scene of John Sebastian Bach and Handel. I might even go back, to oblige some of my friends and enthusiasts, to Monteverdi: that would be just. In fact I might go back to the time of the Greeks! But when I speak of modern music or music generally, I am now speaking of that volume of music which is understood by and liked by musical people, not specialists. I once heard a famous judge in England say, 'There are three kinds of witnesses—good witnesses, bad witnesses, and experts.' I am not dealing with experts and specialists. You are the sort of public I mean.

Now, taking Bach and Handel as a jumping-off point: just examine what these men did and under what conditions they lived musically. You can't take any score of an opera of Handel or an oratorio of Bach or Handel—in fact you can't take anything—except the clavichord pieces, violin sonatas and so on—*that is not imperfect*. No synthesis had been arrived at by that time between the use of the conjoining factors. Look at the score—the autograph score of a piece like the great B Minor Mass: it is recognised to be a masterpiece. Well, I'm not quite sure what a masterpiece is. In the eyes of so many people it is generally a rather large monstrous overgrown and tiresome affair—like the Choral Symphony, the last movement of which has been pronounced by everyone to be a nuisance—or the *Götterdämmerung* of Wagner, where all the tunes you heard the week before are repeated one after another—like certain plays and Greek drama, of which nobody knows the meaning. So many things are masterpieces, ladies and gentlemen, as taught to you, because nobody knows what they're about. If you want to secure immortality, or partial immortality, write something in phrases that nobody else can understand, and get them published if you can. You would achieve a rapid celebrity, and it may last a long time. People are still wondering what Hamlet meant, pretending—either pretending or actually going mad. They're still wondering what some of the plays of Euripides meant. They're still wondering what a great part of Dante meant in the *Divine Comedy*; and what all the Russian plays and novels are about. Of course no one has ever discovered: some of them nobody ever will. The secret was *not meant* to be discovered. This kind of vague delightfully misty meaning, you see, is artfully calculated just to throw sand in the eyes of credulous Anglo-Americans. They have succeeded very well.

Now to return to the subject of Bach and Handel. The '48' of course we know; the Suites we know—French, English and any others—but what about the big works? Are they ever done exactly as the composer wrote them? They are not. Nobody would dare to give a performance of a Handel oratorio just as it is written; or an opera just as it is written. It's a physical impossibility. Anyway, it's been tried: it hasn't *done*. Take a famous piece like *Messiah*. Look at the score. Half of it is figured bass: very few instruments. An equally great composer, Mozart, when this score came into his hands, said, 'This will never do.' So he added accompaniments. Mendelssohn saw it and he said, 'Oh, we'll add something more.' Then a lesser composer, Robert Franz, added some more; and every musician in the executive world of every country in Europe has from time to time added something to a Handelian score. This is very unfortunate, and it may seem to you to be very presumptuous, but I'm going to ask you to take it from me that you cannot play these pieces at all to the satisfaction of the music public of today, or even a hundred years ago, just as written down by the composer. And the reason is very simple.

In those days—250 years ago—there were no orchestras, not as we understand them today, no regularly constituted orchestras, with an equation of wind instruments, stringed instruments and brass instruments. You could find orchestras—I know one example which had sixteen trumpets, and fourteen trombones, a few piccolos and perhaps one double-bass—a charming collection like that. Or you had at the court of Louis XIV an orchestra with sixteen celebrated fiddles, and little else. But an orchestra composed of flutes, oboes, clarinets, bassoons, horns, trumpets and so on, and strings, *did not exist*. They were collected together *ad hoc*, but they did not exist as permanent bodies. It is very difficult to think of that, and believe it, but it is so. Here you have orchestras of seventy-five, eighty and one hundred musicians, tremendously overpaid, and maintained by the unwilling generosity of rich people—characteristic of our modern life—everybody doing something out of conscience and duty that they don't want to do—and every one of these men earns as much in three months or six months—employed in the orchestra—as Mozart made in the whole of his life. Thrilling thought, isn't it? All right, they did not exist, these orchestras. Therefore you will find, in the case of every large composition, that then the kind of synthesis or combination of forces that you are to meet with later, in perfection, did not exist at all.

Now as you know, these gentlemen, Bach and Handel, for whom

I have a great admiration and respect, and for one of them a great love indeed, wrote little sonatas, little suites, little concertos and so on, and sundry small pieces. Very good: that is their complete and final production. Of course the other works, like the St Matthew Passion, are grand and marvellous—and many oratorios of Handel—but I'm speaking now of artistic production, not intentions: because we all know that both these gentlemen sat down at the organ—and Handel at the harpsichord—Handel was the greatest *improvisatore* of his day—and he filled in himself as it went on, and what he didn't hear he put there—and he did it on the organ or the harpsichord or any other instrument that was handy—Bach did the same thing on the organ. *But we have not got in print any edition in the world* of what these men did fill in. We are left with an imperfect combination of forces, and only the *possibilities* of concertos and suites or symphonies.

Now then, the situation remained like that more or less for any practical purpose—I underline the word *practical*—or *vital* purpose—and I underline that too—until the eventful year of 1756 when there was born into the world the most gifted musician it had yet seen. He lived thirty-five years, and what happened during those thirty-five years? For the first time we had real symphonies—*real symphonies*; for the first time we had really *first-rate*—underline it again—string quartets. We saw the birth of the genuine concerto for instruments of all kinds, and orchestras. We saw something more in a variety—an immense variety— greater than anyone has ever conceived—of combinations—light pieces, marches, minuets. Hardly any of them are known, but you can take it from me they all include marvellous little tunes, enchanting little bits of humour, grace—and then something which was perhaps more important than anything for the salvation of the time.

What had Opera been in Europe? Or anywhere else? Where was it? Apart from very interesting experiments, and some solid achievement, but in a very singular fashion by one Italian composer at the beginning of the seventeenth century, the opera of Europe by 1750 was dead. The operas of Handel, with their enchantresses of the Middle Ages, and their heroines, and their heroes like Caesar and Alexander, Epaminondas and so on—sung by *castrati*, of all people—they had already been forgotten. Handel it was true, had invented the music drama, so proudly vaunted by Gluck as a discovery, and revived unsuccessfully by Richard Wagner. Music drama is a form of opera in which the music is of less consequence than the scenery and the costumes and the libretto and the movements and the orchestra. I myself have an old-fashioned prejudice for opera itself. When I go and I read that an opera such as *Aïda* is about a King of Egypt and his daughter, and the King of Ethiopia and *his* daughter, and one or two other people, you know, who are singing the principal roles—just as Hamlet and Ophelia and Polonius and company are the actors in *Hamlet*—I go to hear them *sing*. Now if they don't sing well, I walk out. But music drama says to me, 'Oh don't bother about what those people are doing: they are really irrelevant: listen to the orchestra . . . that's the thing to listen to. Look at the beautiful effects of cloud and light and fire and storm and so on.' That's music drama. Well, Handel had tried this on, you know—he had tried everything. Then Gluck came along and tried to persuade the people of Europe that melody was not very important in an opera: what he called 'dramatic effects' were really of far more serious consequence. Well, you know what dramatic effects are in my experience? It's making loud thumps on a percussion instrument, *sforzandi* in the strings—constant *sforzandi*—a few pathetic whinings on the wind, and sudden blasts on trumpets on trumpets and trombones. That's really what it is, dramatic effects. When you can't write a tune, now you know what to do, ladies and gentlemen. Those of you who are thinking of writing a music drama or a new opera, don't bother about tunes—it's true your work won't have a very long life, because even taxi-drivers like to whistle tunes, you know. Boys in the street—I know little boys in the street in various towns, singing all sorts of tunes—strange people—I heard one singing a tune of Delius the other day—a *tune*, mark you. However, don't you bother about writing tunes: just throw in those thumps and bangs and things, and you'll have a real music drama in the style of Wagner and Gluck. All right! And mind you repeat whatever little phrase you have—I won't call it a melody—whatever you have, don't forget to repeat it 250 times. The so-called Death Theme in *Tristan and Isolde*, a work for which I have a great affection—I've conducted it three hundred times—is played forty-nine times. I don't think you will find that sort of device—let's call it device—in the works of Mozart.

Well, opera was virtually dead: it was dying, anyway, and the opera of 1600–1760 for your general purposes, the purposes of the entire world, save one or two enthusiasts, is that. You can't play an opera of Handel just as it was written. There always has to be, let us say, latter-day co-operation.

Well, 1760—this extraordinary individual, about that time at the age of six or so, began writing operas, and believe me, from almost the very beginning, they differed. They differ materially— childhood efforts differ from what had been heard before. It would require an essay to indicate very clearly where they differ, and the differences are very minute, but they are already there, like seeds almost hidden.

Now I will take you through the extraordinary course of this inventive life. It may be true, and it is true, that by the year 1776 when Mozart was twenty-seven—twenty-one—or twenty-two— that a few people had written a kind of symphony. It is true that they had written symphonies which differed very considerably from those written before, for the reason that the framework of the symphony as you understand it today is there; but the first great European symphony, complete, with absolute mastery, with perfection of structure, with charm of melodic invention, was written by Mozart in Paris, known as the Paris Symphony of 1777 —or 1778—I forget which—and that I am playing tonight in this institution—the Paris Symphony, the first masterpiece among symphonies, the form of which he was not to develop but to carry forward; which Haydn was to accept and carry forward; and which Beethoven was to accept and enlarge; and which Schubert would vary slightly; but which all subsequent composers have accepted as the ground-work and the model: everything is contained in that, the model.

As Tennyson wrote, 'All can raise the flowers now, for all have got the seed.' The seed was deposited there. Now before this fellow had written this symphony, I would like to draw your attention to the fact that he had written something like 200 works before he reached the age of twenty—yes, rather more—and among these 200 so-called early works are some very delightful compositions. He wrote a piece that I am playing tonight too, a divertimento, when he was fifteen. There is no instance in the whole world of art, except perhaps the two cases in painting of Raphael, and in poetry of Milton, of a first-rate piece of work being turned out by a boy of fifteen. This is a first-rate piece of work. It differs entirely, it differs absolutely from anything that had been heard before. In the first place it contains humour, it contains wit. I don't think you will find much of those qualities in the composers that came before Mozart—anyone who does, I shall be very glad to hear about it.

Now it is commonly known or re-asserted that Haydn founded the string quartet. In a sense it is true. But also bear in mind that the writer of the first masterpieces—complete masterpieces in this way of string quartets, was Mozart. It has also been alleged that Haydn invented the symphony. Right, in a way he did. But also remember that Haydn did not write the symphonies that you know and like, and which are accepted by the world today as real symphonies, until several years after the death of Mozart, and none of them until ten years after Mozart had written his three last symphonies.

But now we will take something that even after 160- 170- 180-years—a branch of his composition which is only just beginning to be understood and appreciated. Mozart, among other things, wrote twenty-eight piano concertos. I have no hesitation in saying that about eleven of them are the most beautiful compositions of their kind in the world. There you get—there you get in unrivalled measure and style, the perfect synthesis, combination and contrasting character of what a concerto ought to be as between piano and orchestra. I only know one other concerto where this perfect union is achieved, and even in that orchestra is not always satisfactory: that is the Fourth of Beethoven. But the use of the orchestra and piano in such concertos as the great C minor, No. 24, of Mozart, 491; No. 23, A major; the one in F major, 19; the one in G major, 17—the perfection of combination, the ingenuity of construction which makes all other symphonic writers seem like amateurs and bunglers, and the amazing inter-relationship of the various sections, the freedom of the sections, all that stands—these ten or twelve—as among the great masterpieces of the world.

Now a final word on opera. It is two hundred years ago since this man was born. It was in 1910 that I gave the first performance in London of one of his great operas, *Così fan tutte*—it had taken only 170 years for that work to get to London. (There's quite a lot of hope for much contemporary music, isn't there? I mean, 170 years is nothing in the life of a composition. I only regret that I won't be there at the time any modern compositions receive their due deserts.) I think it reached the United States about thirteen years later. So we had a little edge on you there. Well, when I first started giving Mozart in great lumps, the world of London knew three symphonies, two operas, two pianoforte concertos, and a miscellaneous portmanteau of little pieces. I plugged and plugged this fellow. Every time I played a symphony other than the three last, the press said, 'An early work, oh, an early work.' It is the fashion to talk about early works. There is only one composer in the world the critics will *not* refer to in respect of his early works, and that's Beethoven. They've given up stigmatising the early sonatas—one like the Pathétique, or the early trios—those 'early works'. They don't even call Symphonies 1 and 2 'early works' now. They're afraid. There's always one thing about people who write about music: their distinguishing features are conventionality, cowardice, timidity—well, I won't say any more about that. Early works—masterpieces—when Mozart was fifteen—eighteen—violin concertos, divine melodies. Very good. I plugged and plugged and plugged; I've given over a thousand performances of his operas, translated them into English —and there we are: today, what are we faced with? A Bicentenary, and everyone *playing* the man. Of course, naturally they're not doing it with a great deal of sincerity: there's some piety in it, you know, and fashion. But that's all right, I've lived through many of those phases. Well, anyway, it is some kind of recognition that in the opera houses of the world Mozart has come into his own.

Six or seven operas—six operas—are played, played as often as those of Richard Wagner; not quite so often, but nearly as often, as those of Puccini and Verdi. They are modern operas in the sense that Puccini and Verdi are modern: they are as alive today in invention, they are as sprightly in characterisation and in subject; they are the great comedies in music of European—the European world: the great comedies in music, just as the great comedies like *Twelfth Night* and *Midsummer Night's Dream* are the great comedies in verse: *that* people are dimly realising.

And, ladies and gentlemen, I am very happy to be here today in this educational establishment to pass on to you a few of the very serious and important truths in respect of this man. He is

7—BR * *

the central point of European music: don't forget it. Before that, the various forms of composition, rich as they were, were growing with some pains because of the lack of synthesis between the various elements that made up their scores. In his brief life everything was accomplished, everything that was to come after. The after-effects in the hands of other people were certainly— let me see—increased grandeur, resonance, tragedy—all the rest of it in the hands of Wagner, Tchaikovsky, Beethoven—but the bridge, the *bridge* was complete between the old world of music and the modern world of music. The man who built that bridge was Mozart; but don't think of him only as a bridge. On that bridge were many lovely structures of his own, as there were built upon the old bridges that you used to see in Florence or London or other places—dwelling-places, churches, and all the rest of it. That is something I have wanted to point out to you—his great position in the world of music, his historical figure, and his great position as an individual creator.

And thank you very much, ladies and gentlemen, for listening to this serious and prolonged discourse of mine: but I thought having been invited here to play Mozart, I might also make hay while the sun is shining—the intellectual sun is shining, I would say—and add a few ideas of my own to the music which you are to hear tonight.

The *Times* Obituary

FRANK HOWES (*Times* leader, 9 March, 1961)

It is hard to believe that the vital spark which for more than
eighty years burned in Thomas Beecham and illumined English
public life with its music and flashing wit has been extinguished.
His life was of the stuff of which legends are made. Like
Toscanini he became a legend in his lifetime, for in this century
it is the conductor who attracts that particular form of adulation
formerly enjoyed by the male soprano of the eighteenth and the
female soprano of the nineteenth. Conductors are more powerful
than sopranos, and there is an element of wizardry in their art.
Even the sound of the self-same orchestra differs from one conductor to another, and no conductor ever had in greater degree
than Beecham the power of conjuring ravishing sounds like
nothing else in this world from his players, such as, to take a
special and memorable example, the melting of Delius's *Summer
Garden* into silence at the Edinburgh Festival some months ago.
This was the Orphic element in the Beecham legend.

He was born in Lancashire but he had the Mediterranean wit
in his make-up. His repartee was Aristophanic. Somehow he
thawed the northern music of Sibelius just as when he played
Mendelssohn's *Hebrides* Overture the latitude of Fingal's Cave
shifted somewhat nearer Sicily. There was a suggestion of Pan
in his appearance: his brown eyes could blaze dangerously with
mischief. He delighted in outrageous speech, attacking the
Philistines with barbed and winged words. He was also a master
of more weighty language, and his prose had a measured and
Augustan tread sometimes criticised for its admirable pomposity.
But always its rotundity was likely to be transformed into something fantastic as he recounted, maybe in his autobiography, *A
Mingled Chime*, or in his biography of Delius, some event more
true and strange than fiction. Things happened to him, and if they

did not, he made them happen. This propensity for the incalcuable and irrepressible added to the legend an ambiguous reputation for irresponsibility that was both covertly admired and openly deplored.

There is little doubt that his wit, which is less congenial to his fellow-countrymen than humour, his benevolent dictatorship in artistic matters, and a touch of aristocratic disdain in manner, contrived during his middle life to create some distrust in the minds of the British public. It was to combat what had become a liability to all his schemes for his country's good that he portrayed himself in his autobiography as a conventionally educated man of the world, a musician who could read a balance sheet as easily as a full score, a hard-headed Lancastrian with no Celtic nonsense about him.

But however irresponsible his methods and his speeches, on one thing he was deeply, even earnestly and passionately serious, the art of music. He spent himself and his personal fortune in its service so that the various operatic and orchestral enterprises which he promoted have transformed our musical life and borne fruit which he lived long enough to see gathered. His sheer genius as a conductor gave delight at home to two generations, and abroad the lie to the lie about the 'Land without Music'.

We shall not see his like again, but he will live in his legend, for the legend itself will be written into the history of our time.

'The Memory Lingers On'

Neville Cardus

(An article in *The Guardian* on 8 March, 1971, the tenth
anniversary of Sir Thomas Beecham's death)

Beecham has been dead these ten years—and the eclipse goes on.
Other conductors shine planetarily in the musical sky, also a
comet or two flashes away into the outer darkness. And one of
them, a master, remains with us: Klemperer. None of these
shares Beecham's secret, his capacity to make music rise and fall
and flow as though fresh-born. He had the gift of improvisation.
A final rehearsal by Toscanini was indeed final; the concert itself
was a sort of tonal photostat of the final rehearsal. With Beecham
a rehearsal was a tuning-up of the orchestra, so that at the concert
he could play on it, even as Cortot could play on a piano. Music
is an art of motion, must go up and down, must not ever be static.
'Look for the melody' was Wagner's advice to conductors.
Beecham, by no means a Wagnerian, followed the advice of a
man who first changed conducting of orchestras from metronomic
control to personal interpretation.

His baton technique, often unpredictable, depended much on
the watchful responses of his first desks. I have seen Beecham's
baton fly from his grip high into the orchestra's Empyrean. I have
seen it entangled in his coat tails. In a symphonic development
passage, when frequently he became impatient (if the music
wasn't Mozart's), he would point his baton rapidly down to the
floor of the platform, like a musical water-diviner.

He was the product and fine fruit of a more leisurely and
aristocratically-minded age than ours. He mingled, in his art,
the amateur or connoisseur relish with professional experience.
Toscanini, at Beecham's extreme temperamentally and by aesthetic,
called Beecham a 'great mountainbank', his translation of

mountebank.[1] Beecham could be naughty. If he didn't like a composer he suffered no pains over him. He was not concerned overmuch with harmonic subtleties; a Hallé player, who adored Beecham, called him a 'top-line' conductor. Beecham maintained that music should sing, should dance, should present itself with style, should appeal first of all to the cultivated ear. He could not involve himself in a polyphonic texture. He was gorgeously outrageous about Bach—'too much counterpoint; what is worse, Protestant counterpoint.'

He was himself, for all his sharp piercing wit, entirely humane. And with music after his heart, he could be as scrupulous as Toscanini. He never was naughty in Mozart. His *Figaro* was champagne; his *Zauberflöte* incomparable for dignity of carriage, and heartfelt poignancy. His interpretation of Verdi's *Falstaff* has a sunny brilliance compared with which Toscanini's treatment of the same young-old masterpiece was brittle. It has been said that Beecham was at his best, as conductor, in composers of the second order. True, he avoided the Ninth Symphony of Beethoven (he called Beethoven of the last movement 'the Mr Gladstone of Music'). He found Bruckner rather a bore. 'In the first movement alone,' he remarked of Bruckner's Seventh Symphony, 'I took note of six pregnancies and at least four miscarriages.'

He seemed to me many times to conduct 'by ear', by born musical instinct. For years he dispensed with the musical score. In his old age he actually used a score for a performance of the overture to Mozart's *Marriage of Figaro*. 'You used a score,' I said to him, with pointed astonishment. 'Yes, my dear fellow,' he replied, 'I have been going through my scores lately. And I find that they hold my interest from the first page to the last.'

His range was wide, in spite of his dislike of music of any didactic implication. His Delius, of course, was as though he had collaborated in the conception of it. Poles apart from Delius, Beecham presented Sibelius powerfully and in the round. His conducting of Berlioz was as authentic as his conducting of Mozart.

---

[1] Originally 'quel pagliaccio inglese!' Knowing both men, I can imagine the scornful tone of the above and the mischievous, dulcet sympathy of Tommy when told that it was Toscanini's eye-trouble that forced him to memorise his scores—'I am sorry to hear it—indeed a double affliction ... when you remember for how many years he has become practically ... tone-deaf.'

He could take a hackneyed piece, such as Sibelius's 'Valse triste', and magically cause it to sound haunting, evocative, original. His Haydn has seldom been equalled for geniality and period graciousness.

He came to British music at a time when it was, as Oscar Wilde said, speaking with a heavy German accent. He transformed music of his period into the 'gay science' of the forgotten Nietzsche's dream. He led us out of the German captivity. When he was in charge of opera in these isles, he produced works of fascinating differences of style, form, and procedure: Charpentier's *Louise*, *Boris Godunov*, D'Albert's *Tiefland*, Delius's *A Village Romeo and Juliet*, Bizet's *The Pearl Fishers*, Stanford's *The Critic*, Ethel Smyth's *The Wreckers* and *The Bosun's Mate*, as well as the customary repertory. Richard Strauss thought that Beecham's conception of *Elektra*, and his deliverance of it, was the most powerful of any in his experience. The Russian Ballet, too—stars danced when Beecham was born. Since his death, as I say, the eclipse has scarcely diminished. One of my most affectionate remembrances of Beecham was his appearance, during his last years, at a Sir Robert Mayer Children's Concert. It really was an audience of children. I sat next to two rosy-chubby-cheeked of the cherubim. Sir Thomas walked very slowly to the conductor's chair. Arrived there, he addressed the children—'Ladies and Gentlemen'—an adorable touch—'my slow progress to the conductor's desk was due not to any reluctance on my part to conduct before so distinguished an audience. My slow progress was due entirely to the infirmity of old age.' A pause, then, 'And now, Ladies and Gentlemen, our first piece is by Mozart. It was composed when he was at the age of—er—at the age of—,' he pointed to a small boy on the front row: 'At your age, sir.'

He was mixed in the elements, kind, generous, recurrently intolerant, witty yet given to most rumbustious humours. By Falstaff, out of Toby Belch. More Oxford than Wadham, but no snob. He would talk to a taxi-driver as to the next belted Earl. Kindly and touchy, aristocratic by emulation. None the less, he was 'Tommy Beecham' as orchestra players call him. He was born, after all, in St Helens, Lancashire, a fact he would recall from time to time, with satisfaction.

Appendices

I. Musicians and Other Colleagues

The following is an incomplete but fairly representative list of conductors, singers and other colleagues associated with Beecham during his long career. All of those here listed (alphabetically) attained, or brought with them into his orbit, outstanding distinction of some kind; a glance over this list and the Bibliography and Discography might well give the impression that no performer in musical history has made so much good music come to life for so many composers, singers, players—and listeners.

CONDUCTORS

Ainsworth	Goossens	Polacco
Ansermet	Gui	Prétre
Badini	Harty	Raybould
Balling	Harrison	Reiner
Barbirolli	Heger	Robinson
Bavagnoli	Kempe	Ronald
Bellezza	Kleiber	Sargent
Bodansky	Klemperer	Schalk
Buesst	Knappertsbusch	Stokowski
Cameron	Mengelberg	Strauss
Coates	Monteux	Toye
Del Mar	Panizza	Walter
Furtwängler	Pitt	Weingartner
		Wolff

SOPRANOS

Aino Ackté	Josephine Delprat	Kousnietzoff
Albanesi	Emmy Destinn	Dora Labbette
Gladys Ancrum	Claire Dux	Marjorie Lawrence
Florence Austral	Edvina	Lotte Lehmann
Isobel Baillie	Desirée Ellinger	Frieda Leider
Erna Berger	Flagstad	Tiana Lemnitz
Jeanne Brola	Margherita Grandi	Doris Lemon
Rosina Buckmann	Joan Hammond	Miriam Licette
Lina Cavalieri	Ilse Hollweg	Félia Litvinne
Maria Cebotari	Gertrud Kappel	Germaine Lubin
de los Angeles	Hilde Konetzni	Zelie de Lussan

Lois Marshall	Thea Phillips	Carrie Tubb
Melba	Lily Pons	Norena
Grace Moore	Elizabeth Rethberg	Eva Turner
Dorothy Moulton	Gilda dalla Rizza	Bessie Tyas
Claudia Muzio	Elisabeth Schumann	Ruth Vincent
Agnes Nicholls	Oda Slobodskaya	Jennifer Vyvyan
Phyllis Neilson-Terry	Stiles-Allen	Edith Walker
Sylvia Nelis	Elsa Stralia	Ljuba Welitsch
Mignon Nevada	Elsie Suddaby	
Graziella Pareto	Maggie Teyte	

MEZZOS AND CONTRALTOS

Louise Berat	Anny Konetzni	Ebe Stignani
Muriel Brunskill	Kirkby Lunn	Conchita Supervia
Clara Butt	Louise Anna	Marjorie Thomas
Edith Clegg	Bahr-Mildenburg	Kerstin Thorborg
Astra Desmond	Maria Olcewska	Edna Thornton
Olga Haley	Gladys Parr	Doris Woodall
Mary Jarred	Gladys Ripley	

TENORS

Caruso	Richard Lewis	Sydney Russell
John Coates	John McCormack	Tauber
Björling	Martinelli	Urlus
Edmund Burke	Lauritz Melchior	Jon Vickers
Dalmorés	Webster Miller	Walter Widdop
Tudor Davies	Frank Mullings	Alexander Young
Walter Hyde	Heddle Nash	Zenatello
Raoul Jobin	Maurice D'Oisly	
Parry Jones	Joseph O'Mara	

BARITONES

Frederic Austin	Gerhard Hüsch	William Michael
Bruce Boyce	Lewis James	Dennis Noble
John Brownlee	Roy Henderson	Robert Parker
Fischer-Dieskau	Marcel Journet	Frederick Ranalow
Dinh Ghilly	Herbert Janssen	Paul Schoeffler
Percy Heming	Herbert Langley	Harold Williams

BASSES

Norman Allin	Hans Hotter	Scotti
Böckelmann	Maguenat	Stevens
Bouillez	Maurel	Giorgio Tozzi
Chaliapin	Pinza	Ludwig Weber
Sir Keith Falkner	Robert Radford	Clarence Whitehill
Fassbaender	Schorr	

COLLEAGUES (professionals, administrators, etc.)

Sir Hugh Allen	Eric Fenby	H. Procter-Gregg
Harold André	Denham Ford	Stanford Robinson
Felix Aprahamian	Berta Geissmar	Edith Rose
Sir Thomas	Percy Heming	Thomas Russell
Armstrong	Maurice Johnstone	Temple Savage
Donald Baylis	George King	Charles Kennedy
Sir Joseph Beecham	Sir Robert Mayer	Scott
David Bicknell	Oliver Messel	Douglas Steele
Eustace Blois	Norman Millar	Geoffrey Toye
George Brownfoot	Walter Legge	Denis Vaughan
Lady Maud Cunard	Alfred Nightingale	Verande
Diaghilev	Victor Olof	'Peter Warlock'
Dr. Philip Emanuel	Nigel Playfair	

INSTRUMENTAL SOLOISTS

Dennis Brain	Katherine Goodson	Pougnet
Gwydion Brooke	Leon Goossens	Rachmaninoff
Jack Brymer	Heifetz	Rubinstein
Adolf Busch	Myra Hess	Sammons
Campoli	Hubermann	Schnabel
Cherniavsky	Betty Humby-	Solomon
Cortot	Beecham	Isaac Stern
Curzon	Iturbi	Szigeti
Feuermann	Kreisler	Tertis
Pierre Fourier	Menuhin	Tortelier
Gieseking	Pachmann	Gioconda de Vito

ORCHESTRAL LEADERS

Paul Beard	Hugh Maguire	W. H. Reed
Raymond Cohen	Thomas Matthews	Albert Sammons
Oscar Lampe	John Pennington	Steven Staryk
Arthur Learins	Jean Pougnet	Charles Taylor
David McCallum		

II. Recordings, Concerts and Operas

The Sir Thomas Beecham Society produced in 1975, as a volume in itself, the complete Beecham Discography, and the English Branch of the Society has compiled a complete Concert List, also monumental! From these the following analyses appear by kind permission of the Society.

(a) Recordings

ADDISON: Carte Blanche

D'ALBERT: Tiefland (excerpts)

ALWYN: Symphony No. 3

ARNELL: Punch and the Child; Ode to the West Wind; Sinfonia

BACH: Christmas Oratorio (Sinfonia); Phoebus and Pan

BALAKIREV: Thamar; Symphony in C

BALFE: The Bohemian Girl (excerpts)

BANTOCK: Fifine at the Fair; Hebridean Symphony

BAX: Garden of Fand

BEECHAM, A.: songs

BEECHAM, T. (arr.): God Save the King

BEETHOVEN: Piano Concerto No. 4; Overture, Coriolan; Symphonies, Nos. 2, 3, 4, 6, 7, 8, 9; Fidelio (complete); Mass in C; Ruins of Athens

BERLIOZ: Overtures, Corsaire, Francs-Juges, King Lear, Roman Carnival; Damnation of Faust (excerpts); Harold in Italy; Requiem; Les Troyens (complete and excerpts); Te Deum; Symphonie Fantastique

BERNERS: Triumph of Neptune

BIZET: L'Arlésienne, Suites 1 & 2; Carmen (complete and suite); Fair Maid of Perth (complete and suite); Patrie Overture; Roma: Carnival (ballet); Symphony in C

BLOCH: Violin Concerto

BOCCHERINI: Overture in D; Symphony No. 3

BORODIN: Prince Igor (Dances, March, Overture)

BRAHMS: Overture, Academic Festival; Alto Rhapsody; Piano Concerto No. 1; Violin Concerto; Song of Destiny; Symphonies, Nos. 2 & 3; Variations on a theme by Haydn

CHABRIER: España; Marche Joyeuse; Overture, Gwendoline
CHARPENTIER: Louise
CHERUBINI: Les Deux Journées (excerpts)
DEBUSSY: Petite Suite; Prélude, L'Après-midi d'un Faune;
Printemps; L'Enfant Prodigue
DELIBES: Le Roi S'Amuse (suite)
DELIUS: Appalachia; Arabesque; Brigg Fair; Dance Rhapsody No. 1
& No. 2; Eventyr; Fennimore and Gerda (Intermezzo); Florida
Suite; Hassan; In a Summer Garden; Irmelin (excerpts); Koanga
(excerpts); Marche Caprice; Mass of Life; North Country Sketches;
On Hearing the first Cuckoo; On the Mountains; Over the Hills
and Far Away; Paris; Piano Concerto; Sea Drift; Songs; Song
before Sunrise; Song of the High Hills; Songs of Sunset; Sleigh
Ride; Summer Evening; Summer Night on the River; A Village
Romeo and Juliet (Walk to the Paradise Garden, and complete):
Violin Concerto
DUPARC: Chanson Triste
DVOŘÁK: Golden Spinning Wheel; Legend, Op. 59; Slavonic
Rhapsody; Symphonic Variations; Symphonies, No. 5 (old No. 3)
& No. 8 (old No. 4)
EASDALE: Red Shoes (film)
ELGAR: Enigma Variations; Overture, Cockaigne; Serenade in E;
Introduction and Allegro; (arr.) God Save the King
FALLA: El Amor Brujo
FAURÉ: Dolly Suite; Pavane
FRANCK: Le Chasseur Maudit; Symphony in D minor
GERMAN: Gipsy Suite; Patriotic Song
GHEDINI: Musica di Concierto
GLINKA: Overture, Russlan and Ludmilla
GOLDMARK: Rustic Wedding Symphony
GODARD: Concerto Romantique
GOUNOD: Romeo and Juliet (excerpts); Faust (complete, and ballet
music)
GRIEG: In Autumn; Last Spring; Old Norwegian Romance; Peer
Gynt (excerpts and suite); Symphonic Dances
GRETRY: Zémire et Azor
HANDEL: Amaryllis Suite; 'Piano Concerto'; Concerto Grosso No.
14; Faithful Shepherd Suite; 'The Gods go a-Begging'; The Great
Elopement; Israel in Egypt; 'Love in Bath'; Messiah; 'Origin of
Design'; Solomon; Suite for Orchestra
HAYDN: Piano Concerto No. 1; The Seasons; Symphonies, Nos. 40,
93, 94, 95, 96, 97, 98, 99, 100, 101, 102, 103, 104; Rehearsals of
Symphonies
HUMPERDINCK: Overture, Hansel and Gretel

JOHNSTONE: Celebration Overture
LALO: Symphony in G
LISZT: Die Lorelei; Faust Symphony; Orpheus; Psalm XIII
LULLY: Minuet
MASCAGNI: Cavalleria Rusticana, Intermezzo and 'Voi lo sapete'
MASSENET: Last Sleep of the Virgin; Manon (complete and excerpts);
Cendrillon Waltz
MÉHUL : Overtures
MENDELSSOHN: Violin Concerto; Overtures, Fair Melusine, Hebrides,
Ruy Blas; Midsummer Night's Dream; Symphony No. 1 (Scherzo),
No. 3, 4, 5; Songs without Words
MEYERBEER: Dinorah (Shadow Song)
MISSA: Muguette
MOUSSORGSKY: Khovanstchina Dance
MOZART: Allelujah; Seraglio (complete and excerpts); La Clemenza
di Tito; Overtures, Cosí fan Tutte, The Impresario; Piano Con-
certos, Nos. 12, 16; Flute and Harp Concerto; Clarinet Concerto;
Bassoon Concerto; Violin Concertos, Nos. 3, 4; Divertimenti, No.
2, 15; Deutsches Kriegslied; Don Giovanni (complete, and
Overture; For Whom the Gods Love (film); German Dance;
Magic Flute (complete, and Overture); Marriage of Figaro
(excerpts, and Act 2); March in D; Mass in C; Requiem; Serenade
No. 13; Symphonies, Nos. 27, 29, 31, 34, 35, 36, 38, 39, 40, 41;
Thamos, King of Egypt
NICOLAI: Overture, Merry Wives of Windsor
OFFENBACH: Tales of Hoffman (complete and excerpts)
PAISIELLO: Overture, Nina
PONCHIELLI: La Gioconda (Dance, and 'Suicidio')
POPPER: Hungarian Rhapsody
PROKOFIEV: Violin Concerto No. 1
PUCCINI: Tosca ('Vissi d'arte'); La Bohême (Act IV ('Donde lieta
usci') and complete)
RESPIGHI: Rossiniana
REZNICEK: Overture, Donna Diana
RIMSKY-KORSAKOV: Coq d'Or (complete and excerpts); Overture,
May Night; Scheherazade; Symphony No. 2 (Scherzo)
ROSSINI: Overtures, Barber of Seville, Cambiale di Matrimonio, La
Gazza Ladra, La Scala di Seta, Semiramide, William Tell;
Pastorella delle Alpi (aria)
SAINT-SAËNS: Omphale; Samson and Delilah (excerpts)
SARASATE: Zapateado
SCHUBERT: Symphonies, Nos. 1, 2, 3, 5, 6, 8, 9
SCHUMANN: Manfred
SIBELIUS: Bard; En Saga; Finlandia; Historic Scenes; In Memo-

riam; Karelia (excerpts); Kuolema: Valse Triste; Lemminkainen's
Return; Pelléas and Mélisande (excerpts); Symphonies, Nos. 1, 2,
4, 6, 7; Tapiola; Tempest Suite; Swanwhite Suite; Oceanides;
Violin Concerto

STRAUSS, J.: Gypsy Baron Waltz; Vienna Life; Vienna Blood;
Voices of Spring; Overture, Die Fledermaus; Morning Papers

STRAUSS, R.: Ariadne auf Naxos; Bürger als Edelmann; Don
Quixote; Elektra; Feuersnot; Four Last Songs; Ein Heldenleben;
Intermezzo; Der Rosenkavalier (excerpts); Salome (dance)

STRAVINSKY: Firebird (excerpts)

SUPPÉ : Morning, Noon and Night; Poet and Peasant

TCHAIKOVSKY: Capriccio Italien; Eugène Onegin (excerpts);
Francesca da Rimini; Nutcracker Suite; Jeanne d'Arc (aria); Romeo
and Juliet; Symphonies, Nos. 2, 3, 4, 5, 6

THEODORAKIS: Lovers of Tereul (film)

THOMAS: Mignon (complete and excerpts)

THOMSON, VIRGIL: Symphony No. 2

VAUGHAN-WILLIAMS: Flourish for a Coronation

VERDI: Aida ('Ritorna vincitor'); Falstaff (complete); Macbeth
(excerpts); La Traviata (excerpt); Otello (complete); Il Trovatore
('D'amor sull'ali')

VIDAL: Zino-zina

WAGNER: Overtures, Faust, Flying Dutchman; Lohengrin (Prelude,
Act 3); Die Meistersinger (Prelude and excerpts); Parsifal (Good
Friday Spell); Ring of the Nibelungen: Rheingold (Entrance of
the Gods into Valhalla); Die Walküre (excerpts); Götterdämmerung
(Rhine Journey and Funeral, Immolation Scene, excerpts);
Tannhäuser (Overture, Overture and Venusberg, Introduction to
Act 3, Entry of Guests); Tristan and Isolde (complete and excerpts);
Wesendonck Lieder

WEBER: Overtures, Oberon, Freischütz

(b) Concerts
(Data supplied by Denham V. Ford, Hon. Chairman, The Sir
Thomas Beecham Society)

While mere statistics cannot convey the essential spirit of Beecham,
a few selected facts and figures can provide some evidence of the wide
range of his career, musically and geographically.

A recently compiled list, by no means complete, of his concerts
and opera performances from 1899 until his death shows that, between
1907 and 1940 he appeared at the Queen's Hall some 210 times.
Between 1923 and 1959 there were seventy concerts in the Royal
Albert Hall while in the comparatively short period of 1951–60

Beecham appeared in the Royal Festival Hall no fewer than 92 times. Outside London, his most numerous appearances were in the Free Trade Hall, in Manchester with 88 concerts between 1908 and 1959. There was hardly a major town in Britain in which he did not conduct, as the following list will show: Aberdeen; Belfast; Birmingham; Blackburn; Bradford; Brighton; Bristol; Cambridge; Cardiff; Cheltenham; Croydon; Dublin; Dundee; Eastbourne; Edinburgh; Folkstone; Glasgow; Halifax; Hanley; Hull; Kendal; Leeds; Leicester; Liverpool; Manchester; Margate; Middlesbrough; Newcastle; Norwich; Nottingham; Oxford; Perth; Portsmouth; Sheffield; Sunderland; Swansea; Wolverhampton.

In Europe, he appeared both with his own orchestras and those of Paris (Conservatoire and Radio Orchestras); Berlin; Vienna; and Stockholm. He also appeared with one of his own or other orchestras in Amsterdam; Ascona; Basel; Berne; Biel; Berlin; Brussels; Budapest; Cologne; Dresden; Frankfurt; Geneva; The Hague; Hamburg; Leipsig; Lisbon; Lucerne; Ludwigshaven; Madrid; Munich; Oporto; Paris; Salzburg; Stockholm; Stuttgart; Vienna, Wiesbaden, Zurich.

The list of American towns and cities is no less impressive, with numerous appearances in New York and Philadelphia as well as Boston; San Francisco; Los Angeles; Chicago; Detroit; Cincinnatti; Seattle and Washington. This does not include the US tour of 1950 when he conducted some forty-nine concerts in almost as many days. He also conducted in Vancouver and Montreal. There was also a notable series of operas and concerts in Buenos Aires in 1965.

During his brief wartime stay in Australia, he conducted the orchestras of Melbourne; Brisbane; Sydney; Adelaide and Perth.

Finally there were nine concerts in South Africa in 1948.

Even in these days of jet-age travel, it is doubtful whether any other conductor could match this list.

Orchestras conducted by Beecham 1899–1960

Adelaide Symphony	B.B.C. Theatre
Baltimore Symphony	Buenos Aires Symphony
Bavarian State	Cape Town Symphony
Beecham Symphony	Chicago Symphony
Birmingham, City of, Symphony	Cincinnati Symphony
Berlin Philharmonic	Cleveland Orchestra
Boston Symphony	C.B.S. Symphony
Bournemouth Symphony	Concertgebouw
Brisbane Symphony	Czech Philharmonic
B.B.C. Northern	Dallas Symphony
B.B.C. Symphony	Detroit Symphony

Durban Symphony
French Radio
Hallé
Helsinki City Symphony
Houston Symphony
Illinois University
Johannesburg Symphony
Liverpool Philharmonic
Los Angeles Philharmonic
London Philharmonic
London Symphony
Melbourne Symphony
Minneapolis Symphony
Montreal Symphony
New Symphony
New York City Symphony
New York Philharmonic
Paris Conservatoire
Perth Symphony
Philadelphia

Philharmonic
Pittsburg Symphony
Queen's Hall Orchestra
Rochester Philharmonic
Royal Albert Hall
Royal Philharmonic (Old)
Royal Philharmonic (New)
San Francisco Symphony
Santa Cecilia (Rome)
Seattle Symphony
Spanish National Orchestra
Stockholm Philharmonic
St Helen's Orchestral Society
St Louis Symphony
Sydney Symphony
Symphony of the Air
Utah Symphony
Vancouver Symphony
Vienna Philharmonic
Washington National Symphony

The orchestras of the Royal Opera House, Covent Garden; Sadlers Wells; the Metropolitan Opera, New York; The Royal College of Music, The Royal Academy of Music and the Massed Scottish Military Bands.

Finally it has now been calculated that apart from some hundreds of recording and broadcasting sessions, Beecham conducted before the public on more than 1,600 occasions.

(c) Operas

The following list is at least very nearly complete of the different operas put on under Beecham's authority, sometimes in syndicate, mostly under his own direction: the majority of them he conducted (* denotes those he is not known to have conducted). The list does not include the numerous revivals, re-productions or new ones in other places.

BACH: Phoebus and Pan
BALFE: The Bohemian Girl
BEETHOVEN: Fidelio

BENJAMIN: The Devil Take Her
BERLIOZ: Faust. The Trojans
BIZET: Carmen, Djamileh*, The Pearl Fishers, The Fair Maid of Perth
BORODIN: Prince Igor
CHARPENTIER: Louise
CHERUBINI: The Water Carrier
CIMAROSA: Le Astuzie Femminili*
CLUTSAM: A Summer Night*
D'ALBERT: Tiefland
DARGOMIZHSKY: Roussalka
DEBUSSY: L'Enfant Prodigue, Pelléas et Mélisande
DE LARA: Naïl
DELIUS: Koanga, Irmelin, A Village Romeo and Juliet
DONIZETTI: Lucia, Don Pasquale*
DUKAS: Ariane et Barbe-Bleu*
FLOTOW: Martha
GLINKA: Russlan and Ludmilla*
GLUCK: Orfeo
GOOSSENS: Don Juan de Mañara
GOUNOD: Faust, Romeo and Juliet
GRÉTRY : Le Tableau Parlant, Zémire et Azor
HUMPERDINCK: Hansel and Gretel (?Cond.)
HOLBROOKE: Dylan
LECOCQ: La Fille de Madame Angot
LEONCAVALLO: Pagliacci.
LEROUX: Le Chemineau*
MASCAGNI: Cavalleria Rusticana, Iris*
MASSENET: Manon, Thaïs, Werther, Thérèse*
MOUSSORGSKY: Boris Godunov, Khovanstchina
MOZART: Figaro, L'Impresario, Entführung, Don Giovanni, Così fan Tutte, Zauberflöte
OFFENBACH: Tales of Hoffmann
PERGOLESI: Pulcinella*
PUCCINI: Bohème, Butterfly, Tosca, Turandot, Manon Lescaut, Tabarro*, Sister Angelica*, Gianni Schicchi*, Fanciulla*
RAVEL: L'Heure Espagnole*
RIMSKY-KORSAKOV: May Night*, Ivan the Terrible, Sadko, The Tsar's Bride*, Coq d'Or
ROSSINI: Barbiere, Cenerentola*, L'Italiana in Algeri*
SAINT-SÄENS : Samson et Dalila
SMETANA: The Bartered Bride
SMYTH: The Wreckers, The Boatswain's Mate
STANFORD: The Critic*, Shamus O'Brien

STRAUSS, J: Fledermaus
STRAUSS, R: Elektra, Salome, Rosenkavalier, Ariadne, Arabella*, Feuersnot
SULLIVAN: Ivanhoe*
THOMAS: Mignon, Hamlet*
VAUGHAN-WILLIAMS: Hugh the Drover
VERDI: Trovatore, Traviata, Aïda, Don Carlos, Rigoletto, Ballo, Otello, Falstaff
WAGNER: Dutchman, Tannhäuser, Lohengrin, Tristan, Meistersinger, Parsifal*, Rheingold, Valkyrie, Siegfried, Götterdämmerung
WEBER: Freischütz
WEINBERGER: Schwanda*
WOLF-FERRARI: Gioielli della Madonna

TOTAL: approximately 111
CONDUCTED BY BEECHAM: approximately 81–86

III. Select Bibliography

RICHARD ARNELL, *Tempo* (London), No. 58 (summer 1961), pp. 2-3.

THOMAS BEECHAM, *A Mingled Chime: Leaves from an Autobiography.* 1944

THOMAS BEECHAM, *Frederick Delius.* 1959

THOMAS BEECHAM, *John Fletcher.* 1956.

ROBERT BOOTHBY, *My Yesterdays, Your Tomorrow.* 1962.

ADRIAN BOULT, *Thoughts on Conducting.* 1963.

RICHARD CAPELL, 'Beecham's Genius', *Daily Telegraph*, 9 April 1949.

NEVILLE CARDUS, *Sir Thomas Beecham: A Memoir*, 1961.

NEVILLE CARDUS, *The Delight of Music.* 1966.

CLARE DELIUS, *Frederick Delius: Memories of my Brother.* 1935 and 1937.

NORMAN DEL MAR, *New Statesman*, 17 March 1961, pp. 445-6. Mr Del Mar dedicated his monumental three-volume *Richard Strauss: A Critical Commentary on His Life and Works* (1962; 1969; 1972) to Beecham.

ROBERT ELKIN, *Royal Philharmonic.* 1946.

DAPHNE FIELDING, *Emerald & Nancy.* 1968.

FREDERICK GAISBERG, *Music on Record.* 1946.

BERTA GEISSMAR, *The Baton and the Jackboot.* 1944.

EUGENE GOOSSENS, *Overture and Beginners.* 1951.

SYDNEY GREW, *Favourite Musical Performers.* 1923.

FRANK HOWES, *The English Musical Renaissance.* 1966.

PATRICK ('Spike') HUGHES, *Glyndebourne.* 1965.

GERALD JACKSON, *First Flute.* 1968.

ALAN JEFFERSON, *The Operas of Richard Strauss.* 1963.

MICHAEL KENNEDY, *The Hallé Tradition.* 1960.

OTTO KLEMPERER, *New Statesman*, 17 March 1961, p. 445.

MIRIAM LICETTE, *Daily Telegraph*, 8 April 1949.

ERNEST NEWMAN, 'The Two Thomas Beechams', *Sunday Times*, 26 April 1959.

IVOR NEWTON, *At the Piano.* 1966.

CHARLES REID, *Beecham: An Independent Biography.* 1961.

HAROLD ROSENTHAL, *Two Centuries of Opera at Covent Garden.* 1958.

HAROLD ROSENTHAL, *Opera at Covent Garden: A Short History*, 1967.

THOMAS RUSSELL, *Philharmonic*. 1942. Several reprints and a fine article in *Le Grand Baton*, 1972.

THOMAS RUSSELL, *Philharmonic Decade*. 1945.

HAROLD C. SCHONBERG, *The Great Conductors*. 1968.

BERNARD SHORE, *The Orchestra Speaks*. 1938.

JAN SIBELIUS, *Daily Telegraph*, 27 April 1949.

ETHEL SMYTH, *Beecham and Pharaoh*. 1935.

RICHARD STRAUSS, *Daily Telegraph*, 2 May 1949.

IGOR STRAVINSKY, *Themes and Conclusions*. 1972.

LIONEL TERTIS, *My Viola and I*. 1975.

It seems fitting to add here some details of the Sir Thomas Beecham Society, founded in 1964. It was formed to honour and preserve the name and work of Sir Thomas, and now has a world-wide membership. Past Honorary Presidents of the Society, were, first, Josef Szigeti, and secondly Rudolf Kempe. All particulars from the Hon. Chairman, Sir Thomas Beecham Society, 46 Wellington Avenue, Westcliff-on-Sea, Essex SSo 9XB.

The American branch publishes a quarterly *Le Grand Baton*. Its Executive Secretary is Stanley H. Mayes, The Sir Thomas Beecham Society, 664 S. Irena Avenue, Redondo Beach, Calif. 90277, U.S.A. The British Hon. Chairman is Denham V. Ford.

Index

Compiled by Alan Denson